FUGUE

Music

Editor
SIR JACK WESTRUP
MA, B.MUS, FRCO, HON.D.MUS
Heather Professor of Music
in the University of Oxford

FUGUE

Roger Bullivant
Senior Lecturer in Music
in the University of Sheffield

HUTCHINSON UNIVERSITY LIBRARY
LONDON

HUTCHINSON & CO *(Publishers)* LTD
3 Fitzroy Square, London W1

London Melbourne Sydney Auckland
Wellington Johannesburg Cape Town
and agencies throughout the world

First published 1971

The eight lines of music which appear on the paperback cover of this book are taken from page 19 of Das Wohltemperirte Clavier—Johann Sebastian Bach, *published by Veb Deutscher Verlag Für Musik, Leipzig, and reproduced by permission of British and Continental Music Agencies Ltd., London.*

This book has been set in Fournier type, printed in Great Britain
on smooth wove paper by Anchor Press, and
bound by Wm. Brendon, both of Tiptree, Essex

ISBN 0 09 108440 7 (cased)
0 09 108441 5 (paper)

CONTENTS

PREFACE

This is not a textbook on fugue. It aims rather to show what kind of a piece (or section of a piece) a fugue is, and to give some account of the way in which fugues have been written since the type emerged in the early Baroque period. The book is intended for the intelligent listener, whether he or she be amateur, student or professional musician. Although for convenience some technical language—such as, for instance, reference to chords and notes by numbers (see 'Abbreviations' below)—is used, it is hoped that the listener without technical knowledge will none the less find some illumination and elucidation in approaching a kind of music which has still not entirely lost the connotation of abstruseness and academicism.

Although in no sense a textbook, the present volume does attempt also to clear up some of the muddles which have arisen from the divergence between academic fugue and fugue as live composition, a divergence which has done harm to the reputation of teacher and composer alike, the former for thinking up fusty old rules and the latter for writing in—supposedly—a fusty old style. Chapter 5, entitled 'Examination' fugue versus 'live' fugue, is devoted specifically to an attempt to clarify matters on this still rather vexed topic, and to a brief investigation of the causes of the apparent conflict between the examination-room and the composer's desk. Already a more liberal attitude, geared to the study of great music rather than to rules for their own sake, is abroad in the academic world, and the ordinary listener in turn is better informed academically than he was in the recent past. It is hoped that the present book may contribute in a small way to these welcome developments.

Acknowledgements are due to the following for the use of copyright material: Peters Edition, London, New York, and Frankfurt from op. 65, No. 6 and op. 81 by Reger; Schott & Co. Ltd, from Ludus Tonalis by Hindemith; Boosey & Hawkes Ltd, from Preludes and Fugues by Shostakovitch and Symphony of Psalms by Stravinsky; Universal Edition (London) Ltd, from Music for Strings, Percussion and Celeste by Bartok; British and Continental Music Agencies Ltd, from Fuge in D Major II, vol. 1, no. 45 by Pachelbel, published by Breitkopf and Härtel, Germany; Galliard Ltd, from *Fugue* by Ebenezer Prout; Oxford University Press from *Studies in Fugue* by Kitson, from Symphony no. 1 by Walton and *The Technique and Spirit of Fugue* by Oldroyd and Rutgers University Press, New Jersey, from *The Study of Fugue* by Alfred Mann.

ABBREVIATIONS

WORKS

Denkmäler der Tonkunst in Osterreich and *Denkmäler der Tonkunst in Bayern*: these volumes ('Monuments of Austrian/Bavarian music') are the chief source for lesser-known music of these countries from the Baroque and early Classic periods.

Abbreviation: 'DTÖ', 'DTB' respectively, followed by the volume number and the number of the piece in that volume.

Historical Anthology of Music by Davison and Apel (Geoffrey Cumberlege, Oxford University Press). In two volumes. I: Oriental, Medieval and Renaissance Music; II: Baroque, Rococo and Pre-Classical Music.

Abbreviation: 'HAMI' or 'II' followed by the number of the piece.

Geschichte der Musik in Beispielen ('History of Music in Examples') by Arnold Schering (Breitkopf und Härtel).

Abbreviation: 'GMB' followed by the number of the piece.

Buxtehude

All references are to Volume II of the Wilhelm Hansen (Copenhagen) edition (published in England by Novello and subsequently by Chester), which contains the organ 'Preludes and Fugues' as they are now called.

Abbreviation: 'Hansen', followed by the number of the piece in this volume.

Bach

The 'Forty-Eight', as they are affectionately known in England, are two collections, each of twenty-four preludes and fugues in all the major and minor keys. The title 'Das Wohltemperirte Clavier' ('the well-tempered keyboard'—*not* 'clavichord', as it is sometimes mistranslated) is by convention given to both collections, although Bach only gave it to the first one. 'Well-tempered' refers to the fact that pieces in the keys remote from C major could only be played on an instrument with equal temperament.

Abbreviation: 'WTC I' or 'II', followed by the number of the piece in each volume (thus the last of the 'Forty-Eight' is 'WTC II.24').

All other Bach works are referred to either by title if well-known (Mass in B minor) or by the number in Wolfgang Schmieder's *Thematisch-systematisches Verzeichnis der Werke Johann Sebastian Bachs* ('Thematic and systematic index of Johann Sebastian Bach's works') (Breitkopf und Härtel 1966).

Abbreviation: 'BWV' followed by the number in Schmieder's index.

Hindemith

'Ludus Tonalis' (literally 'A game with keys') is a complete work comprising a prelude, twelve fugues, one in each key (but without major-minor distinction) interspersed with interludes, and a postlude.

Abbreviation: 'LT' followed by the number of the fugue. Hindemith's titles are all in Latin—thus LT 12 is called 'Fuga duodecima'.

Shostakovitch

The 24 Preludes and Fugues for Piano op. 87 are equivalent to one volume of Bach's WTC except that the order of keys is not by ascending semitones, as in Bach, but in cycles of fifths, each major key followed by its relative minor (no. 1 C major, no. 2 A minor, no. 3 G major and so forth).

Abbreviation: '24'. Fugues referred to by number.

CHORDS AND NOTES

In referring to chords the conventional designations I, II, III (large Roman numerals) will be used, with the conventional use of an Arabic numeral to indicate a discord and a, b, c, d to indicate root position, first, second and third inversions respectively. A ♭ or ♯ after the Roman numeral indicates that the note is flattened or sharpened *in relation to the normal scale* (in minor, the descending melodic version or Aeolian mode). Thus in B♭ major IV♯b would be the chord G–B♭–E♮: in D major the triad of F would be III♭a. In D minor the chord E–G–C♯ would be VII♯b.

It is also desirable to refer to individual *notes* of the scale—indeed in fugue this is if anything more important than reference to chords. For this purpose, therefore, small Roman numerals will be used, with again the same use of ♭ or ♯ when necessary. Thus in B♭ major the note E♮ would be iv♯: in D major the note F♮ would be iii♭. In D minor C♯ would be vii♯.

I

WHAT IS FUGUE?

Probably no type of musical composition has ever been graced with so many different definitions, or had so many words written about it, as fugue. From joke definitions ('the voices enter one by one as the audience leave one by one') the range extends through almost every possible kind of description, fugue being listed by different authorities as a piece of imitation, a complete movement in ternary form with strict rules, a contrapuntal procedure, a method of motivic development, or even merely as a texture. Such vagaries of definition are not really to be wondered at when it is realised that terms are not always consistently used by composers or by theorists, and that linguistic muddles do not necessarily imply any difficulty in our recognising certain purely musical phenomena which may be differently described by different writers at different periods. Fugue has become a controversial topic largely because, in addition to its live usage by composers throughout more than four centuries, its study has for long featured in the academic pursuit of music: this is, indeed, probably why so much has been written about it. The academic treatment of fugue has had two very unfortunate results: first, it has led to the idea—also partly fostered by the unfamiliarity of the fugal idiom in periods when it was no longer a normal means of expression—that fugue is a dry and excessively learned type of music; and, secondly, oversimplifications of fugal design and procedure originally intended to make matters more readily understandable to the student have produced a clash between theory and practice which has given rise to the false idea of the great composers of fugue 'breaking the rules'. ('In the next example Bach seems to have confused the issue,' wrote Kitson in a famous passage in *The Elements of Fugal Construction.*) The whole sad story of the relation between the academic teaching of fugue and live fugal practice must be examined a little further in a later chapter, where it will be seen that many of the rules which composers are supposed to have defiantly broken were in fact invented—sometimes for quite good reasons—by theorists of an age much later than that in which the composers themselves flourished.

Despite all the seeming obscurity and controversy as to what fugue really is, however, as far as our everyday usage at any rate is concerned it is the first part of the joke definition that comes nearest the mark. (The second part has become less and less true with the gradual revival of popular interest in Baroque music.) For a fugue, to most people, is recognised specifically by the entry of parts one after the other with a recognisable theme, the first to enter being (normally) unaccompanied and the second usually entering at the fourth or fifth (or more rarely at a compound of one of these intervals) to the first. Normally, at least one other part enters with the theme, and there is as a rule a more or less contrapuntal texture in evidence. Once such a procedure has occurred we tend to register 'a fugue' and are not particularly worried by what follows: what follows may sometimes be a continuation of theme-entries in the existing, or in additional, parts for varying durations of time and at varying time intervals; sometimes the continuation of counterpoint without further theme-entries; sometimes the introduction, in similar fugal manner, of a new theme or themes; and so forth. It is also possible that something quite different may follow, often a return to non-contrapuntal material previously heard.

A good example of how fugue strikes us during the course of a well-known classic-period work is evident in the last movement of Beethoven's C minor Piano Concerto (see Example 1). This passage stands out from what has gone before, despite the fact that its theme derives directly from the first subject of the movement, for the very reasons just given, namely: (a) parts enter one after another with a recognisable theme, the first to enter being unaccompanied; (b) the second part enters at the fifth to the first one; (c) two further parts enter with the theme; (d) there is a more or less contrapuntal texture in evidence.

It is worth noting, with regard to (d), that the 'more or less' is no idle phrase but an essential part of the stipulation. The contrapuntal texture is far from strict, and is hardly of the kind that a student would be encouraged to imitate: the violas, for instance, enter not with the theme but merely in unison with the cellos; also, when the fourth entry occurs it is taken by violas, cellos and basses in unison, while the first and second violins go into octaves and the woodwind introduce a new thematic fragment. After only a few bars of fugue we have clearly entered upon the standard dominant preparation passage common to

Ex 1 Beethoven, Piano Concerto in C Minor op.37: last movement, bars 228–45 (reduced score)

almost all classic sonata-style movements as a means of preparing the return of the first subject: the fugue has ended—or, rather, has passed directly into something else.

How essential to fugue are the four features just mentioned? Examples 2, 3 and 4 illustrate what, in general usage, would be deemed to be fugues. In the first of these the initial statement is accompanied by harmonies, and the surroundings are not homophonic as in the Beethoven but contrapuntal, so that the texture of the fugal part stands out much less. The effect of a fugue beginning is none the less obtained by the introduction of voices[1] and the appearance of a definite theme only partially foreshadowed by what went before.

In the Haydn example the initial entry is not accompanied by harmonies and the fugue stands out from previously homophonic material as in the Beethoven: also (as not in the Beethoven) the theme is quite new; but the second part enters at the octave, not at the fourth or fifth, to the first one, the third and fourth entries being at the upper fifth and upper twelfth respectively to the first entry, and at the octave to each other.

In the well-known Bach D minor toccata for organ the entry of parts with a new theme again characterises the opening, and we again have an unaccompanied initial statement; but it can hardly be said that there is much in the way of contrapuntal texture here, and some of the parts (see, for instance, the middle part accompanying the third entry of the theme) would hardly get a student through one of the more conventional fugue examinations. It may also be noted in passing that the second part here enters at the upper fourth to the first, not at the upper fifth or lower fourth as in the first two cases; and also that there is a quite substantial interlude between the entry of the third and fourth parts (bars 41–51 of the whole—not shown in the example).

These four examples have shown the difficulty of trying to work out an exact definition of fugue: for it will surely be agreed that from a purely *musical* point of view they all belong, despite their divergencies, to a single basic type, so that it is desirable that they should all share the same generic name; yet from these very examples we are obliged to observe that despite the stipulations laid down from time to time by theorists we cannot insist on either (a) the initial statement being unaccompanied, (b) the second entry being at the fourth or fifth to the first, or (c) contrapuntal texture, at any rate in the strict academic sense.

Three characteristics, however, do stand out as common to all four

1. To avoid confusion it will probably be best to refer to the contrapuntal strands of a fugue as 'parts', the term 'voices' being reserved, as here, for human voices as such. Conventional terminology is, as so often, unhelpful here.

Ex 2 Bach, Cantata 17: first chorus, bars 25–52 (reduced score, words and accompanimental parts omitted)

Soprano

examples, and, with many other fugues in mind, these may reasonably be regarded as essential to fugue: there is a definite theme stated at the outset; there is imitation in that the theme is taken up by other parts; there is contrapuntal texture to the extent that the theme may appear in an upper, a middle, and a lower part. That these three characteristics—particularly the first one—are vital ones is suggested not only by present day usage, but also by the history of the term 'fugue'. It seems to have been first used in the fourteenth century, where it appears to

Ex 3 Haydn, *The Seasons*: last chorus, bars 74–86 (reduced score, words omitted)

mean simply 'imitation'. This of course is the basic and original meaning of 'fuga'—'flight', the idea presumably being of one part pursued by, or fleeing from, another. It became conventional to distinguish 'fuga per canonem' (fugue according to the rule) from 'free' fugue: in the former, strict imitation went on right through the passage concerned, whereas in the latter it ceased soon after the opening, the continuation being free. The unqualified term 'fuga' gradually attached itself to the second type, the abbreviated term 'canon' becoming normal for the first. Even at this early stage in the history of the word we can detect the essential idea of a *theme* coming to the fore: with canon all is theme, in the literal sense that all the parts involved must follow the same pattern: the listener's reaction to this must inevitably be that nothing is theme, for the thread is soon lost; fugue, by contrast, recognising, so to speak, the listener's inability to follow strands for ever, or to concentrate for more than a limited time on a single extended piece of material, discontinues the strictly thematic portion at an early stage, thus making this portion shorter and more memorable, and also making

Ex 4 Bach, organ toccata in D minor BWV 565: fugue beginning bar 30

the entry of more parts with the theme not only practicable (a matter purely for the composer) but also more perceptible to the listener and thus aesthetically more desirable. Of the two types, therefore, fugue has naturally the more potentialities: canon, because of its very strictness, has never been a very expressive resource except when incidentally or subsidiarily used, and composers, with their instinctive understanding of what the listener can and cannot hear, have never given it the important place in live music which it has always had—until quite recently—in academic work.

At an early stage, also, another step was taken towards the establishment of the term 'fugue' as referring essentially to a *thematic* procedure. This was the insistence that a criterion for fugue, as opposed to other kinds of imitation, was that the parts should enter at the perfect fourth, perfect fifth or octave to each other at the outset, a definite preference being felt for the fourth or fifth between the first two.[2] This important stipulation, which we have seen to be obeyed in all four examples already examined, arises from the fact that only at these positions of entry can the all-important thematic portion of the material preserve, at least to a reasonable extent, its tone and semitone steps within a single diatonic scale[3]—such a scale being, of course, the underlying basis of all music during the period of history when fugue was establishing itself. Thus C–E–G is faithfully imitated within the C major scale as C–E–G (in another octave), F–A–C, or G–B–D; but at any other position either the triad outlined is changed from major to minor, or a foreign note has to be introduced (e.g. A–C–E, A–C♯–E; E–G–B, E–G♯–B). The preference for entry at the fourth and fifth rather than purely octave entries was almost certainly due to the greater variety—variety yet consistent with a unified effect—obtained by these positions, and also to the fact that such entries fall easily within the natural compass of the different human voices. Later, when fugues came to be written for keyboard instruments, the available compass of the player's two hands would again tend to suggest entry at an interval less than the octave if more than two parts were to be employed. As fugue progressed towards its 'classical' period (1700–50) a further, and cognate, advantage of entry at the fourth and fifth came to the fore—namely the frequent ability of these positions to assist tonality by causing stress on the tonic and dominant notes at the outset of the fugue. Thus, to take C major again, if the first part to

2. 'Fourth', 'fifth' and 'octave' are here understood to include compounds of these intervals, although the first two entries are commonly at the simple interval (fourth or fifth) to each other. In the normal case the sum of the intervals between entries would always be an octave, e.g. if the second part entered at the upper fourth to the first the third would probably enter at the upper fifth or lower eleventh to the second: first and third entries would thus be at the octave to each other.

3. The phrase 'preserve the tone and semitone steps' is taken from that most famous of all fugal theorists, Johann Joseph Fux (see Chapter 5), and it will have to be used a good deal in the section of Chapter 2 dealing with the Answer. It refers to the preserving not only of tones and semitones themselves but also of the *quality* of any interval, e.g. the representing of minor third by minor, not major, third, perfect fifth by perfect, not diminished, fifth, and so forth. The phrase does not, however, exclude the representing of a given interval by a *different interval of the same character*—e.g. semitone by minor third, perfect fourth by perfect fifth, etc. On the important distinction involved here see Chapter 2, p. 61.

enter stressed the note C the second could stress G (entry at upper fifth or lower fourth): if the first part stressed G the second might stress C (upper fourth or lower fifth): in either case the key of C is clearly defined. Not surprisingly, in view of this important additional advantage, the practice of entry at the fourth and fifth became a normal procedure at the height of the 'classical', tonal development of fugue—namely in the work of Bach and his contemporaries, where it is most common for the opening entries to alternate strictly between fourth-fifth and octave positions in relation to the first one. Before and after this period the procedure was also common, but by no means invariable, as one of our examples (Example 3) has already shown. Until the modern period, however, it is distinctly unusual for at least one of the entries not to be at the fourth or fifth to the initial one.

The entry of the second part with the theme at the fourth or fifth to the first one became known in English terminology as the Answer. Largely because of certain alterations sometimes made to the theme, when it is functioning as an answer, in order to preserve the tone and semitone steps within the tonic scale and/or to define the tonic key by stressing the tonic and dominant notes, the answer has become one of those problematical aspects of fugal technique which have helped in the bad work of giving fugue a reputation for abstruse academicism: it has also become the bane of the examination candidate in fugue, in whose work the devising of a 'correct answer', often to an awkward theme, sometimes seems to have been valued more highly by examiners than almost any other facet of technique. All this has magnified an interesting detail to the size of a dominating feature, to the extent that chapters on 'the Answer' in books about fugue tend to be longer even than those dealing with complete fugal design. In the present book the principles of answer are, it is hoped, elucidated rather more clearly and concisely than is common in textbooks, but even here a substantial proportion of Chapter 2 will be necessary for this purpose, if only to try to clear up some of the muddles which have so long surrounded this awkward member of the fugal community.

All that has just been said with regard to position of entry is, it should be stressed, relevant only to an essentially diatonic, and later a diatonic and tonal, era of musical history. With the advent of more modern styles the importance of tonality has declined again, and the diatonic scales have been replaced by more or less complete chromaticism. Now that considerations of diatonic scale and key are no longer valid there is of course no reason why any position of entry should not be employed without in any way excluding the piece from the category of fugue, and we find in fact entries at positions such as the third or the diminished fifth, the intervals of the theme being preserved by free use of chromaticism.[4] There is no magic about the fourth and fifth, nor, as some textbooks have seemed to imply, is their use part of some ancient and hallowed, but meaningless, fugal tradition; they are simply the obvious intervals for scalic, tonal and thematic unity, when these qualities are desired.

So far, then, all we possess towards a description of fugue is the idea of parts entering in turn with a definite theme in a more or less contrapuntal style. There is no indication that a fugue need be more than a merely temporary or incidental event in a larger piece. In general earlier writers do not seem to go beyond this concept; nor is there anything in music before about 1600 to suggest any other use of the term. This use, indeed, was never to become out of date, as is evidenced by the fact that we commonly refer, for example, to the Beethoven passage quoted in Example 1 above as 'the fugue in the last movement of the C minor Concerto'. Clearly, however, once granted the principle involved in such examples, it would be possible to write a complete and self-sufficient piece based upon it without the use of any further resource save the periodic entry of the theme in one or other of the existing, and/or possibly in new, parts. In the case of the Beethoven example, for instance, we could forget all about the rest of the concerto and begin at the beginning of Beethoven's fugue, taking our tonic as F minor: after Beethoven's fourth entry we could continue in more or less contrapuntal vein for a bar or two and then introduce further entries of the theme, keeping to the original two positions (i.e. beginning C–D♭ or G–A♭)[5] but employing a different order of part-entries and/or a different disposition of parts accompanying the theme, and perhaps a different octave for some of the entries. After the last entry a short continuation could lead to a definite cadence in F minor. Example 5 shows a possible version. What we have here is in fact a short complete fugue which constitutes a piece in its own right, instead of, as in the original, a mere section of a much larger movement. For a piece to be regarded as a complete fugue we need require, additionally to what has already been stipulated, only that in a basically contrapuntal style the theme heard at the outset—or at the very least

4. A good example occurs in Bartók's Fifth String Quartet: in the fugue beginning at bar 368 of the last movement the entries begin on E♮ and B♭, i.e. they are at the augmented fourth or diminished fifth to each other (see bars 380, second violin; 390, first violin; 400, cello). Bartók is here almost certainly influenced by the dual tonality of the whole quartet, in which the tonic B♭ (the note on which the whole work begins and ends) is constantly being challenged by E♮, which later occurs actually in the main theme at bar 5. The theme of the fugue is derived directly from the main theme, and it too stresses both notes (see the A♯ at 374, E♮ at 384, etc.).

5. For the change of initial G into F in the fourth entry see Chapter 2, p. 89.

a recognisable part of that theme—shall continue to make its appearance regularly enough for it not to be forgotten by the listener. If these conditions are not fulfilled the essentially *thematic* character of fugue is of course lost and to give the whole of such a piece—as opposed to its opening procedure only—the title 'fugue' is unhelpful, although it is not entirely unknown. The fugue as a complete piece seems to have evolved towards the end of the sixteenth century, and from this time onward the two different types—we may call them the 'complete fugue' and the 'incidental fugue'—run concurrently through musical history, although the complete type was not to become really common until the latter part of the seventeenth century.

As always when types of composition are distinguished one from the other it becomes necessary to take into account a continuum of grades by which the one type is seen gradually to merge into the other. At the extreme of 'completeness' is the (surprisingly rare) separate fugue with no prelude or succeeding movement of any kind. One or two of Bach's organ fugues are of this type, but even here it is not unlikely that he intended such pieces to be preceded by a prelude, but had simply not got around to writing or allocating suitable preludes for them. At the other extreme we have examples such as the Beethoven one already discussed, where there are only three or four entries of the theme and virtually no continuation in fugal style: such cases are sometimes referred to as 'fugal expositions' since the passage consists of what in a complete fugue would conveniently be called the 'exposition' —the opening section in which the parts enter in turn;[6] but this is a little misleading in that the use of the term 'exposition' tends to presume the existence of a complete fugue. The normal 'prelude and fugue' as exemplified by Bach's '48', and other similar types such as 'toccata and fugue', 'fantasia and fugue', and so forth, show the coupling of fugue with a single piece of different character, both pieces being however complete in themselves. A step nearer towards the incidental fugue is evident when, as occasionally happens, the prelude ends on an inconclusive chord, thus leading more directly into the fugue:[7] also, when by way of conclusion to the fugue a return is made to the more decorative writing characteristic of the prelude: this latter occurs in the well-known Bach 'toccata and fugue' in D minor already mentioned, which Bach actually entitled simply 'Toccata', it being understood in the later seventeenth and early eighteenth century that a toccata might contain fugal sections. Still nearer to incidental fugue are the fugal sections of many pre-Bach toccatas, which usually contain

6. See Chapter 2, p. 31.

7. As, for instance, in the fairly well-known Bach organ Prelude and Fugue in C minor BWV 537.

Ex 5

Entry in Tenor
tr
Incomplete
entry, bass
tr

two or more such sections (either on different themes or on variants of the same theme) alternated with non-fugal decorative material. In general the further one goes back before Bach in the history of the toccata, the greater is the tendency towards many short sections rather than few long ones: thus in the toccatas of Froberger (1616–67) the fugues are more 'incidental' than in those of Buxtehude (1637–1707).[8] In vocal work the incidental fugue retained throughout the Baroque period the pride of place which in instrumental music it tended gradually to surrender: in the cantatas and masses of Bach, in fact, can be found fugues of all conceivable grades on the continuum between incidental and complete. In the classic period, with the decline in contrapuntal writing, instrumental music was again to adopt the incidental fugue; we have already seen an example from Beethoven's C minor Piano Concerto, and there are many others in Beethoven's work (e.g. the one in the slow movement of the seventh symphony). Sometimes an incidental fugue may be used as one or more of the main subjects in a sonata-form movement, as in the last movements of Mozart's String Quartet in G, K.387, and Beethoven's in C, op. 59 no. 3. The last movement of Mozart's 'Jupiter' symphony is another, and more famous, example. Once the distinction between incidental fugue and complete fugue is appreciated, the supposedly miraculous nature of this 'fusion of fugue with sonata-form', spoken of with such awe by many writers, particularly when speaking of the 'Jupiter', is seen in fact to be a perfectly reasonable and natural procedure. The 'Jupiter' is indeed great music, but not because of this.[9]

Academic teaching has for long concerned itself mainly with the complete fugue, though in musicological work it is not unknown for the incidental type to be treated also; but the greatest musical, as opposed to musicological, interest must inevitably tend to attach to the complete type, since here we have to deal with the unified form of a piece standing in its own right: constructional problems clearly have their main application here rather than in the incidental fugue. It will thus be with complete fugue that the present book, designed for the intelligent listener rather than for the musicologist, will properly concern itself, although, since every complete fugue begins like an incidental fugue, only the type of continuation distinguishing the two, the procedures of the incidental type must also receive some mention. One

8. As was the case with the Bach D minor toccata, the Buxtehude toccatas are designated in modern editions with the double title 'Prelude and Fugue': Buxtehude apparently used the single title 'Präludium'.

9. The researches of Warren Kirkendale, *Fugue und Fugato in der Kammermusik des Rokoko und der Klassik*, have revealed numberless uses of fugue in the rococo and classic periods which parallel the Mozart and Beethoven instances just quoted.

important fact has already emerged from the present preliminary discussion—the fact that the *fugue is not a form*. This statement, so commonly heard since Tovey, does however need further clarification, as it can easily be misleading, and indeed misled Tovey himself. What it means is that to say that a piece is a fugue is not to make, except in certain very general ways, any prescription about what the form of the piece will be. In this the word 'fugue' differs from the word 'sonata' or 'symphony' in their classic-period sense, since these terms do make more precise prescriptions about the form of the pieces to which they refer. It is of great importance to realise, however, that when we say 'fugue is not a form' we do not mean 'fugues do not have forms'. The forms of the complete fugues are admittedly not 'forms' in quite the academically conventional sense, and it is perfectly true that in some cases it is barely possible to speak of a form at all; but the construction of the complete fugue constitutes none the less one of the most fascinating fields of study, and it is in the work of Bach that the enormous formal possibilities of this type of fugue are most thoroughly explored. The confusion between the two statements about fugue is the greatest weakness in Tovey's constant insistence that 'fugue is a texture': it has already been seen that texture is to a certain extent an attribute of fugue, but to pretend that there is no more to it than that is to ignore the structure of the complete fugue altogether, to say nothing of the essentially thematic nature even of incidental fugue.

So much, then, for preliminaries. It is already beginning to become clear that in approaching fugue we shall have to discard, or at least alter, many of the conventional ideas about form and about musical 'rules' in general, upon which so many of us have been educated. In the succeeding chapters, and particularly in the final one in which the relationship of academic to live fugal practice is examined, it is hoped to show in more detail how many of the confusions about the nature of fugue and its forms and features have arisen—how, as has already been briefly suggested, some of them were due to an anachronistic outlook on the part of writers steeped in later styles (most commonly that of the classic period) while others came into being because of the need to simplify matters for the student, an originally purely academic rule coming later to be falsely regarded as a fundamental principle of art. Today, with the great revival of interest in Baroque music, and with the enormous widening of the stylistic bounds of our appreciation consequent both upon developments in modern music and upon vastly increased knowledge of the remoter musical past, we are in a far better position to understand and appreciate fugal writing than were the listeners, and for that matter even the theorists, of the nineteenth and early twentieth century. Here, perhaps, a word may be said on behalf of those earlier theorists, with many of whose views the following pages must inevitably disagree. They were not stupid men, pedants who delighted in taking inspired composers to task for breaking their petty rules: nothing could be sillier than the tendency on the part of certain recent writers to paint such a picture of them. True, there are many weaknesses and even inconsistencies in their work, but in general it constituted a serious attempt to teach fugue to students whose whole background and requirements of technique were stylistically alien to the true fugal idiom. If their writings are accepted in this spirit instead of being tossed aside as useless nonsense much can be learnt from them: Kitson's 'Bach seems to have confused the issue', for instance, can lead the perceptive student straight to the heart of one of the problems of fugal answer by showing an aspect of Bach's procedure which clearly did not tally with later ideas, and the ink spent on deriding Kitson as a pedant could have been more profitably used in pursuing this line of approach and finding out *why* an early twentieth-century theorist should find himself in disagreement with the procedures of an eighteenth-century composer. And, after all, the spirit of unbiassed enquiry was by no means absent even in what it has become fashionable to regard as the bad old days of nineteenth-century theory. The following words were written not in 1971 but in 1891:

> The farther [the author's] researches extended, the deeper became his conviction of the necessity of placing the laws of fugal construction on an altogether different basis from that hitherto adopted. The results of his investigations will be found in the following pages. In the words of the Psalmist, he may say, 'I believed, therefore have I spoken'. A great deal to be found in this book will probably horrify old-fashioned musical conservatives; but not a single new rule is propounded for which warrant is not given from the works of the great composers; and if he shrank from the logical consequences of the examination of these works, the author would be untrue to his own convictions.

This excerpt is taken from the work of another theorist who has come in for his fair share of derision—derision which in this case arises from simple ignorance of his work: for Ebenezer Prout's *Fugue*[10] remains, after eighty years, still the most enlightened book on fugue ever written in English, and probably in any language. The aims of the present book are far more limited than were those of Prout: but if it can be said to recapture at all the spirit in which the older volume was written, and to apply that spirit to the vastly increased knowledge available to the present-day writer on the subject, it will have more than achieved its purpose.

10. The excerpt is taken from the Preface, p. iv.

2

FUGAL EXPOSITION

It has already been suggested that it is the opening procedure, in which the parts enter in turn, that gives fugue its most readily noticeable characteristic. It has also been mentioned that large numbers of fugues can be called 'incidental fugues' in that they consist of a fugal 'opening' with a non-fugal continuation. It is thus worth devoting a chapter purely to the opening procedures, which are, of course, also of vital importance in the 'complete fugue'.

Conventionally the opening section is called the 'Exposition'. Academically, the exposition is supposed to comprise the section in which all the parts enter in turn with the theme, these entries employing only the permitted positions of subject and answer as already described, and employing them in strict alternation—subject–answer–subject–answer, etc. Such a definition is too narrow for the understanding of fugue as live composition. In real life a part may enter with the theme but may not follow the strict subject–answer sequence: the fugue may not be in any definite number of parts: an entry may occur in an already existing part but may nevertheless follow the subject–answer pattern and may be musically inseparable from the 'official' exposition: conversely, the first entry of a part may occur after a substantial break and thus be musically separate from the opening entries; an entry may give the impression of a new part without actually adding to the number of parts present: and so forth, all these being possibilities actually found in fugue as live composition.[11] It will be more helpful, then, if

11. On indefiniteness of the number of parts see below, p. 90. All the other possibilities can, conveniently enough, be seen in WTC I: if the reader examines the openings of I.1, 5, 12, 14, 19 & 21 he will notice the supposedly 'exceptional' features, which can also be found in many pre-Bach fugues. It is rather amusing to find scholars (Hermann Keller and Brandts Buys, for instance) interpreting the

we say that the exposition of a fugue is 'the opening set of entries in which the theme is first propounded'. In a majority of cases, particularly in the 'classical' period of fugal writing, we may say in addition that the exposition 'will be essentially tonic in tonality', since all tonal music is based upon the principle of a key established at the outset and reaffirmed at the end.

Many incidental fugues, as has been remarked, consist entirely of exposition. Nor is this necessarily true only of incidental fugue: a complete fugue may continue throughout its duration to deliver the subject and answer in primarily tonic tonality without any noticeable break, and in such a case it is, of course, meaningless to speak of an 'exposition section'. The use of the term 'exposition' presupposes some kind of 'working-out', some use of resources other than that of the entry of subject and answer in their original positions. It will be the purpose of Chapter 4 to try to give some account of these 'working-out' resources. Meanwhile we may note that a fugue can still be a true 'complete fugue' and yet make use of no resource except counterpoint and the entry of the theme from time to time, nor need we waste our time, with such examples, desperately trying to decide 'where the exposition ends'.

The features of the exposition may be most conveniently discussed in the order in which they are most commonly heard.

The Subject

In fugue the first thing to be heard is the theme, or 'subject' as it is usually called in English terminology.[12] In a majority of cases the initial announcement of the subject is unaccompanied; in fugues occurring during the course of a movement it is indeed the cessation of everything but the one part that makes the knowledgeable listener predict that a fugue has begun—although he may not always be right in this prediction. Moreover, it has already been seen that the subject, even in its initial announcement, may be accompanied by harmonies, the accompanying material varying from a single continuo part to full

subject–answer–answer–subject exposition of WTC I.1, as Bach defying the fusty old rules and showing at the very outset of his collection that he was going to do just what he liked. Such a Beethovenish attitude had no place in the Baroque, and had either of these writers examined pre-Bach fugues or read Fux, they would have seen that in fact Bach was merely following one of the possible procedures of his day.

12. English terminology unfortunately uses 'subject' to mean both the theme of the fugue in general, and also 'subject' as opposed to 'answer' when discussing the opening entries and similar occurrences later in the fugue. Little can be done about this except to clarify what is meant as far as possible. German terminology makes things clearer by using 'Thema' for the subject generally, and 'Führer' and 'Gefährte' for subject and answer respectively in the second sense.

orchestral and/or choral chords. Such accompaniment used to be called 'free', the idea being that fugue must necessarily be in a specific number of parts each delivering the subject at its first entry. Again, in some fugues two or occasionally more themes are delivered together at the outset, and it was conventional to term such a fugue a 'double (or triple, etc.) fugue' and to speak of the fugue as 'having two (or three, etc.) subjects'. In fact such a definition is not helpful, for there is always one theme which stands out, on grounds of strength of melodic characteristics, as being the main theme to which the others are subordinate, and it is much better for this to be known as the subject. It is true that the other themes may be heard very frequently during the course of the fugue—even perhaps more frequently than the subject, in that they may be employed in development—but they do not usurp the function of the subject as the dominating main theme. Moreover such later prominence given to subsidiary themes does not only occur when these other themes appear at the very first entry; themes which first appear against the second or even later entries can take an equally prominent part in the development of the fugue, yet conventional terminology does not call them subjects but countersubjects. The latter word is best applied to all such themes, whether or not they accompany the initial entry.

Fugue, as we now know it, originated from three types of composition which flourished in the late Renaissance and early Baroque periods. In each type there would be a series of entries of parts, each entering with a 'point'. A 'point', or 'point of imitation', is simply a phrase of a few notes which would be the same in all the parts. The three types of composition are: (a) the sixteenth-century motet; (b) the sixteenth-century French chanson; (c) the seventeenth-century keyboard toccata.

(a) A large number of sixteenth-century motets may be called 'fugal' in that they use the procedure of voices entering in turn with a 'point'. In the cases most relevant to fugue there is a succession of 'points' each associated with a given phrase of the words. No 'point' ever enters with words other than those with which it is first associated. The construction of the whole is thus effectively a succession of what in Chapter 1 we called 'incidental fugues', each dovetailed into its successor. One of the most perfect examples is quoted in full by R. O. Morris in his *Contrapuntal Technique in the Sixteenth Century*.[13] It is the four-part motet 'Veni, sponsa Christi' by Palestrina (see Example 6).

The kind of fugue that originated from this type of motet was known as 'Ricercar' or 'Fantasia', and examples for keyboard instrument appeared in the latter part of the sixteenth and early seventeenth

13. Morris's musical examples, no. 192.

Ex6 Palestrina, motet 'Veni, sponsa Christi': opening

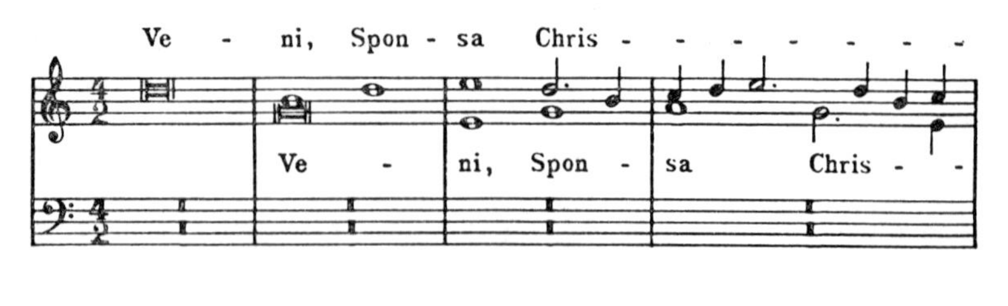

century. The word 'ricercar' literally means 'searching out' (i.e. learned) and 'fantasia', of course, ought to mean a piece in which the composer indulges his fancy. Neither of these two meanings must be taken too seriously: composers are notoriously vague in choosing titles for their compositions, and whereas ricercars are indeed sometimes 'learned' fugues, employing devices of various kinds, they need not be, and there is nothing particularly 'free' about a fantasia. 'Ricercar' can also mean a set of variations, and even as early as Andrea Gabrieli (1510–86) we find a canzona (see immediately below) entitled 'ricercar'. Later on in the seventeenth century Purcell called his polyphonic pieces for viols 'fantazias' whether or not they were in a motet-like style—indeed most of them show a mixture of styles, as would be expected of a somewhat later period in the development of fugue. In general the Italians use the term 'ricercar' while English composers prefer 'fantasia' (or 'fancy' in English). Both terms appear in Germany.

The ricercar and fantasia were, as would be expected, slow and solemn, with a strong tendency towards strict polyphony—as already

Ex7(a)Erbach, *Ricercar I Toni*
(b)Andrea Gabrieli, ricercar
(c)Sweelinck, fantasia
(d)Orlando Gibbons, *Fantazia of Foure Parts* (Schirmer, Early Keyboard Music, vol. I p. 46)

seen, not a *necessary* requirement for fugue. Some typical openings are given in Example 7. The Gibbons piece is typical of English fantasias in that it is built almost entirely on motet principles, a succession of 'points' being heard in turn. German and Italian composers, however, soon adopted the idea of a single theme being heard throughout the piece in various guises, as will be seen in Chapter 4.

(b) The French chanson was a popular type in the fifteenth and sixteenth centuries. It was essentially secular and thus gave rise not to slow and solemn openings of the motet type but to something much faster and more dance-like. The polyphony was much vaguer and less strict than in the motet—indeed homophonic passages were common.

The type of fugue to which the chanson gave origin was called 'canzona' (the Italian for 'chanson') or 'capriccio' (which, like the earlier terms, must not be taken literally as meaning that the composer writes according to his own caprice). These inherited the dance-like rhythms and the lack of strict polyphony characteristic of the chanson. Some typical openings are given in Example 8.

(c) The toccata arose originally from keyboard extemporisation of a more or less brilliant kind. Earlier examples, particularly of English composers, who call it 'preludium', consist of little more than brilliant scalic passages based upon simple chord sequences. Examples for organ often used long-held pedal notes against which the manuals have brilliant passages. German composers, however, soon inserted fugal passages into the toccata in order to avoid the continuous bravura style of the earlier examples. Such fugal passages might be based upon ricercar or canzona type themes, but in other cases a bit of the bravura material might itself be made into a 'point', thus giving rise to a type of theme in continuous quick movement with little or no rhythmic interest often involving arpeggiated harmonies. Two instances are given in Example 9.

Chapter 1 asked 'What is fugue?', and it might here be asked 'What is a fugue subject?'. The sixteenth-century 'point' is usually little more than a formula, and is often imitated so closely at its first appearance—the 'Veni, sponsa Christi' motet is a typical case—that it is hardly the readily recognisable theme required for true fugue. The borderline here is, of course, indefinite, and some pieces actually entitled 'fugue' even as late as Bach have themes which are only just within the category of true subjects rather than 'points' (WTC II.3 is rather near the mark). On the other hand a true subject need not be in any way striking or original—Prout's demand (*Fugue*, ch. II, §54) for 'good striking melody' betrays a nineteenth-century attitude, though to do him justice, Prout is one of the few writers to point out (ibid., §50) the unsuitability for fugue of 'many beautiful melodies'. Many ricercar and ricercar-type subjects are not only shared by a number of composers but are little more than melodic formulas (WTC II.9, for instance, mentioned under 'Answer' below and in Chapter 4).

As the Baroque period progressed all three types of subject tend to become longer and generally more prominent. With greater length comes also the tendency for the subject to end with a definite cadence to which the whole latter part of the theme leads in a strong progression (a point, incidentally, of much importance in considering the Answer). The cadence is, however, by no means an obligatory feature, even as late as Bach, or for that matter even later, and even when a

Ex 8 (a) Gombert, chanson 'Hors, ennuieux!': opening
(b) Maschera, canzona for instruments (HAM I 175)
(c) Frescobaldi, *Canzona quarti toni dopo il postcommunio* (*Fiori Musicali* Peters 4514 no.35)
(d) Froberger, Capriccio IX (DTÖ Jahrgang, X/2, Band 2)

Ex 9 (a) Froberger, Toccata VII, bars 3–033 (DTÖ Jahrgang IV/I Band 8)
(b) Froberger, Toccata I, bars 18–23 (ibid.)

cadential progression is present there may be no perceptible break in the contrapuntal flow. Another development is that one type of subject begins to influence another, and there are also influences from other sources, e.g. the dance suite. Towards the late Baroque, for instance, a number of gigue-type subjects appear (see Example 32). Gigue-like variants of ricercar or canzona themes had already been used in the final sections of these pieces, and actual named gigues in the suites quite often, by the late Baroque, had fugal openings to each of the two sections of the binary form. At this stage in the history of fugue two matters—tonality and chromaticism—acquire considerable importance in the design of the subject and it may be as well to mention them here in some detail.

Tonality

As the Baroque style emerged out of that of the sixteenth-century tonality generally grew in importance. The full definition of tonality could well occupy the rest of the present book, but in dealing with fugue it is necessary that we should be clear about certain aspects. Basically the idea of tonality is surely the domination of one note over others. In most conventionally tonal pieces this domination is shown by the fact that the note concerned, usually reinforced by the chord of which it is the root, appears conspicuously both at the beginning and end and at many points during the piece. Tonality is assisted by prominence given to the nearest acoustic relation of the note concerned—the note (and, of course, in conventional tonality its chord) a fifth above (fourth below), namely the dominant. In that a diatonic scale is clear and a chromatic progression confusing to the ear[14] the use of diatonic scale is also of assistance to tonality, though it should be stressed that neither of these last two requirements is in any way *essential* to it. Stress upon the one note is the *sine qua non*—a point of considerable importance in much chromatic music, both Baroque and modern. It will be noted that this definition is rather different from the conventional 'one sharp means G major' idea. There are, of course, very good reasons why in a particular style one sharp often does mean G major—the diatonic scale and the major chords on tonic and dominant obviously point this way—but it will not do for fugue, and has in fact caused a lot of confusion in dealing with certain fugal features.

If it is agreed that tonality is the domination of one note it can

14. Despite modern developments this is probably a matter of common aural experience to the true naïve listener (to use Tovey's phrase). See also the present writer's 'The Nature of Chromaticism' in *Music Review*, May and November 1963.

clearly exist in melody without harmony. The idea of *melodic tonality* is essential to the understanding of the fugue subject—particularly, but by no means exclusively, that of the Baroque. In most live as opposed to academic fugue, indeed, the initial announcement of the subject, normally completely unaccompanied, none the less has a definite tonality—a melodic tonality which it retains whatever 'harmonisations' it may later be given. It will be seen (Chapter 4) that in later entries this melodic tonality, while it may agree with the prevailing harmonic tonality, may also to a greater or lesser extent oppose it.

As the Baroque period progressed, then, the subject gradually acquires melodic tonality by stress on the tonic and dominant notes. In particular, the first note of the theme itself is very commonly either i or v. By Bach's time this is virtually a rule except where the fugue begins during the course of a movement or follows a movement ending in some key other than the tonic, or is accompanied. If the subject ends with a cadence, this will commonly be on i or v, although there is less strictness here, weaker cadences or iii or even some other note (vi, vii) being found. The cadence, important though it was, does not seem to hold for the Baroque the degree of importance it acquired in academic fugue. After all, any tonal ambiguity at the cadence will soon be redressed by the entry of the answer, whose first note again was governed by strict rule, as will be seen.

A well-known problem in academic fugue has its origins in a type of Baroque subject which in ending on the dominant note actually digresses to the dominant key. The term 'digression' here (and hereafter) is used for a use of the scale of a key without any feeling of a genuine shift of tonality. The academic term is, of course, 'modulating subject' —a most misleading description in that the whole point of a v ending is to help in setting up the *tonic* key (see Example 10).

Ex 10 Buxtehude, *Präludium, Fuge und Ciacona:* fugue subject

One further tonal feature, particularly common in Bach's choral works, may be noted here—the subject which begins in a melodic tonality of the dominant. These cases occur when the fugue follows upon a cadence in or on the dominant (in one exceptional case in Bach, the final fugue of Cantata 68, the previous movement is in the relative of the dominant, C major from D minor). Under the influence of the dominant chord, the opening melodic tonality itself becomes dominant, the subject then either remaining in the dominant throughout or ending in the tonic. Well-known examples of the latter are 'Cum sancto Spiritu' in the Mass in B minor and both fugues ('Let Zion's children' and 'All breathing life') in the motet 'Sing ye to the Lord'. The former is less common, but may be seen in the fugue in the overture of the D major Partita for clavier—incidentally a rare case of an unaccompanied subject opening on the mediant of the dominant (vii of the tonic scale). (See Example 11 for the more common procedure.)

Ex 11 Bach, *Ouverture* ('orchestral suite') no.3 in D, overture: fugue subject

Chromaticism

The chromatic subject is another typical product of the Baroque. Chromaticism was, of course, employed in the Renaissance in madrigals, although the motet style—particularly that of Palestrina—limited its use considerably, and a chromatic 'point' in a motet would be a considerable rarity. In considering the chromatic subject another slight digression into musical theory is necessary. Conventional theory lumps together the major and minor scales as 'the diatonic scale system'. In fact the minor scale cannot properly be called diatonic at all. If diatonic is to mean anything at all useful it must mean the series of notes found (by transposition if necessary of course) on the white keys of the piano—the series of intervals which the ear finds clear and unambiguous. The sharp seventh degree (vii♯) of the minor scale breaks this series—it is, whether we like it or not, a non-diatonic note. It is not too far-fetched to trace all chromaticism—not only in the Baroque but generally—from this one note. The confusion of the ear characteristic of chromaticism exists whenever the vii♯ is brought into close contact with either iii, vi or vii♮. Such relationships were, of course, the very ones that were kept in the background in the old polyphonic style. It was the Baroque style which brought them out and used them deliberately, often for word painting; the diminished seventh leap from vi to lower vii♯ becoming a particular favourite toward the late Baroque, and after. ('And with His stripes' in *Messiah* and WTC II.20 are well-known instances.) Our clumsy listing of the minor as a 'diatonic' scale covers up the genuine chromatic effect of these juxtapositions, seen nowhere more conspicuously than in the initial unaccompanied announcement of a fugue subject.

Not satisfied with these resources the Baroque also employed vi♯ for chromatic purposes. This was basically a note from the Dorian mode, and retained in order to approach vii♯ in what we now call the 'melodic minor scale'—i.e. it originally served the exactly opposite purpose to that now under discussion. vi♯ would now be juxtaposed to vi♮, and together with vii♯ and vii♮ a complete chromatic scale from i to lower v now becomes possible. (It is typical of our muddled use of terms that we call this a 'chromatic' progression despite the fact that all the notes used are in the minor scale!) Imitation of this chromatic scale progression at the upper fifth (lower fourth) soon produced the genuinely chromatic notes iii♯ and iv♯. As if this were not enough the note ii♭, retained from the Phrygian mode, would also be used sometimes in imitating the chromatic figure at the lower fifth (upper fourth) and also for its own sake in juxtaposition to, for instance, vii♯. This array of chromatic notes meant that the minor was employing nothing less than all twelve notes of the chromatic scale—a development of obviously epoch-making significance, although contemporary composers can hardly have realised its ultimate effects! All these developments can be seen in the Baroque fugue subject, as the examples show (see Example 12). As would be expected, the vast majority of chromatic subjects—and indeed chromatic themes generally—of this period are in the minor. There are occasional examples of chromatic major-key subjects, and in Bach two instances of major-key countersubjects, one of them caused by word-painting, but in such cases the chromatic notes used are only those that belong to the minor of the same tonic, so that in fact the major can be said to be 'borrowing' from its own minor (this applies to all chromaticism in the Baroque, and indeed for some time afterwards). Up to Bach the chromatic notes used were limited to one function: e.g. E♭ in a piece in D would always function as E♭, not as D♯. With Bach however we find the beginnings of more remote chromaticism in two uses of v♭. Thus in Example 12(e), D♭ is added to the chromatic resources of G minor, resources which already include C♯. The word 'Elend' ('want') is effectively depicted.

It will no doubt be said that this last instance exemplifies a 'passing modulation to C minor' and one could follow here with a long dissertation on where modulation ends and chromaticism begins. The real point is again that the majority of supposed 'modulations' in unaccompanied and many (like this) in accompanied fugue subjects produce not the slightest feeling of change of key, and in cases like this one the foreign notes are much better described chromatically. Much better justice is done to the effect of the sudden D♭ in the subject quoted by calling the note v♭ than by saying that 'a modulation to C minor is effected by means of the neapolitan sixth of that key'—even if we admit the idea of a chord chromatic to both keys effecting a modulation!

By the late Baroque the variety and complexity of the subject had reached a level which seems incredible when one compares the rudimentary 'points' of the late Renaissance. It is of course in Bach that the greatest variety is found. Bach, admittedly, continued to write 'ricercar'

Ex 12(a) Sweelinck, *Fantasia Chromatica* for organ (GMB 158)
(b) Frescobaldi, *Ricercare Cromatico post il Credo* (Fiori Musicali, Peters 4514, no.31)
(c) Frescobaldi, *Ricercare dopo il Credo* (ibid. no.44)
(d) Froberger, Capriccio VIII (DTÖ Jahrgang IV/I Band 8)
(e) Bach, Cantata 39: first chorus, fugue beginning bar 45 (accompanimental parts omitted)

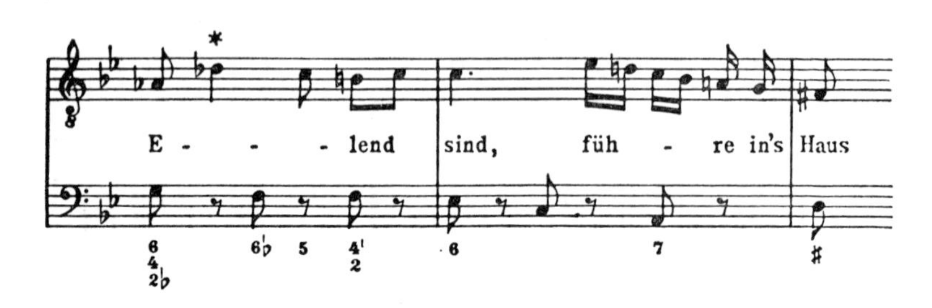

and 'toccata' subjects: he is, indeed, perhaps the last composer to write either of these types unadulterated by any other influence (see Example 13). There are also a number of 'quasi-ricercar' subjects in Bach—themes which while keeping to the slow unrhythmic movement of the true ricercar none the less show a more angular and characteristic melodic line, and are often longer. These are also popular with Handel,

Ex 13(a) Bach, WTC I.22
(b) Bach, organ fugue in A minor BWV 543

particularly in choral fugue. Despite the 'allegro moderato' marking —*how* 'moderato', one wonders—the subject of the 'Amen' chorus in *Messiah* is really one of this type—perhaps even nearer to a ricercar than some of Bach's examples (see Example 14). But it is in the subjects

Ex 14 Bach, WTC II.7

which derive from the canzona that Bach's greatest originality and subtlety of theme is shown. There are so many types even within this one category that justice cannot really be done to them here. Often more than one characteristic type of movement is used and the subject may thus consist of two phrases. Others develop a single rhythmic figure in one musical sentence, while yet others begin with a 'head' as it is sometimes called—a very short phrase followed by a rest—and then proceed to some further material (see Example 15). In general the

Ex 15 (a) Bach, WTC I.21
(b) Bach, WTC I.2
(c) Bach, WTC I.23

mature Bach themes are not of great length, nor leisurely in style. Leisureliness of style, as exemplified, for instance, in the subject of the fugue concluding the well-known C major organ Toccata BWV 564 'usually known as 'Toccata, Adagio and Fugue') is generally an indication of early Bach. Here the theme has four phrases all separated by rests, the final one ending with a digression to the dominant, this last also being an 'early' feature.

One very important feature of the mature Bach subject is its phrasing and rhythmical structure. This is always designed so that four-square phrasing is avoided and the theme will thus fit into the continuous style which is a particularly marked characteristic of the mature Bach fugue. The various ways in which rhythmic subtlety is achieved would again be a matter for a long dissertation; briefly the following devices can be mentioned:

(a) use of an absolutely irregular phrase (WTC I.8, II.14);
(b) omission of first beat and/or prolongation of cadence (both shown in WTC I.23);
(c) use of tied note(s) in the middle of the theme to destroy possible square accentuation (WTC I.1, I.14);
(d) the phrasing of the subject appears four-square at its first few entries, but as the fugue proceeds it becomes clear that the main accent occurs before the subject starts. (WTC I.2, last movement of concerto for two claviers in C major. In each case the initial effect is of a main accent on the third note of the theme, and a resultant four-square phrase. Gradually it becomes clear that this note is the second, not the first, beat of the bar, and the phrasing loses its apparent four-squareness.)

Bach's name has been coupled with these devices because his subjects show them most frequently and to best effect; but to some extent they are evident in the late Baroque generally. The really four-square subject is certainly a rarity in the late Baroque, although paradoxically one of the most extreme cases is by Bach—the subject of the fugue in the early keyboard Toccata in G, BWV 916.

In the classic style fugue subjects become more rigid and less subtle, particularly rhythmically, than in the Baroque. Some of the Baroque formulas survive, notably the diminished seventh (see Example 16)

Ex 16 Haydn, String Quartet in F minor, op.20 no.5: last movement, fugue subject

and occasionally the chromatic scale figure (see Example 17). To chromatic resource is added the sharpened auxiliary note (Mozart, Fugue for two pianos, K. 426). In choral fugue particularly, the subject seems to go through a very dull phase—though this is not to say that the fugues themselves are dull, though many are conventional. Generally speaking the designing of the fugue as a whole seems to become the main aim of the composer and the subject itself more of a

Ex 17 Mozart, String Quartet in D minor K. 173: last movement, fugue subject

brick from which a building is constructed than a feature of much character in itself. As will be seen, fugues in this period began to take on the 'exciting' character reflected in stereotyped form in the 'examination fugue' with its cumulative use of device, and this no doubt tended to a view of the subject as a mere part of a larger design. The 'ricercar' subject always had this function, but the classic themes do not share the ricercar subject's amenability to alteration and its ability to fit into the flow of the counterpoint.

With Beethoven the idea of a personally characteristic subject begins to be seen. On paper the subject of the opening fugue of the String Quartet, op. 131, looks like a ricercar type, but the string tone, the associations of the desolate key of C♯ minor and the *sforzando* on the note vi show a completely different emotional world from any Baroque fugue—this despite the interesting fact that this opening and to some extent the whole quartet are really in the Phrygian mode of C♯! The brilliant type of subject—vaguely, perhaps, the equivalent of the old toccata type—is seen in the finale of the 'Hammerklavier' sonata, op. 106, dramatically contrasted, it may be noted, with a subsidiary subject of utterly different character. Beethovenian humour comes into fugue (albeit incidental fugue, as part of a sonata form design), in the subject of the finale of the String Quartet in C, op. 59 no. 3. ('This subject is abnormally long and is not given for imitation' is the dire warning given by Kitson in *The Elements of Fugal Construction*, pp. 14–15.) The *Grosse Fugue* subject shows what would probably be called a 'passing modulation to the supertonic'—the use of the sharp note B♮ (from B♭). 'Modulation' or not, this is analogous to the generally increasing use of sharp notes in chromaticism as we proceed further away from the Baroque.

Towards the romantic period, it is also possible to see the gradual decline both in strong melodic tonality and in what may be called 'self-sufficiency' in the fugue-subject. We find Schumann for instance in a *separate* fugue in F minor (op. 72 no. 3) beginning the subject on B♭, the subdominant (see Example 18(a)). Even with a prelude this would be unthinkable in the Baroque: a subdominant first note would be used only when the fugue occurred during the course of a piece and started in temporary subdominant tonality. The effect of Schumann's opening, of course, is to give the impression that the fugue is in B♭ minor, the subject ending on what appears to be the dominant F. The fact that the answer ends on C certainly weakens the B♭ melodic tonality, but is insufficient to destroy it (in actual practice the ending of an answer on ii is not unknown, despite what 'the rules'

Ex 18(a) Schumann, Four Fugues for Pianoforte op.72: subject of no. 3 in F minor
(b) W. F. Bach, Fughetta in E♭

prescribe), and almost immediately the third entry makes its appearance, apparently confirming B♭. In fact it will probably be about ten bars before the listener is convinced that the tonic is F. This is where lack of melodic tonality helps to produce the lack of self-sufficiency just mentioned. However chromatic a Baroque subject may be, there is no doubt at the very outset—certainly by the first note of the answer—of what the key is: whereas to understand Schumann's opening we must *know in advance* that the key is F minor—the music is not of itself enough to tell us. Such lack of self-sufficiency can take other forms as well, e.g. the use of a progression whose whole point lies in the relation of the theme to a prevailing harmony. This can be seen as early as W. F. Bach, son of Sebastian (see Example 18b). The example shows notes which really only make sense either as appoggiaturas or with 'dominant seventh' type harmonies which lead directly to resolution on the appropriate chord (see the rest of the fugue). Another

Schumann example, the D minor, op. 72 no. 1, has similar progressions. Lack of self-sufficiency is at its worst, however, in academic fugue, and it is perhaps worth quoting one example here, if only to drive home the point at issue (see Example 19). Kitson's subject is intended here to be in G but in fact sounds—indeed is—in E minor in its initial entry.

Ex 19 Kitson, *Studies in Fugue*, p. 40

These tendencies have their parallel, of course, in music generally. There was a critic who insisted on speaking of 'Beethoven's Ninth Symphony—the one in A'. It sounds a silly remark, but to the true naïve listener there is until bar 15 not the slightest hint that the key will be anything but A. Even the crashing main theme at 16 (last note) does not destroy the feeling of A immediately, as can be tested by replacing bar 19 with a chord of A minor. Our judgement that the opening is 'on the dominant' is due to advance knowledge, just as is our judgement that Schumann is beginning his subject on the subdominant of F and not the tonic of B♭. Similar arguments apply to many well-known romantic works—Chopin's B♭ minor Piano Sonata and Rachmaninoff's Piano Concerto in C minor, to name only two. As for the lack of self-sufficiency in an opening unaccompanied theme, there is no better instance than Schubert's 'Great' C major symphony, whose opening sounds to the naïve listener like a curious modal A minor. Ironically all these features, both in and outside fugue, stem from increased academicism, the listener having to know in advance such things as the key of the piece, the likely 'implied' harmonies of an unaccompanied melody and so forth. It is paradoxical that in all these things Bach, whom the romantics regarded (and revered) as the most learned of all composers, is much more readily understandable to the ordinary listener than the fugues the romantics themselves produced.

Curiously enough there seems to be a lack of genuinely romantic (in spirit) fugue-subjects. This is presumably because composers who wrote fugues were on the whole those interested in the Baroque and particularly in Bach, by now regarded as a towering figure of the past.

Probably Schumann's subjects come as near to romanticism as any. Reger's themes are in many cases—e.g. op. 59 no. 6, op. 65 nos. 8 (compare Buxtehude F major Hansen 15) and 12 (that rarity, a post-Bach ricercar)—obviously modelled on the Baroque. The chromatic subjects are nearer to romanticism but even here the Baroque chromatic theme is a powerful influence (note, however, the opening notes ii♭ and vi, though in each case these are really 'appoggiatura' notes to i and v respectively. See Example 20). César Franck also shows, in

Ex 20(a) Reger, organ fugue in A minor op.65 no.6
(b) Reger, *Variations and Fugue on a Theme of Bach* for pianoforte, op.81

Prelude Chorale and Fugue for piano, a very Baroque-like chromatic subject, with the well-known chromatic scale figure descending from iv to lower v with omission of ii♭ and vi♯. The start on iv is again noteworthy, although here the fugue begins during the course of the piece, the subject being in fact the continuation of a figure which appeared over the final dominant pedal of the 'chorale' section. Exactly which note begins the subject is not clear to the listener until the answer has been heard, when it is evident that the three notes heard over the final V–I cadence of the 'chorale' section are the first three of the subject.

The modern subject has, as perhaps might be expected, returned to something much nearer to the Baroque idea of a theme with its own tonality and characteristics, self-sufficient in its initial entry and subsequently standing in its own right amongst and sometimes against other parts, rather than being dominated by and dependent upon harmonic progressions. Some themes are still very near to the Baroque in spirit, as for instance that of the fugue opening the second movement of Stravinsky's *Symphony of Psalms* (see Example 21). This at first hear-

Ex 21 Stravinsky, *Symphony of Psalms*, no.II: fugue subject

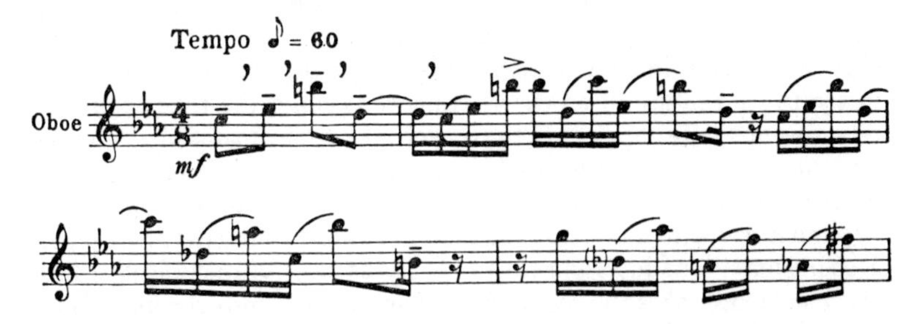

ing has a 'modern' sound, but it is in fact very much C minor: the unfamiliar sound is due only to the fact that Stravinsky goes from iii to *upper* vii♯, whereas a Baroque or classic composer would have gone down to the lower one (e.g. WTC I.4). Chromatic notes are D♭ and F♯, used, Baroque-like, as part of a chromatic scale figure in the arpeggiated two-part progression which is the basis of the theme. Yet again we are reminded of the highly complex and chromatic (in the true sense) nature of the minor scale. Bartók, in the fugue opening *Music for Strings, Percussion and Celeste* (see Example 22), deliberately

Ex 22 Bartók, *Music for Strings, Percussion and Celeste*: first movement, fugue subject

uses the chromatic progressions which are most confusing to the ear. His chromaticism certainly exceeds that of earlier periods, but the rhythmic subtlety of the theme shows a return to Bach's principle of the subject being rhythmically designed to fit into the continuous flow of the counterpoint. Despite the chromaticism the melodic tonality of A is maintained by the all-important first and last notes, and also by the first note of the second phrase. The next most conspicuous note is E♭, which foreshadows the tritone relationship of the main keys of the work, a favourite relationship with Bartók (see above, p. 24 (note 4) and below, pp. 129–30 and 173–4).

A feature seen in some modern subjects (as in much modern music generally) is the use of an exact sequence keeping the tone-semitone relationships of a figure strictly by means of chromaticism. A well-known example is perhaps the most 'catchy' fugue-subject ever written—that from the finale of Walton's Symphony no. 1 in B♭ minor. Walton starts with a more or less diatonic progression (the fourths are a characteristic of his style harmonically as well as melodically) but exact sequence takes the theme further and further into chromaticism, the melodic tonality however being maintained by a strongly tonal beginning and ending (see Example 23).

Ex 23 Walton, Symphony no. 1 in B♭ minor: last movement, fugue at figure 112

The two modern collections of fugues—Hindemith's 'Ludus Tonalis' and Shostakovitch's '24 Preludes and Fugues'—show completely differing attitudes to the fugue-subject. Hindemith is much nearer both to the modern idiom generally and to the Baroque. It must be remembered that unlike Bach and Shostakovitch, Hindemith does not distinguish major and minor—he writes a single fugue in each key. He uses no key-signature, and thus his themes often appear more chromatic than they are. Thus the subject of no. 1 in C is Phrygian apart from a quaver G♭ (see Example 24(a)), that of no. 4 in A is pure Phrygian, and those of nos. 9 in B♭ and 12 in F♯ are major with a flattened sixth degree (and later in the F♯ a flattened third: the subject here overlaps the answer). While the major scale with flat sixth is not a diatonic scale, its use is very common in the romantic period and even in the late Baroque it is not unknown, although it does not seem to find its way into fugue-subjects until later. Some of the other subjects are more chromatic than this (e.g. no. 5 in E, Example 24(b)), but only that of the B canonic fugue (no. 12) drastically so. All the subjects

Ex 24(a) Hindemith, LT 1 in C
(b) Hindemith, LT 5 in E

but one have a clear melodic tonality obtained by stress on tonic and in many cases dominant (nos. 1, 3, 5, 6, etc.) notes. Only the A fugue breaks this rule: its opening phrase is in F melodic tonality but the whole theme does end on A, and Hindemith brings the answer in at the third, not the classical fourth or fifth, so that its first note is E, confirming the A at the end of the subject. Hindemith's work, it must also be remembered, is intended for consecutive performance—the fugues are not separate pieces.

By comparison with Hindemith, Shostakovitch's themes seem very retrospective. Many are diatonic and carry melodic tonality to the extent almost of becoming static. The extreme case of this is the A major subject which consists of nothing but the notes of the A major chord! In other cases the static quality may perhaps relate to Russian folksong, as in nos. 10 in C♯ minor, 20 in C minor, 24 in D minor and, despite its rhythmic complexity and profuse decoration, no 16 in B♭ minor (see

Example 25(a)). A subtlety in no. 21 in B♭ is a prominence of G melodic tonality in the third bar, which leads the composer to bring in the answer on G—as with Hindemith, the classical answer rules (see below) are broken only rarely, and for an obvious reason. Only three of the subjects are chromatic. No. 8 in F♯ minor introduces E♭ (true E♭, not enharmonic notation for D♯) as 'appoggiatura' to D: this theme also is very static and perhaps the most Russian of them all.

Ex25(a)Shostakovitch, 24 no.16 in B♭ minor
(b)Shostakovitch, 24 no.15 in D♭ major

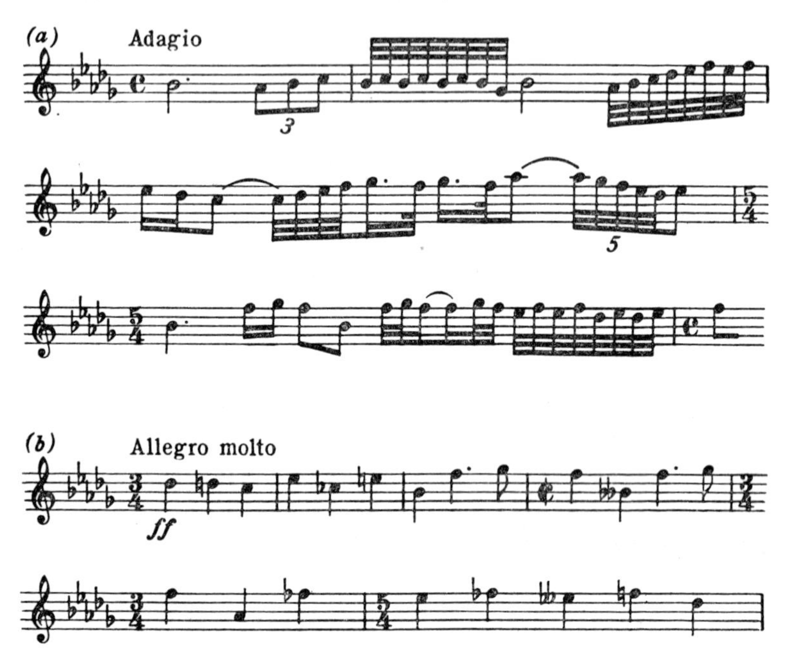

No. 19 in E♭ uses ii♭ and iii♭ (Phrygian mode borrowings, but ii♭ is deliberately juxtaposed to iii♮ and vi♮ to give a fairly strong chromaticism). The most chromatic example is no. 15 in D♭ (see Example 25(b)), a kind of 'Wedge' theme based on two chromatic scale progressions outwards from the tonic. Owing to the opening and ending on i and the fact that the lower chromatic scale figure ends on v, the melodic tonality is quite strong. The opening paragraph of the Preface (by Irwin Freundlich) is thus wide of the mark in speaking of 'atonal tendencies' here: there are no more 'atonal tendencies' than in any strong chromaticism. As so often, commentaries ignore the all-important melodic tonality.[15]

The Countersubject will be discussed below, since in the majority of fugues it makes its first appearance in accompaniment to the First Answer.

Codetta after the initial Subject entry

The name 'codetta' is one of the silliest in conventional fugal theory. By analogy with sonata form it tends to suggest some kind of cadence. A codetta in fugue is the opposite of a cadence—it is a link connecting two entries in the exposition. Such a link is occasionally found between what is obviously the end of the subject (marked by a clear cadence in such cases) and the counterpoint accompanying the answer (see Example 26). In fact, however, a codetta at this point is much less

Ex26 Bach, WTC I.7

common in live than in academic fugue. Almost certainly the reason lies in the academic theory (see below) of the answer being 'in the dominant key', which led to the idea of some kind of link being desirable to bridge the (supposed) gap between the two keys. Such 'modulatory' codettas are even rarer in live fugue—indeed some academic examples give an unfortunate effect of discontinuity at the very point where the relation between two entries is by tradition very close indeed. The 'just wait a minute while I get into the dominant' effect of these is sometimes unintentionally comic. Even Bach produced one example in that rather enigmatic work, the *Art of Fugue* (Contrapunctus VIII). Paradoxically the Bach instance illustrated above occurs in the one case where in academic fugue it would be unnecessary: if the subject 'modulates from tonic to dominant' the answer should 'modulate from dominant back to tonic'.

Codettas at this point are rarely of thematic importance in the fugue as a whole. The example quoted is an exception—it features in several of the episodes.

15. See the Leeds Music Corporation edition of the 24 and also Chapter 4, p. 173

The First Answer

The answer, as has been stated, is an entry of the theme at the fourth or fifth to the initial entry: in a large majority of cases the first answer will be the second entry, but occasionally (as in the Haydn example in Chapter 1 for instance) it will be the third, and even more rarely the fourth one.[16]

This first answer needs a somewhat lengthy treatment in relation to its importance, for the reasons already given in Chapter 1. The difficulties of answer-procedure are often supposed to be due to the complications of 'the rules': in point of fact, however, 'the rules' are drastically simple, and they have already been mentioned in Chapter 1. They may conveniently be given here in the order in which, historically speaking, obedience to them became general practice:

Rule 1: the answer will preserve the tone and semitone steps of the theme within the tonic scale. (Purpose: thematic and scalic unity at the outset of the fugue.)

Rule 2: the answer will give tonic note in reply to dominant note and vice versa. (Purpose: clear tonality at the outset of the fugue.)

Rule 1 can really be divided into two parts: (a) the preserving of the tone and semitone steps (thematic unity); (b) the preserving of the tonic scale (scalic unity). This division will help to make clear some of the difficulties which arise.

With regard to Rule 2, the question of key at this stage in the fugue still refers, as it did in considering the subject, to *melodic* tonality, not to the more conventional idea of harmonic tonality, and even less to scale. Nowhere more than in considering answer-procedure can confusion between tonality and scale create difficulties.

First a few words about 'the exceptions'. When a composer chooses not to follow a common procedure this will mean one of two things. Most probably it will mean that the end to which the procedure was designed was not desired by the composer: thus if he gives an answer which deliberately alters the theme unnecessarily, he will sacrifice a degree of thematic unity at the outset of the fugue, and if he unnecessarily introduces a foreign note, he obviously does not want complete unity of scale—and so forth. Alternatively, and more rarely, the breakage of a rule might mean that the composer had not understood its purpose, and either thought its obedience did not matter, or was deliberately disobeying it because he thought it stupid or unnecessary.

16. One can, of course, talk of an 'octave answer' if the second part enters at the octave (or compound) to the first; but it is probably more convenient to reserve the term 'answer' for an entry at the fourth or fifth.

This latter type of disobedience is, of course, likely to be a feature of a period when the type of composition was no longer a natural means of expression and when its rules had become purely academic. It also might be said to be symptomatic of a lesser composer, or of a weakness in a great composer, since the appreciation of the point involved depends upon academic knowledge, and it is thus not evident to the true naïve listener. In the case of fugue this kind of attitude applies mainly to Beethoven and the early romantic period. As far as the results of disobeying the rules of answer are concerned it may be said that (a) tonal and scalic unity at the outset are in no way essential to fugue: they are, certainly, features which are exceedingly common in all fugue, and are of course the mainstay of 'classical' fugal procedure: but their absence cannot cause exclusion from the category of true fugue; (b) thematic unity *is* essential, but there are degrees of it. Some fairly substantial alterations in the answer can be made without making the theme unrecognisable. And in the last resort recognisability, as has been seen, is the essential criterion of fugue.

Let this section on the answer be itself an exception to a general rule in that it begins with some examples of exceptions instead of dragging them in rather apologetically at the end. These may themselves help to make clear how the rules work (see Example 27).

Finally on the matter of exceptions it should perhaps be made clear that many of the examples quoted in textbooks as 'exceptional' are listed in this category only because of misunderstanding of the rules. You can, of course, prove anything to be exceptional by designing the rules in such a way as to exclude it. Many such examples turn out to be instances either of answer at the lower fifth/upper fourth (the so-called 'subdominant' answers, mentioned below) or of alterations to the tone and semitone steps of the theme in order to preserve the tonic scale. Of the eight 'exceptional' answers quoted by Prout in *Fugue*, only three—one of them the Beethoven just mentioned—are really exceptional,[17] although Prout, being as usual more faithful to live practice than most theorists, did recognise both the 'subdominant' answer and the alterations for Rule 1, though his explanations of both are anachronistic (see Chapter 5).

To turn now from exceptions to the regular procedure, it has been seen that the rules are of themselves very simple. The difficulties of the

17. *Fugue*, ch. IV, §§ 155: (d), (e) and (f) are exceptional. (b) is a 'subdominant' answer, the harmonic tonalities mentioned by Prout being irrelevant (see note 18 below); (a), (c), (g) and (h) are all cases of alteration of the tone and semitone steps in order to keep the tonic scale, a practice too common to be deemed 'exceptional' (see below). In (c) a slight decoration is introduced to avoid a repeated note.

Ex27(a)Bach, Sonata in C for violin alone: fugue
(b)Beethoven, Mass in C major: 'Cum sancto Spiritu' (words omitted)
(c)Beethoven, *Grosse Fuge*, op. 133
(d)Walton, Symphony no. 1 in B♭ minor: last movement, fugue at figure 112 (opening of theme only: cf. Ex 23)

answer lie not in them but in two other factors, namely, the asymmetrical nature of the diatonic scale and the character of the melodic line of the subject. A moment's thought will reveal that owing to the irregular distribution of tones and semitones and the uneven intervals at which the tonic and dominant notes occur only the simplest of themes can be answered in complete accordance with both rules. It was a principle laid down by Fux, the first great theorist of fugue, that the subject must be designed to be 'answerable' in accordance with both rules, but even he breaks his own principle in the fugue in the A mode, in which the subject requires alteration in order to do so.

The answer problem is best approached, in fact, from the point of view of the *suitability of the subject*—something that examiners in fugue, alas, do not always consider.

In real life very few subjects are suitable for answering in accordance with both rules. Such a case is shown in Example 28. Bach's subject

Ex 28 Bach, WTC II.9

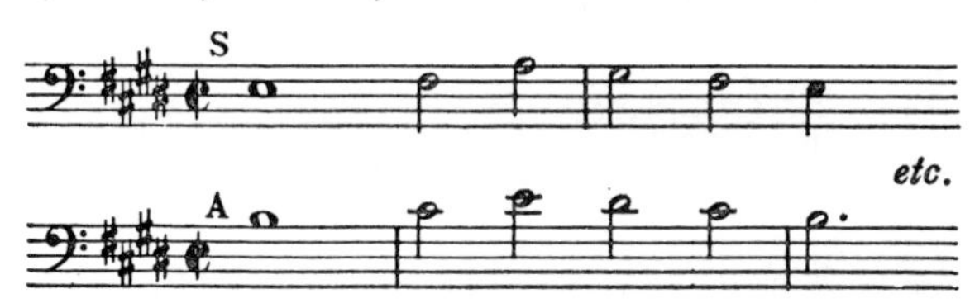

contains here only one of the two tonally important notes—the tonic occurs but not the dominant—and only one of the two semitones of the diatonic scale—that between iii and iv. Significantly, this subject, like those in Fux's elementary fugal examples, belongs to the ricercar type, mentioned above as being the simplest possible kind of theme. The choice of position for the answer gives dominant in answer to the two tonic notes and preserves all tone and semitone relationships without introducing any note foreign to the scale.[18] Such a subject might be said to be a 'perfect' one from the point of view of the answer.

Consider the imaginary themes in Example 29. Here the tonic note again occurs without the dominant: there thus appears to be no problem as regards Rule 2. Obedience to both rules is, however, made awkward by the existence of the semitone C–B: for Rule 1, C–B should really be answered F–E (A1), but this will cause disobedience to Rule 2, and the opening of the fugue will sound as if it were in F. To give G–F would change tone to semitone (A2), while G–F♯ preserves the semitone but introduces a foreign note (A3).

18. It must be stressed that answer-procedure is concerned only *with the notes of the answer itself*—not with anything that may occur in any voice *accompanying* the answer. That the combination of answer and another voice here may be said to 'go into B major' at the fourth crotchet of bar 3 does not affect the essential fact that the subject and answer themselves preserve between them tonic tonality and scale. This point has sometimes caused misunderstanding.

Ex 29

In example 30 both tonic and dominant notes occur in the theme and it is obvious that Rule 2 cannot be fully obeyed: of the two available positions, that at the upper fifth (lower fourth) is the better here (A1) since there is more emphasis on i than on v in the subject, and a momentary ii in the answer is better than two very emphatic iv's (A2).

In both these cases, however, it will be found that it is possible to alter the theme when it becomes the answer in such a way as to satisfy both Rules without serious damage to the melodic line. These answers are shown as A4 in Example 29 and A3 in Example 30 respectively. We thus have here what might be called a 'second-best' type of subject for answering purposes, namely that which, with the assistance of alteration, will yield an answer in accordance with both rules without serious damage to the melodic line of the theme. By convention such an altered answer is called a 'tonal answer' because in a very long stretch of fugal teaching the only purpose of alteration was believed to be tonal—Rule 2, in fact, Rule 1 having since Fux gradually been forgotten. Even then the term 'tonal' is a poor one in that an unaltered answer may well be 'tonal' in the sense that it obeys Rule 2, as our first example shows. By convention an unaltered answer is called a 'real' answer, whether or not it obeys Rule 2.[19]

Here an important point arises, which has tended to add to the already plentiful amount of confusion concerning the answer. For is it not nonsense to speak of *altering* the theme in order to obey the rules when Rule 1, the basic and original rule of answer-procedure, is specifically designed towards *preserving* the theme's original characteristic intervals?

Surprisingly, the fact is that alterations of the type just seen in the last two examples do not, in aural experience, destroy the character of a theme to anything like the same extent as changes in the tone-semitone relationship or other alterations, and it is only the latter which Rule 1 is designed to preserve. In other words, to answer semitone by tone and perfect fourth by augmented fourth would noticeably change the character of the theme (depending, of course, on the prominence and duration of the notes concerned), but to answer semitone by minor third and perfect fourth by perfect fifth alters it very much less. Rule 1, then, is not concerned to preserve every interval exactly, but rather to preserve the *quality* of the intervals, avoiding changes of tone to semitone, major to minor third, perfect to augmented fourth, etc. This apparent paradox is seen at work in innumerable answers from the sixteenth century down to, and beyond, Bach, and as will be seen it applies not only in the exposition but in the fugue as a whole.

Even the 'second-best' type of subject, however, must clearly be a fairly simple theme, easily amenable to alteration in perhaps several places. Let us now turn to two further themes, which at first sight might seem to be of the same category (see Example 31). Although these can both be answered in accordance with both rules by means of alteration (A1 in both cases), the character of the end of the theme is in both cases completely changed: the iii–v progression of the answer can hardly be said to reproduce the effect of the original vii–i of the subject. The difficulty lies not in the tone-semitone relationships, but

19. Listing the number of tonal and real answers which occur in any composer's fugues is, of course, meaningless, for the reason just given.

Ex 31 (a)
(b) Bach, organ fugue in E♭ BWV 552

(a)

S

A1

A2

A3

A4

(b)

S

A1

A2

A3

A4 (Bach)

rather in the function of the last two notes of the subject, which form a definite melodic cadence on the tonic note, whose effect is destroyed by the change of semitone into minor third. We see here for the first time instances of the second cause of answer difficulties, namely an unalterable progression in the melodic line of the subject. The melodic line is at this point such that an alteration would destroy an essential feature of the theme, and the answer would thus begin to approach some of the 'exceptional answers' quoted at the beginning of this section in its failure to preserve thematic unity at the outset of the fugue. The unalterable progression in both these cases consists of a simple cadence of the vii–i type. A cadence is indeed the simplest and most obvious instance of a strongly characteristic progression, although it is by no means the only one. Here, then, we have a third class of subject, even more 'imperfect' from the answer point of view: that which cannot, even with the assistance of alteration, be answered in accordance with both rules without a sacrifice of thematic unity. Annoyingly enough this third class is by far the most common; and the problems of the answer arise from the order of priorities given by different composers to the various factors involved. 'Is key more important than melodic line? Is such and such a progression unalterable? Is thematic unity more important than scale?' These are the kind of questions that come up, and of course different composers and different periods answer them differently. Thus with the two themes just studied there are three other possible ways of dealing with the 'awkward' cadence: end the answer on the subdominant, obeying Rule 1 but not Rule 2 (A2 in both cases); end it on the dominant but preserve the tonic scale by changing the characteristic semitone to a tone (A3); or end it on the dominant, preserving the characteristic semitone by means of a foreign note (A4). It is the last possibility which, as will be seen, is most commonly adopted in the 'classical' period of fugue, scalic unity being sacrificed for unity of theme and key. Since many subjects from this period begin and end on the tonic with some use of the note vii at or near the cadence, it is clear how the conventional idea of the answer as being 'in the dominant key', found in most textbooks on fugue, gained ground.

One special kind of difficulty with the answer, particularly in the 'classical' period of fugue, concerns the minor scale. As was noticed in dealing with the subject, the minor scale is a very difficult and complex affair: the notes vi and vii have two versions—♮ or ♯—according to the context in which they occur. vi♯ and vii♯ occur in many cadential contexts and in some (but not all) ascending melodic phrases. Clearly the difficulty of reproducing the tone-semitone relationship within the tonic scale—Rule 1—is in many cases insuperable and the composer is faced with the alternative of preserving the tone-semitone relationship by introducing foreign notes or changing the nature of the theme, sometimes quite substantially. The former course is again most commonly adopted; and again, since many subjects begin and end on the tonic, the tendency for the answer to be 'in the dominant key' is stronger in minor than in major.

In the sixteenth century, as might be expected, attention was given chiefly to Rule 1 and rather less regularly to Rule 2. This reflects the fact that tonality was not a strong factor in much of the polyphonic music of this period, and more attention was given to the keeping of the mode. In many cases both rules were obeyed automatically by the choice of position of answer—this happens, for instance, in the Palestrina motet 'Veni, sponsa Christi' mentioned above. The mode here is Mixolydian (G) and the answer gives G in answer to D as well as preserving all tone-semitone relationships. In passing, it may be noted that the position of answer is that a fifth below the subject, i.e. what would later be called a 'subdominant' answer. The sixteenth century did also use altered answers—mainly it would seem to answer v by i rather than to answer i by v. (The 'points' are often so short that it is anyway difficult to say what part of the answer is 'normal' and what 'altered'.) It must be said, however, that the answer was not a feature in which the sixteenth century was very strict. There are cases both of altering the tone-semitone relationship to preserve the mode and of preserving the theme by introducing foreign notes—to say nothing of half-way cases where a note might well have been sharpened or flattened on *musica ficta* principles. Although the vast majority of answers obey at least one part of Rule 1 there are a few 'exceptional' cases and some where the whole attitude to the 'point' seems so vague that one can hardly speak of an answer-procedure as such at all.[20]

The gradual growth in the importance of tonality as the seventeenth century proceeds is reflected by increasing obedience to Rule 2, alterations to give v in answer to i now being added to those giving i in answer to v. The first note of the subject, as we have seen, becomes more and more restricted to tonic and dominant, and it is this first note, even when short, that seems to be judged most important from the answer point of view. The cadence of the subject, when present, seems to be a secondary consideration until nearer the late Baroque (see Example 34(a), where the tonic cadence of the subject is brought on to the subdominant in the answer). There is as the century proceeds an

20. Morris, in *Contrapuntal Technique in the Sixteenth Century*, gives a good selection of answers in his musical examples Exx. 158–67. Of these Exx. 161 and 167 are exceptional. (We are concerned only with the *first* answer in the present section—Morris quotes later ones as well.)

increasing disregard of Rule 1, although it remains an important consideration until and including Bach. Disobedience to the rule seems at this stage to be equally divided between preserving tones and semitones by the introduction of foreign notes and preserving the tonic scale by changing tones and semitones.

Towards the late Baroque, of course, subjects became longer and gradually became less amenable to alteration: the cadence is more frequently present and grows in importance. Chromaticism and the use of the minor key (see above) also tend to make Rule 1 less and less applicable. At this stage one of the most interesting composers from the answer point of view is Buxtehude, for he seems to catch these developments just at the point where although the themes are often of fair length they are still amenable to alteration. It is worth analysing in detail one fascinating answer—that of the separate gigue fugue in C (Hansen 3. See Example 32). The example is marked in five sections

Ex 32 Buxtehude, organ fugue in C (Hansen 3)

A to E. Buxtehude answers as follows:

A	lower fourth	Rule 2 (i answered v)
B	lower fifth	Rules 1 and 2 (v–vi–v answered i–ii–i).
C	lower fourth	Rule 1. The chromatic (really Mixolydian) note vii♭ is answered in the tonic scale by iv.

C

D	lower fifth	This long section contains both iv and vii—and also iv♯ (a momentary digression to the dominant), so that the answer cannot be perfect. Rule 1 is obeyed throughout except for the single iv which is answered vii♭ (preserving the tone-semitone relationship at the expense of the tonic scale—but only for one quaver). Rule 2 is only obeyed with regard to v (answered i): i is answered iv, but the melodic tonality depends much more on the opening and end of the theme than on these notes in the middle.
E	lower fourth	Rule 2 takes charge here for the cadence, i answered v, the cadential progression employing F♯ as it must.

There is probably no other answer in the history of fugue with so many conspicuous changes from one position to the other, and yet there is, owing to the pliable nature of the theme, no feeling that the changes are niggling or fussy.

Buxtehude's fugues also contain good examples of the 'subdominant' answer—now, of course, beginning to become rarer and eventually to be listed as 'exceptional'. Two A minor fugues (Hansen 4 (first fugue) and 5 (first fugue)) show minor subjects with cadences on vii♯ and iii respectively with subdominant answers obeying both rules except for a passing tonic note in the first case. vii♯ is, of course, not a diatonic note anyway and is as appropriately answered by iii♯ (as here) as by iv♯. There are also a number of so-called 'modulating' subjects—those ending with a dominant cadence with digression, and we now arrive at the stage where the cadence gains in importance and is usually answered in accordance with Rule 2 (see Example 33). If one *is* interested in what Tovey once called the 'vexatious minutiae' of answer-procedure Buxtehude is one of the best composers to study. Yet in the academic textbooks, with the honourable exception of Prout, there is barely a mention of him in this connection.

Ex 33 Buxtehude, *Präludium, Fuge und Ciacona:* fugue

The different approach to the answer by different composers is shown in the next example, where Pachelbel and Fischer hit upon virtually the same subject: the former allows the opening, in which v is answered by i, to 'pull' the whole answer, cadence and all, into the 'subdominant' position, with several uses of vii♭ in answer to iv♮ (preserving the theme at the expense of the tonic scale: conventional theory would say that the answer was 'in the subdominant key') whereas Fischer gives an altered answer which obeys Rule 2 for the cadence as well and is also better for Rule 1, although a small tone-semitone alteration is made (see Example 34).

Ex 34(a)Pachelbel, clavier fugue in D (DTB Jahrgang II/1 no.45)
(b)Fischer, *Ariadne Musica* fugue in D major

It is in Bach that the strictest attitude to the answer is found—indeed the academic strictness about the answer probably stems as much from Bach as from Fux, much though both of these were misunderstood by the theorists who made the later rules. 'Strictness' here, however, does not mean obedience to both rules—which we have seen is rapidly becoming impossible owing to the changing nature of the subject—but rather a predictable attitude to both rules. Rule 2 now becomes almost absolute for the first note of the theme, except in accompanied fugue (see immediately below). There is only one definite exception—the fugue from the clavier toccata in E minor BWV 914: the subject, a toccata type, is unalterable, and answering of the initial semiquaver v by i would result in considerable subdominant bias—

virtual subdominant harmonic tonality, in fact, since the theme features an arpeggiated harmonic progression.

Tonic and dominant notes *near* the opening may often be tonally answered with alteration if necessary. The case where Bach 'confused the issue' was one of these—WTC II. 21, where the dominant seemed to Kitson a mere accessary of 'tonic harmony' and thus not to be tonally answered (see Chapter 5). Bach unobligingly confuses the issue the other way round in the G minor organ fugue BWV 578, where v is answered by ii. Obviously the second note was considered less important than the first, and its answering is more a matter of the individual subject and how far it is considered alterable.

Bach produces some interesting alterations near the opening for Rule 1—he is indeed probably the last composer to do this, the themes being amenable to alteration at the appropriate point (see Example 35). The I.18 answer is well-nigh perfect—the foreign note iii♯,

Ex 35 (a) Bach, WTC I.18
(b) Bach, WTC I.23

answering the already 'foreign' vii♯ (cf. Buxtehude's A minor, above). Some occurrences of i near the opening of the subject are brought on to iv in the answer, but first note and cadence obey Rule 2. (Notice how Bach, like students of today, 'failed to understand the implied harmonies of the subject': the 'implied subdominant cadence' (end of first to beginning of second bar) fails to materialise, the countersubject having A♯ at this point.)

In the main body of the subject Bach's chief consideration is for the theme, the tone-semitone relations of which are preserved by introducing foreign notes where necessary. In a large number of cases, of course, this in effect means the use of the dominant scale.

As far as cadences are concerned, Rule 2 is mostly obeyed. Answers ending on iv are confined to cases where the first two entries overlap and the cadential effect of i in the subject is to a large extent nullified (e.g. WTC II.3). Cases of v answered by ii, less harmful to the initial tonic tonality, are a little more common. The 'half-close' on v is, in mature Bach, answered on ii, Rule 1 having priority over Rule 2 (WTC I.17). There is also WTC I.10, where it is always said that the cadence on ii is due to the fact that this is a two-part fugue and there is thus no third part to enter on the tonic afterwards. More likely this is simply an unalterable 'toccata' type subject, and bringing the cadence on to ii is preferable to opening the answer on a full subdominant arpeggiated chord. Increasingly, of course, the commonest cadence is becoming that on the tonic or sometimes the mediant (iii) and tonic in close association. The strong progression towards the cadence tends more and more to pull the greater part of the answer into dominant position. In one important case, WTC I.24, a similar exceptionally strong and unalterable progression leads to a *dominant* cadence in the subject, so that the opposite occurs—the whole latter part of the answer is pulled into 'subdominant' position. The subject already contained a digression into the subdominant scale, so that the answer now contains a digression to the subdominant of the subdominant (A minor)!

Not all cadences are on i or v, however, and it is important to realise that only these two notes are the concern of Rule 2. In the well-known early and possibly unauthentic D minor toccata fugue, BWV 565, quoted in Chapter 1, the cadence is a weak one on iii, as it is also in the very short subject of the concerto-fugue in the Sonata in G minor for violin alone. In both cases the strong dominant preponderance in the subject causes a completely 'subdominant' answer, all the dominants being answered by tonic. Both answers are also the best for Rule 1: the violin example is a 'perfect' answer.

Generally speaking any alteration of the tone-semitone relationship becomes very rare in mature Bach. An occasional auxiliary note near the beginning (II.1, II.21) and sharpening of vii♮ to vii♯ in minor cadences (II.22) represent the extent to which this is usually done. But there is certainly greater laxity in this matter in fugues from cantata and mass choruses: two well-known instances are 'Sicut erat in principio' from the *Magnificat*, and 'Cum sancto spiritu' from the Mass in B minor—the latter case surely the worst example of fugal answer in

Bach, and difficult to sing for this reason (significantly he uses it only once!).

By Bach's time two kinds of fugal exposition had come into being which affect the subject-answer relationship. One is the exposition with 'free' accompanying continuo harmonies. The presence of harmonies does affect substantially the clarity of tonality at the outset of the fugue and it is not surprising to find that composers here waive the rule (as it had now become) that an initial dominant must be answered by tonic. Well-known examples are 'And He shall purify', no. 7 in Handel's *Messiah*, and the second movement of Bach's sonata in E for violin and harpsichord.

The accompanied fugal exposition indeed behaves much more in accordance with academic answer rules than the unaccompanied: there are fewer tonal alterations for small notes, less account of Rule 1 (though Bach still alters near the opening for this rule in the first chorus of Cantata 171) and much more effect of dominant and tonic keys answering each other. The link with examination rules is significant, since as will be seen (Chapter 5) examination practice in the answer is based upon ideas of harmonic progressions (supposedly) underlying the unaccompanied subject. But curiously enough in the matter of the initial note just mentioned the academic rules are contravened—it did not occur to theorists that the note v could 'imply' a harmony of I and thus be answered by ii 'implying' V!

The other kind of fugal exposition that affects answer practice is that following a cadence on or in the dominant (very occasionally the relative of the dominant), or occurring during the course of a movement. Again these examples are common in choral work and, in the case of a preceding dominant cadence, in French overture fugues. The influence of the dominant chord can produce a subject in dominant melodic tonality, as has been seen, and by an obvious extension of Rule 2 this is answered by tonic melodic tonality. If such a subject forms a cadence on the tonic the answer will probably be 'tonal', i.e. altered to bring the cadence on to the tonic (Bach, final fugue of motet 'Sing ye to the Lord'); but cadences on the mediant are not the province of Rule 2 and alteration is not usually made for them (Bach, fugue from Orchestral Suite no. 3 in D—a wholly 'subdominant' answer.) Fugues which begin during the course of a movement sometimes occur in temporary tonalities. In many cases the temporary tonality will again be the dominant, answered by tonic, but another key is sometimes found, and the answer-procedure may be related entirely to the temporary key. This is the position with the fugue in the opening chorus of Bach Cantata no. 102: the overall tonality is G minor, but the fugue (beginning at bar 71 last crotchet) starts in a temporary tonality of C minor and the exposition is entirely in that key. Prout (*Fugue*, §73–5) makes almost incredibly heavy weather of this example—he was perhaps confused by the fact that the subject starts on the dominant note and digresses to the dominant key at the end, with a passing digression to the dominant of the dominant (caused by the high C♯ on 'Fels', rock) in the middle—a description which betrays the ineptitude of the 'scale' view of tonality in comparison with the simple statement that the overall melodic tonality of the exposition is C minor. Another slightly confusing factor is that G minor, here serving very much as a dominant, is also the overall tonic of the piece. Bach's answer is a 'perfect' one for both rules apart from its second note (i answered by iv). After Bach, as would be expected, answer-procedure tends more and more to the 'dominant key' idea, alterations being on the whole restricted to prominent dominant notes at or near the beginning answered by tonic. The young Mozart, however, can still obey Rule 2 in the middle of a theme, and a chromatic one at that (see Example 36). We have already seen Beethoven perhaps

Ex36 Mozart, String Quartet in D minor K.173: last movement

deliberately giving 'exceptional' answers in the Mass in C and the *Grosse Fuge*: but that Beethoven fully understood the 'classical' answer-procedure is shown in the very interesting answer—arrived at apparently after many attempts[21]—of the fugue opening the C♯ minor String Quartet, op. 131. This is an almost 'perfect' answer given that the piece is in the Phrygian mode—the only foreign note, E♯ (iii♯) answers the non-diatonic vii♯, as we have seen in Buxtehude and Bach, and Rule 2 is also obeyed except for the single i, third note of the theme, answered iv. But why the Phrygian mode? Tovey[22] has pointed out that the D♮, the characteristic note of this mode, dominates the whole work: it recurs at the end of the fugue (the stretto of bars 110–114 and after) and is not only the tonic key of the second movement but also that of the recapitulation of the second subject of the finale (bar 220)—at least at first: and the whole quartet closes (bars 350–end)

21. Kirkendale, *Fuge und Fugato in der Kammermusik des Rokoko und der Klassik*, p. 305.

22. *Essays and Lectures on Music* (OUP, 1949): 'Some aspects of Beethoven's Art Forms', pp. 288–97, especially p. 290, 294–5.

with what amounts to a prolonged elaboration of the classical plagal cadence IV–I major which was always the traditional ending of Phrygian pieces. A much less serious affair is the answer in the fugue of the 'Eroica' Variations for pianoforte, op. 35, followed also in the fugue in the last movement of the 'Eroica' itself: Beethoven's v–i–i (octave below)–iv in answer to i–v–v–i shows the opening of the theme having, as it did in the early Baroque, more consideration in the answer than the cadence. To have answered v–i–i–v would have been tonally stronger but impossibly static.

The idea of a melodic tonality defined by the initial notes of subject and answer in turn now gradually begins to fade. We have already seen the opening of a subject on iv by Schumann, and in Mendelssohn's organ fugue in D minor (Peters III) the answer opens on iv: the opening progression, a prominent i–ii–v (below) in the subject becomes iv–v–i in the answer, the obeying of Rule 1 as regards the third note having priority. From the harmonisation of the third entry it would seem that the composer had in mind a IV–V–I cadence in the dominant answered by a similar progression in the tonic: but the ear does not hear an initial i as anything but the home tonic, so that this may well be a case of lack of self sufficiency in the answer similar to those already observed in the subject.

Although in this period the 'dominant key' idea of the answer is increasingly prevalent, it is still not unknown for the tone-semi-tone relationship to be altered in order to keep the tonic scale, as in the fugue 'Lord, Thou art worthy' concluding no. 6 of Brahms' Requiem, where C–B♮–G is answered G–F♮–D. This is just the kind of case where a Baroque composer might have made an alteration for Rule 1, but such alterations seem not to be found after Bach (there would anyway be difficulties here since an opening G–E–C would cause bad tautology). Two of Schumann's fugues, the piano fugue, op. 72 no. 2, and the second of the Six Fugues on the Name B-A-C-H for organ, op. 60, also show conspicuous alterations of tones and semitones, though these are concerned with digressions to the dominant in subjects which are not easily amenable to alteration at the right place.

In modern fugue, as would be expected, the use of positions other than fourth or fifth for the answer appears for the first time since its rare occurrence in the sixteenth century (p. 64 note 20). The case of Bartók's Fifth String Quartet (fugue beginning bar 368 in the last movement) was mentioned in Chapter 1: a B♭ subject ending on E♮ is given an answer opening on E♮ and ending on B♭, the note E♮ representing a tonality which recurs at several points in the whole work. Hindemith in LT answers one subject (no. 3 in F) at the lower minor third and another (no. 4 in A) at the upper major third. It has been mentioned that in the latter case the answer is able to stress the dominant note at the outset, only the very last note of the subject here referring to the tonic A at all. One Shostakovitch answer, no. 21 in B♭ major, appears at the lower minor third, again for a reason suggested above when discussing the subject. In all these cases except (significantly) the Shostakovitch the theme is preserved exactly by means of chromatic notes—the exact opposite procedure to the Tallis example quoted by Morris (p. 64 note 20).

Despite these cases, however, it is surprising how often in fact the traditional positions are still kept. Of Hindemith's twelve fugues in LT, for instance, only the two just mentioned answer at a position other than fourth or fifth. Of the others five—nos. 1, 2, 5, 6 and 11—have 'subdominant' and five—nos. 7–11 inclusive—'dominant' answers. These are all made in broad obedience to Rule 2 except no. 2, where the 'subdominant' answer gives iv as repeated initial note in answer to i: the effect here is of C tonality until the third entry rectifies matters. There are no 'tonally altered' answers—thus in no. 1 the initial v–i is answered i–iv: the first note however is by far the more prominent. There is some vagueness about the answering of the cadence, when present, comparable with that observed in pre-Bach fugue: thus neither no. 3 nor no. 5 reproduce the cadence in the answer, no. 3 altering the line completely and no. 5 reproducing the progression on the 'wrong' notes with diminished cadential effect.[23]

Shostakovitch, whose subjects are for the most part diatonic, knows only the dominant answer, 23 out of the 24 answers using this position —the exception being of course no. 21. There are conventional 'tonal' alterations at or near the opening much in the manner of Bach. Also following Bach, an opening i–v may or may not have its second note altered for Rule 2: no. 1 in C does not alter. An altogether retrospective feature is the occasional altering of the tone-semitone relationship in order to keep the tonic scale. In no. 16 in D♯ minor the first 36 bars of the fugue are in pure Æolian mode,[24] and thus ii is answered vi♮ with change of tone-semitone relationship. The same occurs, though not for a specific reason, in no. 24 in D minor. Even where Shostakovitch adopts a 'modern' position of answer, in no. 21, he alters the tone-semitone relationship, giving G *minor* in answer to B♭ major.

On the other hand the pure diatonic nature and simple scale-struc-

23. In studying the answers of a typical modern composer it is important to remember to ignore enharmonic notation. In Hindemith's E♭ fugue, for instance, the notation of the answer conceals the fact that it is an accurate representation of the theme. In bar 7, E♮=F♭, B♮=C♭, A♮=B♭♭, answering C♭, G♭ and F♭ persectively.

24. Compare the pure major of the whole of no. 1 in C.

ture of many of the themes often makes complete obedience to Rule 1 possible in the answer, not only in major (nos. 1, 5, 7 etc.) but also in minor (nos. 4, 10, 18: no. 8 also obeys the rule, the extraneous notes in the answer being extraneous also in the subject).

Interesting though these features are, they are on the whole untypical of modern fugue, which is by and large interested chiefly in preserving the theme's intervals (part (a) of Rule 1 above) and secondarily in a degree of obedience to Rule 2.

It is hoped that this section may have helped to clarify some of the problems concerning the answer in live fugue. The academic attitude to the answer will be discussed in Chapter 5, where some reasons for the obvious divergences between the rules as generally taught and live practice will be suggested. The main trouble over the years since Fux's teaching has of course been due, firstly, to the failure to recognise Rule 1, and secondly—a matter perhaps in the end even more vital and certainly more relevant to modern music—to the failure to understand melodic tonality. These two errors having been rectified, it is possible to trace a common thread in the procedures used in the answer from the beginnings of fugue until the present day.

The Countersubject

The term 'countersubject' means simply 'a theme which accompanies the subject'. Some teachers use the term of the continuation of the first part against the first answer, whether this material recurs or not. It is probably more helpful to reserve it for any theme heard against the subject a sufficient number of times to become recognisable. It has been mentioned that such a theme, or even more than one, may accompany the initial entry itself, the strength of melodic characteristics distinguishing the true subject from its subsidiaries, which are, despite common usage, much better called countersubjects. In most cases, however, the first time a countersubject is heard will be against the first answer.

There seem to be two historical origins of this feature. In discussing the 'Veni, sponsa Christi' motet of Palestrina it was noted that the material of the first and second parts overlaps, i.e. the two parts are in canon for some bars. We could call the material heard unaccompanied in the first part 'A' and that heard against the answer 'B'. 'A' is in this case a single note. As the 'point' gradually developed into the fugue-subject proper, however, 'A' would become longer, and eventually, as we have seen, it became common to have a definite cadence before or as the answer enters. Even so, the idea of continuing the same material still survived, and 'B', originally inseparable from 'A', now becomes a countersubject, a theme in its own right. Buxtehude shows a half-way case where it could be said that 'A' was a short subject and 'B' a countersubject (see Example 37). Even as late as Bach such cases are not unknown (see Example 38). It will be noted that in Example 37 what is officially the 'codetta' after the answer consists in fact of 'B' without 'A', i.e. the codetta could be said to consist of a statement of the countersubject (see below).

Ex 37 Buxtehude, Präludium in A minor (Hansen 5): fugue beginning bar 17

Ex 38 Bach, organ fugue in C BWV 547

From another direction the idea of a countersubject stems from the ricercars and fantasias of the early Baroque period. When the principle of a series of separate themes being heard in turn was replaced by that of varying treatments of one single theme, resources had to be found to provide variety, and one of these was the combining of the one theme (perhaps in augmentation) with another theme or themes subsidiary to it (see Chapter 4). In such cases the combination would probably occur in the first entry of the section concerned, thus originating the procedure where the countersubject is heard against the initial entry of the fugue. It is also the origin of the addition of new countersubjects later in the fugue (resource 5(b) in Chapter 4). The countersubject heard against the initial entry was usually a more prominent affair than that originating from the overlap of the first two entries, but later this distinction gradually faded, and by Bach's time the latter type had become equally prominent.

In live practice it should perhaps be stressed that a countersubject is in no way a necessity to fugue. A great many fugues have either no countersubject at all, or else an inconspicuous one, sometimes appearing only in the exposition and subsequently being forgotten. Not only this, but the subsidiary nature of the countersubject in comparison with the subject has been insufficiently emphasised in textbooks. It is true that countersubjects often have prominent characteristics and that they may feature in 'development' episodes (Chapter 3); but compared with some of the complex themes thought up by writers of academic fugue the countersubject in live practice is generally a much simpler and less obtrusive affair. It is an interesting exercise to take one of the most conspicuous countersubjects written—say that of WTC II.16—and then think of writing a fugue on it as subject: the difference between main and subsidiary theme soon becomes clear. The idea of the compulsory and conspicuous countersubject comes chiefly from academic fugue.

Before Bach the exposition countersubject, with which the present section is concerned, is usually a formula of little thematic character of itself (see Example 39). As early as Sweelinck, however, we can see already an important point—that the countersubject has an essentially *contrapuntal* relationship to the subject: the two parts make contrapuntal sense as a two-part passage, just as the subject in its initial entry was seen to make sense as a one-part passage. The self-sufficiency of the answer/countersubject combination is comparable with the self-sufficiency of the initial entry. Moreover, the combination does not readily suggest any harmony, a point that will be of importance when we come to consider the academic attitude to this question (Chapter 5). Commonly the countersubject will contain a characteristic tied note, often a suspension (see the examples), but the sense lies in the two-part combination itself, not in imaginary chords 'accompanying' it. A common manifestation of contrapuntal relationship is the use of the interval of the sixth where a more harmonic approach would have resulted in a fifth, third or octave.

Normally the subject-countersubject combination is designed to be 'invertible', that is to say either part may be used as the lowest part at a

Ex 39(a) Sweelinck, *Fantasia Chromatica* for organ (see Ex 12a)
(b) Sweelinck, Fantasia (Peters, Alte Meister des Orgelspiels II, no.26)
(c) Buxtehude, Präludium in C (Hansen 2): fugue beginning bar 55
(d) Buxtehude, Präludium in F♯ (Hansen 13): fugue beginning bar 29

given time. This has reference to one matter only—the fact that in the 'classical' period of fugue a fifth is a consonance whereas its inversion, a fourth, is treated in the manner of a dissonance when it occurs to the lowest part present. This means that fifths in the combination must be used in such a way that the fourth which results when the parts are inverted will be correctly treated. A full explanation of dissonance treatment in the periods concerned cannot be entered into here, but generally speaking if the fourth is part of a downward stepwise movement, or is tied backward and then falls by step, all will be well. Or, of course, the intended inversion may be at an interval other than the octave, a technique to be described in Chapter 4 (see p. 117) since it concerns later use of the themes. Buxtehude's countersubject (see Example 39(d)) is invertible at the twelfth (the commonest interval after the octave) so that the fifth, last beat of the first complete bar, which would hardly have made a 'good' fourth, becomes instead an octave.

The countersubject with a definite melodic character of its own seems to appear only in the late Baroque, and in instrumental fugue it is very much the prerogative of Bach. The early Bach countersubjects, which go with the characteristically early, rather leisurely subjects, are often in the nature of rhythmic 'filling-in' themes, the rests in the subject coinciding with movement in the countersubject, as in the C major toccata for organ, BWV 564, and the D major organ fugue, BWV 532. The shorter and more pregnant subjects of mature Bach give rise to simpler and more flowing countersubjects, and again it is common to find a long note as the focal point of the theme (WTC I.3, I.7, I.14 etc.). Often again there is a characteristic contrapuntal feature such as a suspension (or more than one) or other dissonance. In I.3, for instance, no student—or teacher for that matter—would ever have thought of putting an accented ninth against what is so obviously 'tonic harmony' (of the dominant key G♯ major—this would be the academic way of looking at it) at the first note of the second bar (see Example 40(a)). Rather similar is the seventh at the last note of the second full bar of the combination in II.10: the dissonance is part of a downward stepwise progression but is none the less conspicuous and unexpected to the harmonically minded. A good example of the use of a sixth mentioned above as a characteristic of contrapuntal relationship is the 'great' G minor organ fugue BWV 542: at bar 5 beat 2 we have such an obvious case of 'implied' dominant harmony, that the sixth on the A seems the more odd to the fugally knowledgeable, quite apart from the fact that the following D in the subject means that Bach has committed the ultimate crime and has produced an 'implied 6/4 chord'. Yet such sixths are typical and present no problem to the listener unless he has

Ex 40(a) Bach, WTC I.3

Ex 40(b) Bach, WTC I.24

the misfortune to have learnt too many rules. The following well-known Handel example (the subject and countersubject appearing together at the outset) is in fact full of 'implied 6/4's' (see Example 41). Yet another symptom of contrapuntal relationship sometimes found is the ignoring of a sequence in the subject. The subject of WTC I.24 would have produced many clever countersubjects in academic fugue, but would anyone have produced Bach's four simple descending

Ex 41 Handel, *Judas Maccabæus*: fugue concluding Part II (words omitted)

minims (see Example 40(b))? (To speak of 'ignoring' a sequence is of course to assume a normal case of 'following' a sequence—but this itself shows the harmonic attitude. To the ordinary listener Bach's four minims sound more natural than anything the clever examination student would have invented.)

The chromatic countersubject to a diatonic subject is not uncommon in Bach. In II.18 again no one brought up on the conventional 'examination fugue' would have thought of Bach's sequentially ascending theme, employing the chromatic scale figure from v to upper i of the dominant key (note particularly the opening of each step of the sequence on a sixth). II.22 is another interesting case in which the complete chromatic scale from iii♯ up to i of the dominant key is employed. Unusually, the descending i–v chromatic scale figure (of the dominant key) features in the major in II.17—instrumental chromatic themes are distinctly rare in the Baroque, though in vocal fugue words can cause chromaticism, as in Bach Cantata 179 where the same figure of the *tonic* key (despite the ending of the inverted answer in the dominant) occurs to the word 'falschem' (false).[25]

The typical countersubject of choral fugue is by convention supposed to be a rather distinctive and often brilliant theme. Also it is usually supposed to carry separate words from the subject. To quote another phrase of Kitson's (not made in the present context), 'Bach shows no consistency in the matter'; nor does anyone else. 'And with His stripes' from Handel's *Messiah* has a neutral countersubject with no words of its own. The above-quoted *Judas Maccabæus* countersubject is a little more brilliant but again has no separate words. The 'Et in terra pax' and 'Pleni sunt coeli' fugues from the Mass in B minor have flowing countersubjects in semiquavers, but they are really less characteristic than those used in instrumental fugue: Bach does not use such themes in instrumental fugue except perhaps as second countersubjects. Again, they carry the same words as the subject, as does the similar flowing countersubject in the 'Kyrie' of Mozart's Requiem. The supposedly 'correct' allocation of words is also used, as two Bach examples show (see Example 42), but clearly there is no rule on the matter as far as exposition countersubjects are concerned. The 'separate words' rule would seem to apply more to second subjects or countersubjects introduced later in the fugue.

With Handel in particular the words of choral fugues do induce the composer to write two or more themes, but these do not necessarily

25. This is a typical example of 'negative word painting': the words say 'See that thy fear of God be not hypocrisy, and serve God not with a false heart'. The word 'falschem' produces its chromatic figure automatically irrespective of the general sentiment of the words.

take the official subject/countersubject form. In the Dettingen Anthem 'The King shall rejoice' (not the well-known Coronation Anthem), for instance, the final chorus starts in fine style with a slow 'Alleluja' accompanied by a brilliant countersubject 'We will rejoice'. Unfortunately the 'subject'—'Alleluja'—is not heard again until bar 18, and one has to decide whether this is a fugue at all.

After the Baroque the importance of the countersubject seems gradually to fade, and certainly themes of the particular individuality of Bach's examples are rarely found in later fugues. As with so many features whose importance is stressed in academic teaching, the 'importance' is chiefly a feature of Bach's work, and is not a general principle. Even in choral fugue post-Bach examples are not very notable. Beethoven's Mass in D provides one well-known instance in the 'Et vitam venturi' fugue (subject and countersubject stated together at the outset). A less notable but definite example occurs in Beethoven's 'other' Mass, that in C, in which the 'Cum sancto Spiritu' fugue has a countersubject, one characteristic of which—the G–G♯–A progression in its first appearance—is fairly regularly preserved. In instrumental fugue Mozart's C minor Fugue for two pianos, K.426, is another case where a single characteristic—three quavers leading to a trill in the second bar—is preserved regularly, although the rest of the theme is very vaguely adhered to. Beethoven's *Grosse Fuge* certainly shows one of the most conspicuous countersubjects ever written, but the circumstances here are rather unusual: had the subject not been previously stated, both in introductory manner and in the 'false start' to the fugue at bars 26–9, it is more than possible that the countersubject would have 'taken over' and appeared to be the main theme. This is especially likely since, unlike any other case where two themes are announced together at the outset, the countersubject begins first. The point here is that, uniquely, in the exposition the subject is already being varied (see Chapter 4, p. 123), having already been made familiar to the listener in the preceding bars.

In modern fugue Shostakovitch, following Bach, is the only composer to make much use of the countersubject. Typically he out-Bachs Bach in that every fugue has a countersubject, regularly used except when the subject is in stretto. The spirit of Bach's subject-countersubject relationship is however lacking in many of the examples owing to similarity of general character between the two themes. Even in no. 15, where the countersubject is chromatic, the subject also is chromatic, so that there is as little contrast as in, say, no. 13, where both themes are placidly diatonic. No. 16's countersubject is rhythmically highly complex—but so is the subject. The true Bach-like relationship, at which one imagines the composer was aiming, is better

Ex 42 (a) Bach, Cantata 47: opening chorus, fugue beginning bar 45 (continuo figuring omitted)
(b) Bach, Cantata 102: opening chorus, fugue beginning bar 45 (continuo figuring omitted)

seen in no. 17 where the countersubject has a characteristic rhythmic drive of its own, different from the subject, or in no. 19 where the long notes of the countersubject give it an easily memorable feature which also has the function of filling in beats of the bar on which the subject has held notes.

Codetta after the First Answer

This is of much more common occurrence than that after the initial entry. From the beginning of fugue it was common for the entries to be in pairs, the first two close in both pitch and time. This is seen in the 'Veni, sponsa Christi' motet and innumerable other cases. Just as the countersubject was originally part of a single melodic line and was separated off when the subject became a definite theme ending with a cadence, so this codetta was originally simply the continuation of the answer, becoming separate when the answer ended with a cadence. Very naturally there are a number of cases of the codetta consisting simply of the countersubject without the subject, as in Example 37 above. In the case of answers tending more and more towards the dominant key, particularly in the minor, another reason for a codetta here would be the desire to restore the tonic key, even sometimes to digress to the subdominant in order to redress the balance of flat and sharp side keys.

As with the countersubject, the first injection of real character into the answer-codetta comes with Bach. To use the word 'beautiful' of so apparently perfunctory a feature as a link between two entries may seem to be over-romanticising Bach, but such examples as WTC II.8 and both the 'Kyrie' movements of the Mass in B minor[26] have a genuine beauty in themselves, and all are used to good effect later in the fugue (in II.8 the last appearance at bars 35–40, after no fewer than nine consecutive entries of the subject, is particularly moving). All these codettas digress to the subdominant key, the fugues being in the minor: the two Kyries are accompanied fugues with consequent increased stress on the dominant key in the answer.

Codettas at this point may be more or less independent or derived from subject or countersubject (if present) or both, or from the subject-codetta (if present). Of the three cases just mentioned the first two are independent, whereas the third derives from the second part of the subject. It must be remembered that 'independent' in the Baroque style does not imply the sharp thematic contrasts of sonata form: it merely means that there is no immediately recognisable quotation from themes already heard. Probably the extreme of 'independence' is the codetta of WTC I.15, with its arpeggiated two-part progression. The well-known I.2 shows a figure from the subject with altered intervals, treated sequentially (note the humorous false entry at the end of the second bar); in I.7 free sequences are made on the original subject codetta. In II.17, rather oddly, the answer-codetta consists simply of the opening phrase of the subject in the dominant, as if another entry were to take place. Tovey in his notes to this fugue[27] says that 'in bar 5 . . . the alto's allusion to the subject must on no account be emphasised' but both Bach and Tovey knew perfectly well that on the Baroque instruments there could be no question of 'not emphasising' a short passage like this.

It will be seen that commonly in Bach the answer-codetta sets the general pattern for some or even all of the episodes. The extreme case of this is certainly the 'Dorian' organ fugue, BWV 538, where an innocuous bit of canon founded on a fragment of the subject/countersubject combination generates the most learnèd and complex set of episodes ever written (see Chapter 4).

26. The fugue in the first Kyrie begins with the voice entries at bar 30 (bar numbers include the four introductory bars).

27. Associated Board Edition.

One case in Bach may be mentioned where a third part is allowed to creep in unobtrusively in the answer-codetta. This is in the fugue from the (French) Overture of the D major Partita for clavier. Bach does not do this kind of thing in movements entitled 'fugue', but evidently regarded 'concerto-fugues' such as this (see Chapter 3) and choral fugues as less deserving of strictness. It will soon be seen that a similar freedom traditionally applies to some aspects of the exposition from the third entry onwards.

After Bach the importance of the answer-codetta, like that of the countersubject, seems to diminish: some composers indeed, such as Schumann and Mendelssohn, commonly omit it altogether, the exposition entries being consecutive. Both Hindemith and Shostakovitch, clearly under Bach's influence, have revived the feature as an entity of some musical importance. In LT no. 4 in A the answer-codetta refers rhythmically to the second bar of the subject, and a more definite development of a conspicuous subject figure (four demisemiquavers) is seen in no. 9 in B♭. In other cases the material is neutral (no. 10 in D♭). Shostakovitch is more deeply influenced by Bach, as in other respects: the independent codetta of no. 10 in C♯ minor sounds as if it has come straight from a Bach fugue, and other independent examples are no. 17 in A (new semiquaver running figure), 20 in C minor (new quaver figure) and, perhaps most original of all, no. 2 in A minor, where the foreign scale of C♯ minor accompanies the prolonged E at the end of the answer. In other cases the codetta is derived from the subject either precisely (no. 19 in E♭, where the opening figure of the subject is freely inverted) or more vaguely. Typically, Shostakovitch uses the answer-codetta in every fugue, and in all cases it is the foundation of the later episodes.

The Third Entry: subsequent Entries and Codettas

With the third entry we enter upon the stage of the exposition where matters are gradually becoming more free. Both tonality (where relevant) and theme have been made clear in the first two entries, and the need for strictness is beginning to lessen. The common use of an answer-codetta, derived from continuation of two overlapping entries, itself reflects the interval of time before the third entry occurs, and in cases where the answer-codetta employs new material or begins to develop material already heard the further tendency to separate the third entry is increased—after all, effectively speaking, such a codetta is an episode, and indeed some writers (Tovey, for instance) use the term episode even though the feature occurs in the exposition.

As has been observed, up till the late Baroque the third entry could consist of subject or answer—it did not matter which. In addition to

Bach's WTC I.1, Froberger's Fantasia 5 and Canzona 4,[28] both show the subject–answer–answer–subject order. The same composer's Capriccio 18[29] is interesting as showing the use of the identical positions to those of Bach's I.1, key and all. Other examples are Fischer, *Ariadne Musica* 4 and 14, Lübeck, organ fugue in G minor (Peters no. 4, final fugue), Handel, *Belshazzar* chorus 'And every step he takes', and (curiously neglected in this context) the 'Credo' fugue in Bach's Mass in B minor.

Another possibility, recognised in few textbooks, is that the third part should begin with a further entry of the countersubject, if present, the next subject (or answer) entry being reserved for the fourth part, as in Froberger Fantasia 2 and Ricercar 2.[30] This procedure seems to have origins in the sixteenth-century motet—Palestrina's 'Gaudent in coelis' and 'Si ignoras te', for instance.[31]

In the chorus 'We have a law' in the *St John Passion* Bach gives a third entry which approximates more to the form of the first answer than to that of the original subject, which is in fact never used again. This is an unusual procedure—could Bach perhaps have been dissatisfied with the original subject, which has initial subdominant melodic tonality but forms a cadence on the dominant?—but it again reflects the tendency to greater freedom at this point. In WTC I.20 the third entry inflects one note from ♮ to ♯ (bar 10 beat 2, bass).

Despite these examples, towards the late Baroque matters were generally becoming stricter and more stereotyped, and the officially 'regular' exposition was becoming more and more common. Bach, in pieces actually entitled 'fugue', is usually 'correct', despite the cases of I.1 and I.20; the latter, incidentally, an early fugue.

When the initial subject entry has opened in dominant tonality following a preceding dominant cadence, it has been seen that the first answer normally opens in the tonic. In such cases Bach normally makes a 'tonal alteration' to the third entry so that it opens not in dominant but in tonic melodic tonality. Such fugues always have an overall tonic tonality, the dominant opening being simply due to the pull of local circumstances. The entry which the first sopranos always fail to get in the 'Cum sancto spiritu' of the Mass in B minor is one of these. The original tenor entry began E–A–E and ended with a D cadence: the first sopranos are surprised to find that their entry begins D–A–D, the second D incidentally accompanied by a dominant seventh of the key of A major—the very chord which according to academic rule

28. DTÖ Jahrgang IV/1 Band 8.
29. DTÖ Jahrgang X/2 Band 21.
30. DTÖ Jahrgang IV/1 Band 8.
31. Edizione Scalera III, p. 121, and XI, p. 105, respectively.

tonal alterations are designed to avoid! (This chord is another factor which contributes to the difficulty of singing this phrase accurately—to say nothing of the leap to the high A!) This procedure occurs in many Bach cases (both fugues in the motet 'Sing ye', for instance), though curiously enough not, apparently, in any other composer.

It is in the third entry that a countersubject which has first appeared against a 'tonal' (altered) answer will probably have to be adapted to fit the subject. If the 'tonal alterations' are only near the beginning of the theme there is little difficulty in this, since the countersubject, as has been observed, has less complete melodic characteristics than the subject, and its opening can be easily altered. In the case of tonal alterations in the middle or at the end it is usually possible to alter the countersubject at an unobtrusive place, e.g. in the middle of a group of semiquavers, as Bach does in WTC I.7 and 'Pleni sunt coeli' in the Mass in B minor (in I.7 compare bar 3, soprano with 6, alto: in the Mass example compare bar 58, tenor, with 64, alto II). Contrary to academic instructions the relationship between the two themes need not be identical at every point: in both the examples just quoted the alteration is made in the countersubject earlier than in the subject, a changed relation (barely noticeable to the listener) existing for a few notes.

Bach's fourth entries are also sometimes of interest. A 'real' instead of a 'tonal' answer is given in two organ fugues in G major BWV 541 and 550 and in the A major, BWV 536. In all cases a further codetta occurs after the third entry and the fourth entry is clearly representative of a move towards dominant tonality. In two of the fugues, BWV 550 and 536, the pedal entry is the one concerned, and this is in many other cases separated from the manual entries by a codetta, as for instance in the well-known D minor, BWV 565, and A minor, BWV 543, in both of which a perceptible move away from tonic tonality (to the subdominant in the D minor) is evident. One could of course argue for ever as to exactly which entries of this type should be included and which excluded from the exposition (the 'codetta' in the D minor is ten and a half bars long!): the important point is to see that there are no fixed boundaries in fugue and that tonic tonality is a relative matter.

Curiously enough the exact opposite case to that just discussed is seen in the fourth entry of WTC I.4 where Bach gives the answer form that is better—perfect, indeed—for Rule 1 but disobeys Rule 2 in bringing the cadence on to the subdominant. In the first answer he had done the exact opposite. It may be significant that the subject, a 'ricercar' type, is four-square, and Bach, obviously at pains to disguise this, shortens the fourth note of this entry to a minim and brings in the fifth entry, its first note (like that of the third and fourth entries) also shortened to a minim, on the last note of the fourth. The fourth entry has the advantage of keeping the tonic scale and making the fifth entry more natural.

Returning to 'Cum sancto Spiritu' in the Mass in B minor, here the fourth entry—that of the second sopranos—consists of an additional entry of the second countersubject (see immediately below), a procedure analogous to that observed above in Froberger. The second sopranos in fact have to wait until well on in the second of the two fugues before they get a look in with the subject. This chorus may well be an adaptation from an original four-part one, now lost. Just possibly for the same reason the second sopranos in 'Pleni sunt caeli' in the same work enter with the contraltos, doubling them a third higher, a practice that would hardly meet with the examiner's approval.

Finally on Bach's expositions there is the question of additional countersubjects. These are mainly a feature of vocal fugue and arises in what is called *Permutationsfuge* in German or sometimes Round Fugue in English. This appears to be a Bach speciality—like many things in the history of fugue. As in a round the plan is as follows, A being the subject and B, C, etc. being countersubjects (the diagram assumes four countersubjects—the maximum number found):

A	B	C	D	E	
	A	B	C	D	etc.
		A	B	C	etc.
			A	B	etc.
				A	etc.

In a round, of course, all entries are at the octave or unison, whereas in fugue they are at the fourth/fifth alternating with octave: in the *Permutationsfuge*, therefore, alterations have to be made at suitable points, but this, like the alteration of countersubject to fit the third entry where necessary, causes little difficulty. One of the most perfect examples is the fugue concluding the first part of Cantata 21 'Ich hatte viel Bekümmerniss' ('My Spirit was in Heaviness') where four countersubjects are used, the whole fugue consisting of nothing but various permutations of the five themes (all of which incidentally carry the same words: 'for He is the help of my countenance and my God') with the assistance only of the contrast between solo and tutti voices and that between the timbre of first voices, then instruments, then instruments doubling voices (Chapter 4, resource 10). A similar *tour de force*, though with only three countersubjects, this time each theme having its own set of words, is seen in the single movement which is known as Cantata 50. The third countersubject here would probably not satisfy the examiners, since it consists almost entirely of a single held note. In the Mass in B minor, 'Et in terra pax' has three countersubjects, though the third is not often heard: the first sopranos will probably remember it since they have it twice, at bars 131–4 (counting from the beginning of the 'Gloria') and 154–6. 'Cum sancto Spiritu' has two. Even the two 'Let him be crucified' choruses in the *St Matthew Passion* show two countersubjects in a total of only four entries! For the reader who knows German, Neumann's *Bachs Chorfuge* is a fascinating study of these and many other examples. In instrumental fugue second countersubjects are sometimes found, but they are much more vaguely treated. WTC I.2, I.21 and II.17 are instances: in the first two a distinctive rhythm is preserved, while in the third continuously flowing semiquavers 'represent' the theme concerned despite the, otherwise, vague way in which it is treated.

After Bach, probably under increasing influence of fugal teaching, expositions tend to become absolutely 'regular'. None the less freedom in the third and subsequent entries is not unknown. In the very first example in the present book, the 'incidental' fugue in the last movement of Beethoven's Piano Concerto in C minor (see Example 1), the first answer is 'real' (opening on ii in answer to v) while the second is 'tonal' opening on i, the opening semitone becoming a minor third. This seems a difficult procedure to explain, but it must be remembered that the fugue is in a temporary tonality of F minor, preceded by a passage concluding in A♭, the overall tonic being, of course, C minor. Beethoven may have intended the 'real' answer as a reference back to C minor, the fugue then moving away more definitely to F minor before making a more definite return to C minor to prepare the recapitulation. The 'incidental' fugue opening the last movement of the String Quartet, op. 59 no. 3, shows the order subject–answer–subject–subject. Beethoven perhaps felt that he was breaking a rule here, little knowing that he wasn't. Schumann, in the D minor fugue for piano, op. 72 no. 2, sharpens all the F's in the third entry, and towards the end employs the scale of G minor, to which key the cadence is diverted by 'tonal answer' methods. The same composer's Six Fugues for Organ on the Name B-A-C-H are also interesting in this connection: the third and fifth entries of no. 1 displace the opening of the subject by one beat, while nos. 2 and 5 have pedal entries (the fourth in both cases) which discontinue the theme before the end.

In modern fugue perhaps the most interesting exposition is that in the first movement of Bartók's *Music for Strings, Percussion and*

Celeste, where the entries are in a cycle of fifths: the initial entry (mentioned above) has a melodic tonality of A, the tonic, and the answer enters classically on E; but after this a gradual move away from the tonic is made with the third entry in D, the fourth B, the fifth G and so on. The fugue is discussed in Chapter 4 (pp. 129 and 173): clearly no one can say 'where the exposition ends' since the whole point is a *gradual* move from the tonic. What Bartók does is in fact only an extension of the idea of the 'lightnings and thunders' chorus in Bach's *St Matthew Passion* (entries B minor, E minor, A major, D major, etc.).

Of the two modern collections of fugues Hindemith's shows a passing appreciation of the classical freedom of entries after the first answer: in the second fugue of LT, in G, the subject begins on G, the first answer on C, and the third entry on D. As mentioned when discussing the answer, a strong bias towards C is caused by the first two entries but the third entry brings the melodic tonality back to G, which key is confirmed by a subsequent G entry. In Shostakovitch's collection, significantly, the conventional methods are used in every example, with the single exception of the above-mentioned G minor answer in the B♭ major fugue.

Before leaving the exposition two further points may well be mentioned, which also concern the whole fugue—the question of counterpoint in a definite number of parts, and the matter of the individuality of separate parts in keyboard fugue. On the first, it has been mentioned that in live fugue not every exposition entry may represent a real new part entering, and it is particularly in entries after the third, and even more after the fourth, where present, that part-writing may often become 'lax', academically speaking. When it comes down to it, it is very questionable whether more than three parts can really be taken in by the listener as genuine entities, particularly on the keyboard. The presence of four and more parts is indeed perceived, but rather as general thickening of the texture than as the addition of separate melodic lines. For convenience, at the beginning of this chapter examples of academically 'incorrect' part disposition in the exposition were quoted from WTC, but Bach is not really the composer in whose work one should look for common occurrences of this sort of thing, for, as in so many other things, it was he who was responsible for a stricter attitude to the matter, which has in turn been adopted by academic fugue. Both earlier and to a lesser extent later fugue writers are frequently much vaguer about counterpoint, both as regards the quality of some of the melodic lines and the number of parts present at any given time. Good composers always have an innate sense of what the listener can and cannot hear, and such vaguenesses as appear do not trouble the listener at all: the only person they will trouble is the student who decides to write the fugue out in 'long score', each part on its own separate line. One pre- and one post-Bach example must suffice here to show what was common practice. In Pachelbel's organ fugue in B minor (Peters, *Spielbuch für die Kleinorgel*, vol. II no. 2) there are three 'correct' entries, but in the fourth one four parts are reduced to three before the end of the theme, and apart from odd moments are never heard together again until the last five bars. In Schumann's F minor Piano Fugue, op. 72 no. 3, there are similarly three 'correct' entries, but the four parts of the fourth entry last for precisely three crotchets; characteristically the post-Bach composer is a little more 'correct', and four parts reappear together at bar 20. The Beethoven Piano Concerto no. 3 fugue quoted in Chapter 1 shows, incidentally, that part-writing need be no more strict in fugues for ensembles, since two instrumental parts can always double each other when the composer requires!

The second question, relevant to counterpoint, concerns keyboard fugue only. By convention we speak of the uppermost part in keyboard fugue as 'the soprano', the lowest as 'the bass', and so forth. It is all too easy to forget that there are no real 'voices', but only one keyboard instrument. All effect of part-writing on the keyboard is really a deception of the listener, engineered by continuity of melodic line and judicious use of pitch. In the average exposition the parts which have already entered continue against the new parts, thus giving the listener the same effect as of voices entering in turn. When in II.17 Bach removes the uppermost part just before the lowest part enters (bar 8, first crotchet) the listener knows by the continuity of the middle parts and the difference in pitch between high A♭ and low A♭ that 'the soprano has rested and the bass has entered'. But when in II.2 people begin to argue as to whether the entry of bar 7 is 'really' that of the bass or whether it is a re-entry of the tenor (the part that originally entered at bar 4), the bass remaining silent until a much delayed entry at bar 19, they are being purely academic, since in this fugue Bach has made a momentary return to the vagueness of part-identification which was characteristic of his predecessors, and has not cared properly to simulate the entry of real voices. The entry of 7 gives the impression of a new part to the extent that it is lower in pitch than the entry of 4, but it is not so much lower that it could not be a re-entry: it differs in this way from the entry of bar 6 of I.19, which coincides with such an unexpected drop in pitch that it does sound like a new part. Once again the academic argument regarding II.2 does not worry the listener, but only the student who thinks that each part in a fugue must have an individuality of its own—'bass', 'tenor', etc. As always, it is Bach's mature practice which is the 'exceptional' thing, not cases like this where he slips back into a habit common in other composers. The full study of ways in which Bach makes his keyboard parts virtually identifiable with true voices is of itself a subject for a substantial piece of research. We are so used to Bach that we take it for granted—until we have to correct a student's fugue in which the only distinction between soprano and alto at some points lies in whether the notes' tails are turned upwards or downwards!

It was said of the Bartók example discussed above that there was no reasonable 'end' to the exposition. In varying degrees this is true of all fugue. The subject and answer were, according to the old rule, supposed to retain their two positions and forms not only at the opening of the fugue but right through, and it will be seen in Chapter 4 that this rule held sway, to a greater or less extent, almost up to Bach's day and indeed was a powerful influence upon Bach. But even when the use of other keys or a substantial gap (episode) between entries separates off an exposition section from the working-out of the fugue, there will be no precise boundaries, and no particular note upon which we may say 'the exposition ends'. In 'incidental' fugue it will of course merge into other non-fugal material, but even here the transition is not usually sudden. For this same reason, half-way cases should not worry anyone. Are the entries of WTC I.8 bars 12–14, bass or the already discussed II.2 bars 7–8, bass 'really' exposition entries? These, in that they vary the tone and semitone steps, are like the above-mentioned 'real answers'—they *begin* a move away, here from the strict thematic form rather than from the key, and it is more important to observe this than to argue over their exact category. Both the student and the listener must try to assess the musical sense, and in fugue the musical sense is always moving forward, pointing the way to the next event.

3

THE EPISODE

It seems that every book on fugue has to have a chapter on the 'episode'. Yet in many ways the whole concept of an episode is a most unsatisfactory one. Conventionally it refers to any passage after the exposition which is not an entry of the theme. The whole idea here is, of course, of a subject ending with a definite cadence entering in specific keys: between the entries in the interest of variety and also to perform the necessary modulations, episodes occur which contrast with the entries (Kitson recommends fewer parts in the episode[32]) but which are at the same time expected to develop figures from the themes already heard. Thus the episode, in conventional and academic terminology, is a separate entity, a kind of miniature 'development section' which contrasts with sections of statement on either side of it. Having developed this concept, the theorists then had to stress that fugal style is continuous and that between entry and episode 'There must be no rough stitches, and hardly the semblance of a seam. . . . One of the chief difficulties in writing an episode is to hide the fact that technically it is an interpolation.'[33]

As with so many features of academic fugue—the regular countersubject, for instance, as mentioned in the previous chapter—the idea stems from what Bach does in a number of the best-known fugues. Even more than the countersubject, the organised episode, in which figures from exposition themes are developed in what superficially resembles the methods used by Beethoven in sonata development sections, is very much the prerogative of the mature Bach keyboard fugue, particularly WTC. The apparent link with sonata form is, of course, another reason for this type of episode featuring in academic

32. *The Elements of Fugal Construction*, p. 55.
33. Kitson, *Studies in Fugue*, ch. 3, opening paragraph.

fugue, since works employing sonata form are, or were until recently, more familiar to the student than those in the 'classical' fugal style.

Apart from Bach, and to a lesser extent other late Baroque composers, this concept of the episode has little application to the main stream of fugal writing, and there are more fugues in Bach to which it does not apply than there are those to which it does. From the style of the vast majority of fugues it is quite evident that even though the subject may end with a cadence (and by no means all do) there was no idea in the composer's mind of 'the episode' as a separate entity. Episodes, or parts of episodes, may, it is true, separate themselves off from their surroundings in various ways, but this may also happen with entries. In Chapter 2 we saw that the idea of the subject as necessarily tied to a set harmonic tonality and a set series of 'accompanying' chords is quite foreign to fugal practice generally, and there is no reason why, say, an important cadence might not be formed in five parts half-way through an entry, after which the number of parts might be reduced to two: variety and relaxation are here present, but they do not necessarily need an episode. It will be seen, moreover, in Chapter 4 that the enormous possibilities of variation of the subject mean that as far as key variety is concerned entries are not even from the melodic tonality point of view bound to a single key, so that the idea that modulation is the prerogative of the episode while the entries represent fixed keys is not true either. The keys employed in most fugues are anyway so close to the tonic as to make any modulatory passage unnecessary. Most important of all, however, is the fact that even if the subject does end with a cadence, this need not mean any perceptible break in the contrapuntal flow. So far from Kitson's 'hardly the semblance of a seam' it is clear that composers in general did not even think of there being any 'seam' whose semblance they must avoid. Academic fugue, tied no doubt by the idea of 'implied harmonies' accompanying the subject, could not get away from the idea that if the subject ended, say, ii–i these would have to be 'accompanied' by some kind of V–I cadence and that therefore great care would be needed in attaching the episode. In real life composers are in fact continually altering subject cadences in order to fit more closely into the succeeding counterpoint, but even if this is not done, firstly ii–i need not be harmonised V–I at all—there are numerous other possibilities, VII b–I in the relative minor or IV–I in the subdominant, to mention only two that are available from a major key—and secondly not every V–I progression sounds cadential: if the parts are continued in flowing movement, or particularly if a part re-enters as the progression is occurring, any cadential effect is nullified even if the chords are root position, which they do not have to be. Many subject cadences, particularly in Bach, whose mature style is probably the most continuous of any composer, are much less definite than ii–i and are thus even easier to absorb into the general flow.

In large numbers of cases, then, the dividing line between entry and episode is a theoretical one. The episode is simply the continuation of the counterpoint and can only reasonably be described insofar as it comprises or contains some definite feature: and even then we must remember that the feature may be one which could have been provided by an entry. Thus in WTC I.6 bars 20–1 are an episode which provides an important cadence in the dominant (see Chapter 4, resource 9, below). But look back to I.4 and you will find the equally important relative major cadence of bars 32–5 provided by an entry, that of the 'alto' (if we so correctly call the third part from the top). In II.22 bars 31–2 are a link, connecting one stretto to another: the number of parts drops to a mere two in order to draw attention to the re-entry of soprano and bass with the succeeding stretto. An equally link-like function is performed by bars 59–60 of the A minor clavier double fugue BWV 904: a definite cadence has occurred in the dominant at 58–9 and the two bars 59–60, with the number of parts reduced from four to three are very much a 'till ready' for the first combination of second and main subjects which is, moreover, to be in the tonic, and thus a climax. Yet not only was the cadence itself performed by two overlapping entries of the second subject (56 last crotchet to 59 first note, soprano: 59 last crotchet to 61 first crotchet, alto), but the link function is itself achieved by the second of these two entries. In fact, of course, we are wrong in talking all this time of 'entries performing . . .' and 'episodes performing . . .' various functions. The contrapuntal parts which partake in the fugue do various things, such as making important cadences, forming link passages, modulating, and so forth: sometimes an entry of the subject may coincide with one of these passages, it may partially coincide with it, or there may be no entry at the relevant place. The entry if present may assist in the process, or may oppose it. In a sense every part not actually engaged in delivering the subject is 'episodic', whether or not it coincides in time with an entry. The vertical view of entries and episodes, stemming from the harmonically based concepts of academic fugue, is here, as everywhere else, unhelpful in dealing with music which is fundamentally contrapuntal.

It will have become obvious from the foregoing that what is technically an episode may well comprise several sections with quite different functions. This is particularly to be found in the two late fugal works of Bach, the *Art of Fugue* and the *Musical Offering*. The first episode of the famous six-part 'ricercar' in the latter work, for instance (bars 29–47), begins with a full six-part passage derived in a very vague way from the descending chromatic figure in the subject (so much for Kitson's reducing the number of parts!). A firm modulation is made to E♭, the relative major, at bar 39 (we are still in six parts). Here, according to theory, the first 'middle' entry, in, of course, E♭, ought to follow. Bach, however, continues his episode, and begins a kind of miniature fugue on the descending chromatic figure: at first only one part is heard (note its omission in the preceding chord) but the others are added in turn (ought there to be a ♮ before the first A of 41?) and eventually a cadence is formed in B♭ (less strong than the E♭ one) at 45. There follows a series of false entries of the subject—B♭, F minor, C minor. A further C minor one in the lowest voice really seems at last to be a true entry—but no, it is the next one, a tonal answer in the next to lowest voice (48), which finally completes the theme, leading it to the dominant G minor. Judged purely as music all this is quite acceptable to the listener, but call it a 'compound episode' and it immediately becomes difficult. It shows, incidentally, how far from the mark is the academic idea of the episode as the vehicle for modulation between entries: Bach's nineteen bars have got us from G minor to G minor—on either side is a tonal answer ending in that key!

Before looking at some of the more organised episodes it might be of interest briefly to survey all the episodes in a single fugue, WTC I.8, one which will also be the subject of mention in Chapter 4. There is no trace of thematic development in the whole fugue—the episodes are simply those parts of the fugue where no entry occurs:

Episode 1 (bars 10(second half)–12): A casually introduced chromatic scale figure. The ii–i cadence of the preceding entry is delivered 'straight', but the flow is uninterrupted. Note the alteration to the opening of the succeeding entry to fit into the line of the bass part.

Episode 2 (15–19): Here the preceding entry, which was in the dominant position but in the tonic scale (see resource 6(b) below, Chapter 4) has its cadence rhythmically changed. The episode makes as if to form an F♯ cadence, but diverts it and later forms one in the dominant A♯ minor.

Episode 3 (22(second half)–24): After echoing the two cadences of the preceding stretto (see Chapter 4, resource 4: note the quaver rest which has now appeared, partly to make bar 21 playable and partly to avoid an unprepared ninth) this episode forms a half-cadence in preparation for the next stretto.

Episode 4 (33–6): The last note of the inverted entry (resource 6(iii), Chapter 4) is tied over. This episode is pure continuation of the counterpoint: neither 34–5 nor 35–6 can be called a cadence within the meaning of the act.

Episode 5 (41 (second half)–44): A good example of a 'compound' episode, though short: 41 delivers the vii♯–i cadence of the inverted subject 'straight' but there is not the slightest break in the flow. 42–3 is a perceptible half-cadence, and the rest, reduced to two parts, is a link to prepare the important entries of 44½–5 (see Chapter 4, p. 151).

Episode 6 (50–2): The rhythmically changed, varied inverted entry starting at 47 last note, soprano, is incomplete, and merges into the episode. Again a half-close is formed to prepare the first three-part stretto.

Episode 7 (56–7): To call this an 'episode' reflects the absurdity of distinguishing such small passages from their surroundings. The previous three-part inverted stretto in F♯ was 'false' (i.e. the theme was not complete). The next entry has its first note cut to a quaver (the second E♯ in bar 57, soprano) to fit into the flow of the counterpoint.

Episode 8 (60–1): Possibly intended as a conspicuous scalic descent (see resource 18, Chapter 4) to draw attention to the first appearance of the augmented subject at 62.

Episode 9 (75–6): No. 72–5 is not episode, but a varied entry in the middle voice, very chromatically 'harmonised'. The episode continues the counterpoint in the same vein.

This survey shows how, although it is of interest to the student of fugue to observe how entries are 'joined on' to what is technically 'free', musically speaking the only features that mean anything are cadences, conspicuous scale figures, etc., which are significant not as parts of episodes, but in relation to the design as a whole. It is by no coincidence that there have been continual references to Chapter 4. And, as has been said, resources of this kind can occur during entries as well.

The tendency toward organised development in episodes appears with the approach to the late Baroque. A number of the Buxtehude organ fugues show sequential treatments of figures—a particularly good example is the gigue-like second fugue of the G major Präludium (Hansen 8) where the third bar of the subject forms the basis of the episodes bars 78–85 and 89–92, as well as playing some part in the later long episode 101–25. Similarly in Pachelbel's C major organ fugue (Peters, *Spielbuch fur die Kleinorgel*, vol. II, no. 1) bars 26–9 treat the figure of the last 1½ bars of the subject: although the intervals are not the original ones the rhythm makes the derivation quite plain. The same way is also pointed by sequences on the complete countersubject in inversion in Fischer's D major fugue from *Ariadne Musica*, bars 13–14.

In mature Bach it is true that the methods of episodic development resemble in some ways those of Beethoven. (How typical it is, incidentally, that academically the middle part of sonata form is known as the 'development' section. Before Beethoven, whether a composer developed themes in this section or not was a matter of choice—there are plenty of such sections where virtually nothing that can reasonably be called development occurs. It was Beethoven who made it a regular practice to use the section for building up new sentences from fragments of exposition themes, and academic teaching has made a 'rule' from Beethoven's practice—very much as in fugue it has made 'rules' from Bach's practice, the difference being that what it has taken from Bach is much less representative of the composer's output as a whole.) The vital difference between Bach and Beethoven lies in the amount of significance given to the thematic figure. Nearly always in Beethoven this dominates the musical thinking, so that the listener is always conscious of the derivation. To give just one instance, the crotchet–four quaver figure in the first movement of the Eighth Symphony occurs many times in the development, but never loses its identity: when the recapitulation arrives this is felt as a culmination of all that has gone before, the figure now being heard again in its original thematic context. Not only are Beethoven's forms essentially dramatic, but the themes themselves are strongly characteristic, so that even with the intention of doing so it would be difficult to develop a figure from one of them to the extent of making it a pure background. Fugue, by contrast, is an undramatic type of music, its main feature being, as we have seen, continuity. Bach's themes, although more characteristic than many of earlier periods, are not the 'personalities' which Beethoven's are. Many of the most strongly characteristic ones are anyway unsuitable for development—the subject of WTC I.12 is an obvious example: development in this fugue is entirely of the more neutral rhythmic countersubject. Still further, the parts of the theme Bach selects for development are often not the most characteristic ones. In WTC I.9, for instance, the section selected for development is not the arresting opening (two notes followed by a rest) but the second bar, consisting entirely of flowing semiquavers (the first two entries overlap, there being no cadence to the subject). What the listener will notice in bars 11–16 will be first of all the upper parts of 11–12 and then the characteristic suspensions of the middle part in 13–16 (these would be very clear on the harpsichord—on the piano they have to be 'brought out'). Of course he will be conscious of the continuation of the semiquaver flow, but he will not regard this as 'the subject being developed' as he would in a Beethoven symphony. Significantly it is only in very late Beethoven, when the composer had again come under the influence of Bach and the Baroque, that occasionally an exposition figure fades into the background in the Bach manner—as, for instance, in the first movement of the last Piano Sonata op. 111, where the first subject figure tends to disappear beneath a new minim theme, itself not unlike a Baroque fugue subject. The 'disappearing' is partly the fault of pianists, but no amount of bringing out the exposition figure (see Tovey's notes[34]) can entirely save it from being dominated by the new one.

Any figure from exposition material may be used by Bach in development episodes. The most obvious one, however, the opening figure of the subject, is not very commonly employed. WTC I.2, always quoted as *the* example of episode construction, is in this way unusual, as are bars 22–3 of I.7. Nearly always something is tacked on to the end of the figure used, and/or the figure may be melodically altered in some way: another possibility is the joining together of two statements of the figure into one unit. Straight sequential treatment of a figure exactly reproduced from the exposition is rare. Despite its one unusual feature, I.2 is a convenient example of the three ways in which the figure is normally treated. Episode 1 (bars 9–11) shows the subject figure in the upper voices unaltered, but with material tacked on, while the bass makes a unit of sequence out of two statements of the descending scale from the beginning of the countersubject. Episode 3 (bars 17–19) is based on a direct sequence on the subject figure (bass) with no material tacked on, but with a melodic alteration, the original fourth becoming a sixth. From this example alone it is clear that the 'material tacked on' to the figure is of the very simplest—indeed in some cases it may amount merely to a prolongation of the last note of the figure, or simply a rest. Most frequently, as in episode 1 just mentioned, the figure is heard in dialogue between two parts, the figure in one part coinciding with the added material in the other. The episode is commonly, also as here, based on a strong harmonic foundation of chords moving in fifths—another reason, of course, why this kind of episode was seized upon by academic fugue as actually showing some real harmonies moving in a nicely regulated harmonic rhythm. In fact these episodes are about the only features in the normal Bach fugue which do show regular harmonic rhythm, always excepting fugues with toccata-type subjects, where a strong harmonic progression may be present in the subject itself. (It is interesting to compare the harmonic rhythm of entries with that of development episodes in the same fugue, and to note the comparatively 'bad' harmony of the entries.) In the case discussed the chords are G–C, C–F, F–B♭, B♭–E♭, E♭–A♭. It will also be observed that not only do these chords follow in regular succession, but the scales of each of the keys of which they are the tonics are used in turn. This digression of key, a common

34. Associated Board Edition of the Sonatas.

feature of development episodes, must be distinguished very strongly from true modulation, and after studying this episode 'the student is recommended', as the textbooks say, to look up bars 32–7 of the 'great' G minor organ fugue, BWV 542, and see what a real modulating episode is like. Another point: the last step of the sequence, E♭–A♭, is of course the beginning of the next entry, which has an E♭ melodic tonality. Even development episodes may be inseparable from entries on either side!

In episode 3 of I.2 it will be noticed that the middle part is effectively a free part: any scalic semiquaver figure *can*, of course, be derived from the opening of the countersubject, but such derivations are liable to end up by proving that everything is derived from everything else. The tied quavers here are quite enough to distinguish this part from the countersubject figure. The other part, the soprano, simply doubles a bit of the subject figure at the tenth. The use of 'free' parts in these episodes is quite common.

The following is a brief survey of the various ways in which Bach creates development episodes.

Two-part development episodes

(a) each part developing different exposition material. I.21, bars 19–21: upper part based on semiquaver figure from the subject with one note altered: lower part based on first six notes of subject, inverted and varied. See also II.1 bars 29–33.

(b) each part developing the same exposition material. I.15, bars 34–7: first two bars based on second bar of answer-codetta (bar 10, lower voice, on inversion of 9 upper voice) with added material—a long scale: 36–7 based on first bar of answer codetta, again with the scale added.

(c) one part thematic, other part free. I.9, bars 17–18: lower voice based on bar 2 of subject with one note altered (first semiquaver of 18). The free upper voice is, significantly, more noticeable than the thematic lower one (cf. above on bars 11–15 of the same fugue). See also I.10, bars 5–9, 24–8.

Three-part development episodes

There are no cases of all three parts developing different exposition material.

(a) two parts in dialogue developing one theme, the third developing another. I.2, bars 9–11, 22–5: for 9–11 see immediately above. In the recurrence of this episode (see Chapter 4, resource 9) bar 22 first beat corresponds not, as would seem at first hearing, to 9 first beat but to 9 third beat, the upper parts having been interchanged, as the disposition of the bass figure shows. In bar 24 the episode is prolonged, the bass figure continuing but the upper parts becoming free. This episode does not digress throughout as the first episode did: with two extra steps added this would have landed it in the remote region of G♭! As always with longer sequences in fifths in the Baroque, at some stage the diminished fifth is used to keep the key within sight of home: the second half of 24 is in fact based on the chord of II with D♮, not D♭, and from the second half of 23 onwards the scale used in C minor. II.1, bars 13–16, 55–80: upper parts develop opening subject figure (not unlike that of I.2) with one note tacked on (the first note of 15, soprano, and corresponding notes) replacing the rest in the original subject. Bass develops end of subject plus beginning of countersubject (the countersubject had begun by continuing the material of the end of the subject—see bars 3–6).

(b) three parts, two in dialogue, all developing the same theme. I.12, bars 10–12: the two upper parts are in dialogue on the opening figure of the countersubject (bar 4, first two beats, lower part) with a considerable amount of added material. The C in bar 10, alto (the uppermost part—the soprano is 'late' entering in this fugue) becomes a crotchet; the part then rests, to re-enter *below* the tenor in bar 11, after which it starts the pattern again, not however to complete it. The tenor, in bar 10 the middle of the three parts, starts with what the alto has in bar 11 and carries on in the same way. The bass is based on the same figure, with simpler added material. This rather unusual disposition sounds on the piano like an uppermost part delivering a sequence in single-bar units with a fill-in in the middle part when the uppermost part has its long tied note. Only on the older instruments is it clear that the E♭, last note of bar 10, middle part, is held over to the first note of bar 11, and the F, first note of 11 uppermost part, is a crotchet against which the middle voice falls to D♭. This tells the listener, in the only way possible on the keyboard, short of putting in 'expression' of an un-Baroque nature (better than nothing, perhaps, on the piano—see Tovey's notes[35]), that the uppermost part in 11 is a different one from the uppermost part in 10. The episode is a wonderful lesson in contrapuntal writing for the keyboard.

(c) three parts in canon all based on the same material. Although the dialogues seen in examples so far constitute canon of a kind they are so strongly harmonically based that the canonic effect does not really come over to the listener. Genuine canon, the effect of which is contrapuntal, is rare in episodes, presumably because the exposition itself is a kind of modified canon (see Chapter 1). Only in one fugue does Bach

35. Associated Board Edition.

employ it episodically, but here he makes of it a *tour de force*. The fugue is the great D minor organ BWV 538, the so-called 'Dorian'. The answer-codetta here, as has been seen, was a canon derived from a bit of the answer/countersubject combination: this is the basis for all the development episodes of the fugue.

The canon, originally at the upper sixth at one minim's distance, will in fact work at many intervals of pitch owing to the large proportion of step progression present. It will also work at the time interval of a semibreve (one bar). Prout, in his useful *Fugal Analysis* (pp. 52–65), analyses the episodes on the basis of various pitch intervals and the two time intervals—half and full bar. In fact, however, owing to the recurrence of the material in the canon, the 'full bar' canons turn out to be identical with inversions of 'half-bar' ones (see Example 43), as the diagram shows:

A B C A B C
A B C A B C

A B C A B C

A B C A B C

Ex 43

Here A, B and C represent the three portions of the material of the canon, each of a minim's duration. The upper part of the diagram shows a canon at the minim (half-bar), and the lower one at the semibreve (full bar). It is clear that no new combinations arise in the latter, the combination A–C for instance being merely an inversion of C–A in the minim canon. It is much more convenient to think of all the canons in terms of the minim time interval, and to list them in terms of the upper pitch interval, since the original appearance was at the upper sixth, appearances at lower intervals being regarded as inversions. In this way the material is much more logically ordered than in Prout's rather confusing array of apparently diverse canons.

Bach, in the whole of the fugue, uses the canon at all intervals except upper third and upper seventh. The difficulty with the former is probably the dissonance occurring in the C–A portion, with the latter the narrowly avoided consecutive octaves in B–A. The upper fourth position gives rise to unresolved fourths in the inversion in the portion $\frac{A}{C}$, and this is therefore not used to the lowest part owing to the fourth to this part being in Bach's style still treated in the manner of a dissonance.

The examples relevant here are bars 67–71 and 138–43. In the former soprano and alto show canon at the upper fourth inverted, soprano and tenor (lowest manual part) that at the upper sixth, and alto and tenor that at the upper fifth inverted. In the latter soprano and alto show the upper second, soprano and tenor the upper fifth inverted, and alto and tenor the upper octave. Both episodes, incidentally, contain other material: bars 64–6 prolong the previous entry, while 144–5 lead to a cadence in B♭ preparing the next entry.

(d) two parts in dialogue developing one theme, one part free. I.7, bars 7(beat 3)–10: the subject-codetta plus the first note of the countersubject (see bar 2, second half–3 first note) is used here, between bass and soprano. The 'tacked on' material differs: in the bass it is two quavers separated by a rest, in the soprano a quaver and tied crotchet. The middle part is free but, this being keyboard counterpoint, its first note in bars 8 and 9 provides the first note of the codetta figure, the sense transferring from the middle part to the soprano at the second semiquaver. This sounds complicated but presents no problem to the listener.

(e) two parts in canon, one free. 'Dorian' organ BWV 538, bars 156–60: the canon is here at the original upper sixth, but inverted. The free middle part is chromatic, linking up with the opening part of the episode which treats a chromatic figure incidentally introduced to divert the subject cadence at 152, lowest manual part.

(f) one part thematic, two free. I.7, bars 22–3: the opening figure of the subject, melodically altered (its first leap now a fourth and two semiquavers in the second group of four sharpened) is used with 'added' material of a minus quantity—the last two notes of bar 1 are replaced by a rest. The lower free part is in semiquavers, the middle in mixed rhythm. II.15, bars 17–19, 31–4, 48–51, 65–8: unusually, the figure from the answer-codetta is here stated in sequence with no added material and no melodic alteration. The two free parts recur with slight variations in all the occurrences mentioned. Note that they are more noticeable to the listener than the exposition material. The combination is in invertible counterpoint.

Four-part development episodes

These are comparatively rare. Most of the development episodes are in keyboard, particularly clavier, fugues, in which the normal number of voices is three. An occasional example is found in WTC, as in I.12, bars 43–7. This is a recapitulation of the episode of bars 10–12 already described. It is interesting that here Bach does not intend the dialogue effect so carefully contrived in the earlier episode. The alto now does duty for both the original upper parts and Bach even puts in an extra semiquaver (the D♭ of 44, alto) to ensure that there is no effect of two parts. The bass is the same, and the soprano and tenor are free. Note the melodious nature of the soprano which tends to dominate over the thematic parts.

Another example is II.22, bars 21–5 (25–7 are clearly a link to introduce the first stretto). Here the end of the subject is in dialogue between tenor and alto, with added material well sprinkled with rests (any crotchets with rests between them tend to recall bar 13, soprano, a second countersubject represented mainly by this rhythm: cf. Chapter 2, pp. 88-9). Bass and soprano are free. It is symptomatic of four parts in an episode that the soprano is rather stationary.

For other examples of the four-part organised episode one has to turn again to the canonic treatment in the 'Dorian' fugue. In bars 95–100 Bach contrives to combine the opening notes of the subject in the tenor with the three-part canon in the other three voices. Canonic positions are soprano-bass, upper second inverted; soprano-alto, upper fourth; alto-bass, upper second. On paper it may seem exaggerated to derive three harmless minims from the opening of the subject, but it must be remembered that by bar 95 the listener has heard many of these canons, but only one of them has so far contained a similar progression —the *four* minims at 38–9, equally intended as a reference to the subject but not sequentially treated and thus less conspicuous. The repetition in sequence here must surely attract his attention, and it must be remembered that the Baroque organ tends to bring out such inner parts far more clearly than the average organ in use today. Other four-part episodes involving the canon are bars 50–5, 88–93 and 124–9: the reader may perhaps seek these out, the principles on which the canon works having been made clear. Bars 124–9 are an excellent example of a passage defying harmonic analysis, explicable only as counterpoint.

Other composers of the late Baroque do use sequential procedures of a less strict kind than Bach. Bars 71–9 of 'And with His stripes' in Handel's *Messiah* show the inversion of a figure from the countersubject (bars 7–8, soprano) treated in something like Bach's 'dialogue' manner, with digressions of key similar to those observed in I.2. In 'He trusted in God' in the same work the phrase 'Let Him deliver Him', which can just about be called 'exposition material' since it appears in the bass at the very end of the fourth entry (bars 18–19), is used in rather free sequential manner (19–20, 33–5, etc.). There is nothing really comparable with Bach's methods, however, and after the Baroque the episode seems to return to its more typical function of prolongation, cadence, etc. It must be stressed again that only in a very limited number of fugues does even Bach himself use the development episode: in most of the organ fugues and nearly all choral fugues it is completely absent, and in WTC such mature examples as II.8, II.14, II.18 and II.23 do not employ it. There is nothing 'good' about the development episode: it is of great academic interest, easy to analyse and a convenient model for students (who hate to be left free to do what they like) and in the history of fugue it really points to a particular stage where organised thematic development had arrived on the scene, but before fugue began to become a stylistically unnatural type of music, a special, conscious excursion into an increasingly unfamiliar style. More and more, fugue came to be regarded as an exercise in counterpoint, and the increasingly exciting device-oriented fugues of post-Baroque composers had little use for the development episode. Even the modern fugal writers have not revived it. Hindemith's notable episodes are of the new material type (see immediately below). Shostakovitch makes his answer-codettas in every case the basis for episodes but most of the episodes are short and refer to the codetta rather than developing it—quite apart from the fact that, as was seen in Chapter 2, many of the codettas themselves are undifferentiated in character from the rest of the exposition.

Two further distinct types of episode must be mentioned here. The first is that which uses definite new material. This is not a very common type, since fugue is essentially monothematic in nature and such new themes as are introduced tend to be either countersubjects or subsidiary subjects, i.e. they make their first appearance either with the subject or in an exposition of their own. Almost certainly Bach's WTC I.13 is the first case of a new theme appearing in an episode: bars 7–11 cannot be derived by even the most ardent supporter of 'functional analysis' from anything in the exposition; the new theme does not accompany the subject—yet—nor can its appearance be called in any sense a new exposition. The style is 'modern' in that these bars might almost have come from an early piano sonata by one of Bach's young contemporaries. Immediately, as if rather perturbed by his daring venture, Bach makes a new countersubject of the figure—freely altered but completely recognisable—and this accompanies many (though not all) of the remaining entries. The figure also regularly appears in episodes and the whole fugue ends with bar 7 extended to a cadence (really a use of resource 21, below, Chapter 4).

Other Bach examples are much less conspicuous, and in some cases can be, but are probably better not, derived from the exposition. The same means of construction are used as have already been noted in development episodes. I.18, bars 21–4 and 28–30 show a typical two-part dialogue on a figure with one 'free' part, the figure not being traceable to the exposition. In I.23 all the episodes (bars 9–11, 13–15, 26–9) are based on the new material. Tovey[36] alleges that the episodes are based on the casual semiquaver figure at the end of bar 7, alto, but this in no way corresponds to the aural effect. It only explains the semiquavers anyway, whereas what the listener notices is the soprano line of bar 9, which is not traceable to anything. In I.24 a pure formula, but not traceable to the exposition, occurs at 16–21, 27–30 and by way of recapitulation (resource 9 below) at 65–9. These passages give one the strange feeling that they have come out of another fugue, and Bach oddly inserts into the first two occurrences the opening figure of the subject (19 and 28, first halves: note the meaningless part-writing in 19) as if to convince the listener and perhaps himself that there is a connection with the present fugue.

Finally in Bach a very mature example in triple counterpoint is seen in II.13, bars 12–20 and 44–52. Tovey is usually very wary of dubious derivations, and elsewhere insists that they have no value unless made clear to the listener: yet he derives[37] these episodes on the strength of four quavers (bar 12 first half soprano) from bar 3 of the subject in defiance of a completely different context, accentuation and position in the scale! The episodes are both in four sections of two bars each, digressing, in the manner we have already seen in other cases, to keys a fourth apart (D♯ minor, G♯ minor, C♯ major, F♯ major in the first one and G♯ minor, C♯ major, F♯ major and B major in the second). The three parts are regular themes, retained, with small alterations, in every two-bar unit, with interchange of parts in invertible counterpoint.

This type of episode does find a continued history in modern fugue. Hindemith, in LT, employs it in fugues 7 in A♭ and 9 in B♭. In the former, despite a momentary use of the rhythm in the third entry at bar 12, it seems reasonable to account episode 1, bars 14–22 as new material in a mainly faster rhythm than was used in the exposition. The lively uppermost part reappears as the bass of episode 3, bars 33–41, in

36. Notes to the fugue in Associated Board Edition.
37. ibid., notes to this fugue.

subdominant relationship (i.e. a fifth—plus an octave—lower). The upper parts are different apart from 37–8 (cf. 18–19). At the last moment Hindemith adds a semiquaver so that at 42 the bass arrives on F♭ instead of the F♮ that would correspond to the C of 23 first note. The following entry there was itself in C, but the entry of 42 is in the subdominant D♭. Fugue 9 in B♭ shows an equally definite use of new material in episode 1, bars 12–15 (all groups of four demisemiquavers recall the end of bar 2 of the subject and also the answer codetta but the line here is very different from either) and 2, bars 22½–4. Episode 1, with a D tonality, is recapitulated at 42–5 a minor third higher, in F, and at the close of the fugue (last five bars) a major third lower, in the tonic B♭. Episode 2, perhaps strangely in view of its distinctive character, does not reappear. (In analysing this fugue beware of retrograde entries (resource 6(d), Chapter 4) which look like episodes!)

Finally, mention must be made of the purely decorative episode in which counterpoint ceases—or is much reduced—giving way to purely bravura material. This is, of course, a direct inheritance from the concerto—not necessarily the solo concerto as such, for such passages occur also in concerti grossi, usually in the first violin part. The term 'concerto fugue' may well be applied to fugues in which many such episodes occur. A good example is the fugue forming the third movement of Alessandro Scarlatti's Concerto in F (HAM II no. 260) where at bars 27–36 the first violin, accompanied only by continuo, switches to purely decorative material, the 'proper' fugal style being resumed at 37 and lasting through to the end. A well-known Bach example is bars 87–120 of the fugue concluding Brandenburg Concerto no. 4: here again the solo violin has the bravura material, but Bach characteristically cannot resist thematic references from 105 on. The fugue forming the second movement of Handel's D major Sonata for violin and continuo is another well-known case, the first episode (bars 13–26) being mainly bravura though the continuo part has unobtrusive references to the subject. Bach's sonatas for violin and harpsichord also show a kind of concerto episode, although it is often a rather contrapuntal bravura that emerges. The second movements of the A major (bars 30–93) and E major (bars 58–91) sonatas exemplify such episodes in the middle sections of ternary schemes (not strict in the case of the E major). The Orchestral Suites also employ the type in the overture fugues, as, for example, bars 42–9 overture of the well-known Suite no. 3 in D major (numbering from the beginning—the fugue starts at bar 24, second time). Under concerto influence many of the organ fugues of Bach also show, in greater or less degree, the decorative episode. The well-known early (if authentic) D minor

Toccata BWV 565 has two passages of pure harmonic decoration (bars 62–70, 73–86) in its fugue, but the classic case is the great E minor ('Wedge', BWV 548) which has, like the violin and harpsichord sonatas just mentioned, a ternary scheme, strict in this case apart from the join between 'B' and the second 'A', the 'B' section (59–173) consisting of bravura episodes alternating with entries.

It is interesting that with Bach, as has been noticed in the cases just discussed, especially the last one, concerto-fugue often employs a degree of exact recapitulation. This resource will be more fully described in the next chapter (resource 9). It is obvious that a new type of fugue altogether is emerging in these examples, but like so many of Bach's specialities it was to have little future after him.

With the Orchestral Suites we come back to the very problem with which this chapter opened—that the same function may be performed by an entry, or series of entries, as by an episode, and that in turn what is technically an episode may be a passage of considerable weight and importance. This could not be better seen than in the fugue in the overture of Suite no. 1 in C major. From bar 22, second half, to 27 is a most important continuation of the exposition which will recur later. At 27 the tutti ceases abruptly, leaving the two oboes and bassoon—the concertino section—developing the subject. Developing? They are in fact *stating* the subject, the oboes once each in A minor (relative minor) and the bassoon giving an answer on the dominant of that key. Thus what is clearly 'exposition' in spirit is technically episode; and what to the listener is clearly 'episodic' is in fact three entries in close succession. The further the reader gets in this book the more he may be tempted to think that we need a completely new fugal terminology. And he would be right.

4

THE COMPLETE FUGUE

Just as the question 'what is fugue?' has received many and varying answers, so, not surprisingly, has the form of the complete fugue often been a matter of controversy. From Prout's idea—attributed by him to Riemann and shared probably by most teachers of his day and many since—that fugue was a definite ternary form we may go to the other extreme of Tovey's dictum that fugue was merely a texture.

It is perhaps helpful to point out that the idea of 'form' is not as simple as the average textbook perhaps implies. 'Sonata form', for instance, tends to be taken for granted as a fairly straightforward concept, but on considering it further we can see that a number of different principles are involved. In a typical 'normal' example of the form these would be:

(a) thematic content: there is supposed to be a first subject, a second subject, a cadence theme, etc. The development is supposed to differ from the exposition and recapitulation in that it breaks up the themes and produces new combinations of them.

(b) key: the second subject is supposed to be in the dominant; the recapitulation must begin in the tonic; the development must avoid tonic and dominant, and so forth.

(c) sectional structure: the exposition has a definite end and is repeated, the rest of the movement (also repeated in earlier examples) forming a second 'half'.

Arguments occur when there is doubt as to which feature to regard as governing the form, or when an event occurs which fulfils only some of the stipulations laid down. Thus the controversy that once raged as to whether sonata form was 'really' binary or ternary was due to a failure to specify the governing feature: by sectional structure the form is binary, with (in the assumed normal case) a definite end to the exposition. By thematic considerations it is ternary—exposition, development, recapitulation. And incidentally by key it is quaternary—tonic–dominant–other keys–tonic—although no one has ever suggested this![38] Similarly when we ask 'Is bar 599 of the finale of Schubert's "Great" C major "really" the beginning of the recapitulation?' the only answer must be 'thematically yes, tonally no' (the first subject appears on the mediant of E♭ major).

When Prout[39] ascribed to Riemann the 'honour' of 'the first discovery that a fugue is written in ternary form' he based his analysis mainly on key—key, moreover, as seen in the entries of the subject. In the first section, the exposition and 'additional' entries (if present), the key is tonic and dominant. There follows—so the theory goes—the 'middle' section, in which the subject would be heard in keys other than tonic and dominant, after which the 'final' section would return to tonic and dominant entries. A small amount of analysis by thematic content also came into this ternary definition in that the middle section was supposed to introduce stretto and the final section would contain a climactic stretto.

When on the other hand Morris[40] says that some fugues may be 'definitely in binary form' while others 'proceed to [their] final cadence without a break of any kind' he is using quite a different basis of analysis from Prout. Morris's 'binary' examples, WTCI.6 and II.21, have a definite cadence in the dominant somewhere about the middle of the fugue, and a similar cadence in the tonic at or near the end. The analysis is here based on a mixture of thematic content (the recognisable cadence), sectional structure (the cadence in the middle gives the impression of a section, although there is, in these examples at any rate, negligible break in the flow), and key—this time key not of theme-entries but of the cadences, which make a dominant-tonic pattern. Similarly Morris's first example of a fugue 'without a break of any kind' is WTCI.7, which happens to be one of the fugues—and there are not all that many—that fit Prout's ternary form based upon key of entries! Morris's references to its continuity refers only to the lack of any sectional structure or of any thematic feature other than the alternation of entry and episode.

Certainly the most familiar method of analysis—both to student and

38. Equally, a five-fold form could be found thematically by the analysis: first subject, second subject, development, first subject, second subject. The coda if present would make the form six-fold.

39. *Fugue*, Preface, p. 5.

40. *The Structure of Music*, p. 89.

listener—is that by thematic content. In the case of sonata form, people who know little about key can grasp the idea of first subject and second subject, and have at least a vague idea about development. With any luck they will recognise a recapitulation, though they will say that they 'didn't know whether it was in the right key or not'. One of the troubles with fugal forms is that it is just this familiar aspect of the analysis which has little application except in the comparatively rare double and triple figures (see below). Morris's binary cadences are, when it comes down to it, very inconspicuous compared with those of a sonata movement—and, of course, only a small number of fugues show this feature. In the average fugue, analysis by thematic content leads to the unhelpful result: Exposition, Episode, Subject-entry, Episode, Subject-entry, Episode, etc. etc.—and even this assumes not only that there are episodes (there aren't, for instance, in WTC I.1) and that there is a reasonably marked distinction between entry and episode which, as was seen in Chapter 3, is often not the case!

The same objection must apply to a more recent theory of fugal construction—Bukofzer's idea of 'continuous expansion'.[41] 'Continuous expansion'—the idea applies not only to fugue—means, apparently, the developing or working-out of a single motive or theme either without a break (as in WTC preludes I.1, I.6 and I.15—the author's own examples) or with 'incisions' in which the motive is 'consistently expanded in modulatory fashion'. In fugue, Bukofzer says, 'continuous expansion' is 'realised in a chain of fugal exposition'. The 'incisions' in this case clearly denote episodes: presumably such fugues as WTC I.1 (with no episodes) would be relegated to the 'radical type' where the motive is worked out without a break. The theory is reasonable as far as it goes, but on the author's own admission hardly a formal principle. It does little to explain, say, the feeling of excitement at the end of WTC II.17 or the enormous sense of design communicated to the listener in Beethoven's *Grosse Fuge*.

Clearly it was the absence of any reasonable thematic or sectional basis for analysis that drove nineteenth-century theorists such as Riemann, and Prout following him, to the ternary analysis by key of entries. Key of entries is certainly *one* method of describing what happens in certain types of fugue, although we can now see that 'ternary' here does not mean what it means in the more familiar sonata context. But when the entries show little or no key variety, or the key 'system' of the entries appears to be no system but a continual alternation of the tonic with other keys in apparently capricious manner, or a lop-sided scheme appears such as ten tonic or dominant entries, one in

41. *Music in the Baroque Era*, p. 358.

another key and then a final tonic entry, it seems clear that as an all-pervading theory of fugal form key analysis will not do.

Paradoxically it is not the strictness of fugal form that makes it a problem but its freedom. Cecil Gray[42] once said, 'After the exposition . . . almost anything may—and generally does—happen with Bach.' The remark—with a few qualifications of the word 'anything'—applies not only to Bach but to fugue in general. The monothematic basis of fugue means that there is much greater freedom of design than is the case with sonata form, with its two themes. Another difficulty in analysing fugue is the fact that it is (largely) contrapuntal and continuous. Some fugal writers are more continuous than others, the mature Bach fugue probably being the most continuous of all. But in hardly any fugal work can it be said that 'the final section begins at beat so-and-so of bar so-and-so'—even if one has decided what the criteria are for a final section. We may find a conspicuous entry of the subject which seems a vital event—say it is the first entry in the tonic key to be heard since the exposition; we mark it as introducing a new section, only to find that against its first five or six notes other parts are still completing a sequence belonging to the previous episode, or are forming a prominent cadence led up to by the whole preceding passage and which now occurs well *after* our entry has begun. Such is the essence of counterpoint—and of fugue.

We return to what was said in Chapter 1—that while fugue is not a form, many fugues do have forms about which something can usefully be said. It will be the purpose of this chapter to examine briefly what it is hoped will at least be a representative number of such forms. Before this is done, however, it will be as well to list the resources available for the construction of a fugue, for the sustaining of interest and (where desirable) for the building up of a climax. A few of these —stretto, for instance—will already be well known to those who have had the misfortune to 'do' fugue; but the number and variety of resources in real life exceeds by a long way anything ever dreamt of in academic fugue.

The resources available for the complete fugue

In each case after the resource has been described a single example is given (occasionally more than one). These have deliberately been chosen from the most easily accessible and best-known fugues so that the reader can see, and, it is to be hoped, hear in performance, how the resource works.

(1) *Pitch-contrast of entries.* The fugue begins, of course, with a num-

42. *The Forty-eight Preludes and Fugues of J. S. Bach*, p. 9.

ber of entries at different positions of pitch. Subsequent entries of the theme may use these positions again, but variety can be obtained by the use of new positions. The use of other keys (q.v. below, resource 7) for entries of course entails this anyway, but even with the retention of the original subject–answer scale-positions use of a higher or lower octave provides effective contrast.

Example: Handel, *Messiah*, no. 25, 'And with His stripes'. Soprano re-enters at bar 25 with the original answer, but at a higher octave than hitherto used.

A very high or very low entry may be used to give an effect of climax. This is particularly true of low entries on the harpsichord, which have a very impressive sound.

Example: High—Handel, *Messiah*, no. 28 'He trusted in God', entry of bar 50 soprano. Low—WTC I.4, bar 73 bass.

(2) *Contrast in 'accompanying'*[43] *parts.* In that fugue rarely exemplifies an exact repeat of any entry of the subject this resource is to some extent always being employed—it is indeed one of the fundamentals of fugue that every subject-entry should be differently 'accompanied'. More conspicuous changes in the nature of the 'accompaniment' may sometimes be made, such as the introduction of quicker or slower movement or, say, the use of dotted notes when the previous 'accompaniment' has been in even ones.

In some cases the change in movement is associated with the introduction of a new theme (resource 5, below).

Example: Beethoven, *Grosse Fuge*, op. 133. Even in the first section four types of movement appear—at the opening, quaver-semiquaver alternation (quasi dotted rhythm); at the viola entry of bar 58, triplets; at the violin I entry of bar 111, two semiquavers-quaver; at the viola entry of bar 139 (itself varied) a new kind of triplet figure.

(3) *Contrast in time-interval of entries.* Academic teaching has always recognised stretto, the actual overlap of entries (see 4, immediately below), but it is not generally realised that the spacing in time of ordinary entries can be an important source of variety. A long passage without entries can give particular point to the entry that follows, the listener beginning to imagine that the subject has been forgotten and then being suddenly confronted with it. Similarly a series of entries very close to each other has an obvious intensifying effect.

Example: A long interval between entries is well illustrated by WTC II.11, bars 25–52. For intense piling up of entries, see WTC, II.8,

43. The word is used merely for convenience: in fugue these parts are, of course, usually of equal importance to that which carries the subject.

bars 15–35 and Hindemith LT fugue 4 in A, whole of last section (45–end).

(4) *Stretto.* Stretto, the overlapping of one subject-entry with another, is well known, if not notorious, as a resource because of its featuring conspicuously in examination fugues. It always seems to be supposed that the student finds stretto 'difficult', but in fact either the subject will work in stretto or it will not: it is only a matter of seeing how it will work, i.e. at what point(s) in the theme the overlapping is to take place and at what pitch interval(s). The subject itself is set by the examiner, and it is his unfortunate task to design it so that it will 'work'!

In the examination-room no doubt the counterpoint between the two or more entries of a stretto is supposed to be smooth and correct. In real life, however, a certain amount of 'roughness' has always been permitted, the fact of the subject being a familiar theme causing the listener to hear horizontally rather than vertically. 'Roughnesses' are certainly evident in some of Bach's stretti, where however some of the dissonance may be mollified by use of appropriate harmonies. In modern fugue, of course, any combination of the subject with itself will do (although not all may be equally effective).

In the examination fugue there is supposed to be a series of stretti, each one closer in time interval than the last, thus producing a gradual heightening of intensity. It will be seen that this 'rule' finds little support in live fugues for the very simple reason that although closeness of entry is *one* way of heightening the tension it is not the *only* way. Increasing the number of parts involved in the stretto is another obvious means, to say nothing of all the other resources which are in live fugue combined with stretto: to give one example only, a very close stretto inconspicuously introduced in a foreign key will have less climactic effect than a not-so-close one dramatically introduced in the tonic. For a stretto in all parts present the Italian term 'stretto maestrale' is used.

False stretto. Very commonly one or more—sometimes indeed all—of the entries in a stretto begin but do not complete the subject. While this may for convenience be called 'false stretto' it is none the less a very telling device: it is, after all, the opening of the theme that the listener remembers best, and, particularly when there is the distracting effect of the subsequent entry or entries of the stretto, the absence of the ending may be of little concern to him. Much of the latter part of Handel's 'Amen' chorus in *Messiah* consists of a mass of false stretto—indeed the complete subject is not heard after the bass entry of bar 38!

In other cases the existence of one complete entry can often create the illusion of true stretto when in fact the other entry is not complete: great composers, if not examiners, know exactly how much the listener can or cannot follow in a complex web of sound.

Example: *Real*—two Bach examples are given in Example 44. To

Ex 44(a)Bach, WTC I.16: stretto
(b)Bach, Mass in B minor: *Kyrie* II, stretto

see how Bach deals with the 'roughness' of the first and the virtually bitonal result of the second, see in WTC I.16, bars 17–19, and, in Kyrie II of the Mass in B minor, bars 35–8, 40–3 and 54–7. *False*—Handel, *Messiah,* no. 28 'He trusted in God', bars 22–7 (bass incomplete, alto complete) and 27–33 (tenor incomplete, soprano complete).

(5) *Thematic combination and contrast.* This is one of the oldest devices of fugue, being used in many of the early ricercars. It can take a number of forms:

(a) As already seen, a regular countersubject or more than one may appear in the exposition and may play a prominent part in the fugue. In addition to accompanying the subject a countersubject may also, as has been seen, feature in episodes, thus forming an important source of contrast with the subject, while never usurping the latter's function of main theme.

Example: WTC II.16—see also immediately below on Invertible counterpoint.

(b) A new countersubject, or more than one, may appear during the course of the fugue. The word countersubject is here used for a theme making its first appearance with the subject, the term 'second subject', 'third subject', etc., being reserved for themes which are given a separate exposition on their own.

Example: Bach organ fugue in B minor BWV 544. Two new countersubjects, bar 28 (soprano) and bar 59 (soprano).

Exceptionally the new countersubject may be formed from material from a preceding episode, as in WTC I.13 (see above p. 105).

(c) Reference to the subject may cease altogether and a new theme appear in exposition (i.e. delivered in all, or at least several, parts in turn). When such a theme is given its own individual exposition it is probably reasonable to refer to it as a 'subsidiary subject' and to use the term 'double (or triple) fugue'. Even here, however, the new themes do not in true fugue usurp the importance of the subject—the main subject, as it may be called in such cases.

Examples: Hindemith LT 1 in C (2nd subject bar 11, combination at bar 35): Shostakovitch 24 no. 4 in E minor (2nd subject bar 47, combination bar 88).

As these examples suggest, subsidiary subjects almost always combine later on with the main subject—sometimes in more than one way, as with the third and main subjects of Bach's well-known E♭ organ fugue BWV 552. Occasionally, however, as in Bach's C minor organ fugue BWV 537, there is no combination, the first subject simply returning, in this case with an exact recapitulation of a whole passage (resource 9, below: the second subject is the chromatic theme of bars 57–60, tenor: recapitulation, bars 105–23, corresponding to 5–23 with some minor differences). Obviously there is a danger here that the piece will cease to be a true fugue, but that is not the case with this example. In another case, the F major organ fugue BWV 540, Bach pretends to be using the same procedure; the second subject disappears and the main subject conspicuously returns in the tonic key without combination (bar 128, alto). This, however, is only a ruse—in all remaining entries both themes are combined. Bach here hit on rather a clever way of avoiding the obvious, one which he was also to use to good effect in some of the later numbers of *The Art of Fugue*.

In Bach particularly the relationship between main and subsidiary subjects is highly contrapuntal rather than harmonic: this has been seen to be true of most subject–countersubject relationships, and it is even more evident in the present cases, the themes sometimes being of different lengths (as in BWV 552 just mentioned) or overlapping each other in the combination. In the *Art of Fugue*, Bach's last fugal work, this contrapuntal tendency is most marked in the combination of the subsidiary themes with the main theme of the work (see p. 159). An interesting test is to confront someone with the main theme and any of the subsidiaries separately, and see if he can guess the way in which they combine.)

Invertible counterpoint: In a number of cases the combination of themes may use the device of 'invertible counterpoint' at intervals other than the octave. This forbidding term refers to a procedure very simple to understand—as with stretto the difficulty lies in composing the kind of themes which will 'work'. In the second line of 'Three Blind Mice', for instance, it is clear that while the first voices are singing 'See how they run' the second voices to enter could sing their 'Three Blind Mice' not beginning on E but on B, a fifth higher or a fourth lower. This would in technical language be called 'invertible

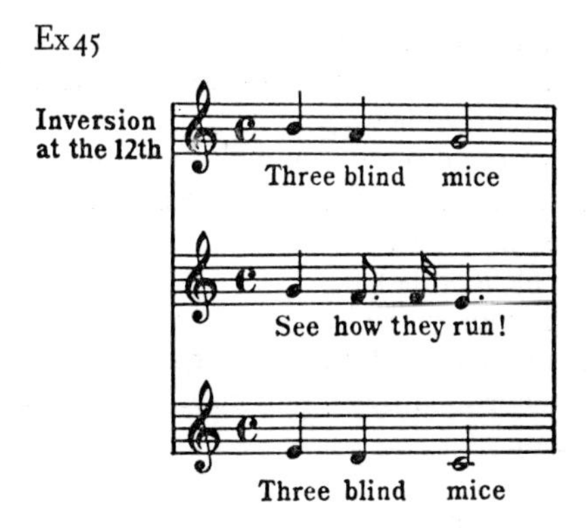

counterpoint at the twelfth', in that the second voices' material could be transposed up a twelfth and put above that of the first voices.[44] ('Twelfth' and not 'fifth' because if inversion is to take place it is more likely to be at the compound interval for convenient layout of the themes.) Clearly two devices are here involved (a) invertibility and (b) ability to combine at more than one interval.

Invertibility at the twelfth is the most commonly used of these special invertibilities because, as our example shows, the commonly used third becomes another third. Also fifth, a consonance, becomes octave, another consonance. Invertibility at the 11th is also not uncommon—here sixth becomes sixth. In both cases the theme concerned is transposed the compound of a fourth or a fifth, thus minimising the amount of alteration to the tone and semitone steps. Other intervals of

44. The invertibility at the twelfth does not work beyond this point!

invertibility found in fugue are the tenth and the thirteenth: in the former an original octave between the themes becomes a tenth, in the latter it becomes a sixth. If the themes are also invertible at the octave the second theme may be doubled in thirds or sixths respectively, an important climactic device (see resource 13, below).

Example: *The* case of the use of special invertibilities is WTC II.16. As this fugue is virtually a textbook on the device (perhaps a more pleasant one than most) the instances are listed here in full. The two themes concerned are the subject and countersubject—see, in the first instance, bars 5–9. The entries where new positions are used are as follows:

bars 28–32	12th.
bars 32–6	10th.
bars 36–40	10th.
bars 45–9	normal and 13th together—subject doubled in thirds.
bars 51–5	normal and 10th together—subject doubled in sixths.
bars 59–63	normal (alto to tenor).
	10th (soprano to tenor and alto to bass).
	12th (soprano to bass)—subject and countersubject doubled in thirds.
bars 69–73	(incomplete entry)
	normal (soprano to bass).
	10th (soprano to alto and tenor to bass).
	12th (tenor to alto)—again both the themes doubled in thirds.

Bach, with unerring judgement as to what the listener will and won't hear, allows himself a good deal of freedom both at the beginning and end of the theme. The crux of the combination is obviously the two conspicuous bars in the middle (first occurrence bars 6–7), and here Bach is always strict. The 'matrix' of the combination in these bars is given in Example 46. At heart it is very simple. One of the positions, that equivalent to inversion at the 12th (see Example 46(d)), is dissonant, but the dissonance has a delayed resolution by step. Step progression, with if possible (as here) an intervening note or notes to avoid the possibility of consecutives, is the answer to most contrapuntal problems in this style. Another position, that of 'inversion at the tenth' (see Example 46(c)), produces fourths, which in Bach's style would cause difficulties if they occurred to the lowest part present. Bach simply avoids the contingency, and in fact characteristically arranges for the fourths to form the upper parts of dissonant seventh chords, again with delayed stepwise resolution (bars 33–4).

Ex 46 Bach, WTC II.16: matrix of subject and countersubject combination

(a) Original, as in exposition (e.g. bars 6–7)

(b) 'Invertible counterpoint at 13th', as at bars 45–6, alto to bass

(c) 'Invertible counterpoint at 10th', as at bars 33–4, upper parts

(d) 'Invertible counterpoint at 12th' (dissonant combination) as at bars 29–30, upper parts

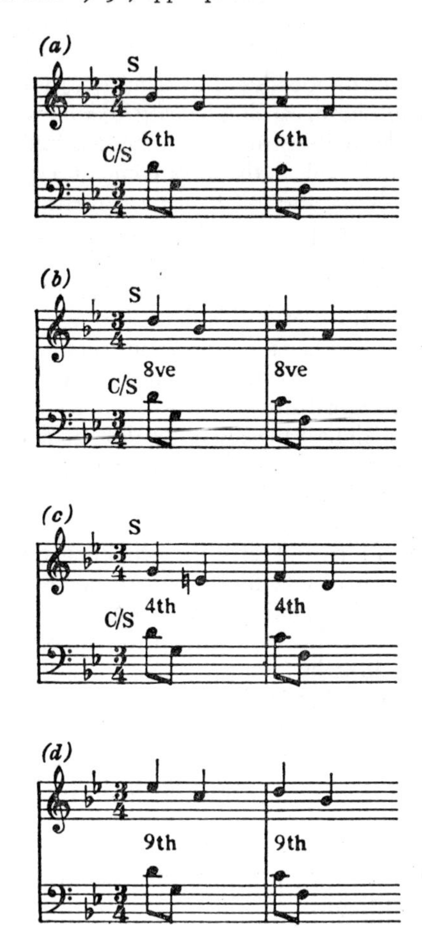

(6) *Variation of the subject.* This important resource is almost entirely neglected in academic teaching except for the devices of inversion, augmentation and diminution. In real life a far greater number of means of variation are used:

(a) 'Tonal answer variation.' In Chapter 2 it was seen that alterations were often made to the theme when it became the answer for scalic and/or tonal reasons. The altered answer form of the theme, by convention called 'tonal answer', can be used later on in the fugue: moreover, other forms which could have been used for the answer in the exposition, but were not, can also be used later in the design. Still further variations based on the idea of tonal answer, but which would be unlikely in the exposition, can still be used later on when the demands of tonality and scale are less stringent. In the 'classical' period of fugue, and perhaps generally, this is the most common type of variation of the subject, probably because, as Chapter 2 suggested, the individuality of the theme seems to be preserved with tonal alterations in a way not apparent with other types of variation.

Example: Of literally hundreds of examples perhaps the best known is the glorious final entry of Bach's E♭ major organ fugue BWV 552, bar 114, pedal. This is in fact the form an answer might have taken had the key been A♭, although the fourth note of the theme is not changed as Bach did in the original answer—this would have given too great a melodic tonality of A♭ near the end of the design. WTC II.8, bars 15–17, bass, shows an answer-form that Bach could have used in the exposition but didn't. (It is in fact a better answer for Rule 1 than the exposition one!)

(b) Alterations of tone and semitone steps. This is self-explanatory. (As has been seen, it is sometimes, though not regularly, found in the first answer.) Such alteration may be used either to avoid or produce chromaticism: the first case arises if the subject is used at a new position in a diatonic scale.

Example: The most drastic change of tones and semitones occurs when a subject originally beginning on i is introduced on vii. Both Bach and Shostakovitch use this position in their first fugue in C: Bach WTC I.1, bars 21–3, tenor: Shostakovitch 24, 1 bars 48–56, bass.[45]

The second is due to the deliberate seeking of chromatic colour, sometimes for 'preparatory' purposes (see resource 17, below).

Example: WTC I.7, bar 34, middle part—G♭ in place of G♮ preparing final cadence of fugue.

A very effective chromatic sharpening of the very first note of the

45. Shostakovitch in fact uses every scale position in this fugue, which is in pure C major scale throughout.

subject is seen in Mendelssohn's organ fugue in D minor (Peters no. 3), final entry, 8 bars from the end, pedal part.

(c) inversion. Here rhythm remains the same but each interval in the theme is turned upside down, the theme being still recognisable. The classical inversion scheme replaces tonic by dominant and vice versa, the mediant remaining the same (thus C–G (above)–E–C becomes G–C (below)–E–G). This scheme has the advantage that inverted and direct versions can be consonantly combined[46] if (as commonly) the subject employs only the first five degrees of the scale, or uses the sixth and seventh degrees in such a way that the resultant discords can be resolved, or at least convincingly used.

Example: Bartók, *Music for Strings, Percussion and Celeste*, first movement bars 68–73, 3rd and 4th violin part. For direct and inverted combined see WTC II.8, bars 43–5, soprano and tenor; Hindemith LT 4, bars 24–5 and later.

(d) retrograde motion. Here the theme (*pace* modern theories) loses its recognisability. It now starts at the end, keeping its note values exactly, and ends at the beginning. Rhythm is completely reversed and is thus unrecognisable, and although the intervals are the same they occur in reverse order and are thus also unrecognisable, since music is an art that moves forward in time. (Comparisons with the reversal of designs in architecture or painting are for this latter reason irrelevant.) It must be remembered that in retrograde motion *everything* is reversed. If one says to someone 'A, B, C, D' and then 'D, C, B, A' the other person can of course recognise that the four letters have been said the other way round. This is in no way the equivalent of the retrograde delivery of a theme: the procedure in music of which it is the equivalent is the delivery of four thematic fragments first in their original order and then in the reverse order, *each thematic fragment, however, still being delivered forwards, and thus being recognisable.* In retrograde motion *each fragment would itself be reversed*—it is as though the letters D, C, B, A were themselves each said backwards, i.e. the 'ee' sound of D coming before the initial 'd' and the 'd' itself being reversed so that it is no longer the consonant we know.

Retrograde motion has, significantly, little use among the classical fugue composers. (Bach uses it in certain canons, but never in fugue.) A famous use is Beethoven's, in the fugue which forms the last movement of the 'Hammerklavier' Sonata op. 106, bars 143–8, lower part, 152–9, soprano, and 159–66, bass. At the end of his life Beethoven

46. In styles up to and including the late Baroque, the fourth (C–G below in the case just imagined) must not occur to the lowest voice if it occurs by leap. A 'free' lowest voice can usually be found at appropriate moments—see the first three notes of the combination in WTC II.8 quoted immediately below.

developed a great interest in the older styles and his fugues of this period are highly academic. There is a chance that the listener may recognise the middle of the theme (as at 146, 147 lower part), but this is only because it is a two-bar sequential pattern with semiquavers, and any such two-bar sequential pattern will tend vaguely to recall the second and third bars of the direct version of the subject. Hindemith, another academic composer, uses retrograde motion in LT: in LT 3 in F, bar 30 is a half-way point: the last beat of this bar corresponds to its first beat (chord of A major) and from this point on the whole of bars 1–30 occurs in retrograde, completing the fugue. Both entries and episodes thus appear reversed, the only difference between the versions being the addition of free parts to retain the three-part texture to the end. Retrograde entries also play a large part in the B♭ fugue LT 9. Bars 30–3 show the retrograde subject in the soprano; at 33–8 bass and middle part are in stretto on the retrograde subject; 38–41 show a retrograde/direct stretto in bass and soprano; at 46–50 bass (later middle voice—the part writing is vague here) and soprano are in stretto on the retrograde inversion of the subject, and overlapping this stretto is one between middle voice and soprano of the 'normal' retrograde subject at one-and-a-half instead of the previous one-bar interval! It would be interesting to play this fugue to an unbiassed listener, not mentioning which devices are in use, and to find out which entries he can detect. Normal inversion is also used at 16–19 bass and in the stretto of direct and inverted subject at 25–9 soprano and bass, so that the piece would make a good test of the relative recognisability of inversion and retrograde motion.

(e) augmentation. Here the note values of the theme are made longer —commonly twice as long. The device is an old one, stemming again from the early ricercars. Its tendency is to make the entry more conspicuous, and it is thus commonly a climax device.

Example: WTC I.8, bars 62–7 bass and 77–82 soprano. Note also tonal answer variation in both entries, and tone and semitone alteration in bar 82, giving E♮ instead of E♯—a singularly beautiful Phrygian mode effect for the end of the fugue.

(f) diminution. Here the note values are made smaller—commonly half their former value. It is not a very common device: while intensifying the movement, it has also a tendency to make the subject disappear into the flow of the counterpoint.

Example: Although on the borderline between being two incidental fugues and one complete one—there is a drastic interruption at bars 108–30—the last movement of Beethoven's piano sonata op. 110 provides probably the best-known case; see bar 146, bass, and subsequently. There is also a change of accentuation and a slight rhythmic change at the end of the theme. Bar 162, soprano, shows an even more drastic diminution of part of the theme—but by now the listener's attention has been diverted by the augmented version (bar 154, bass) and it is doubtful whether the 'diminished' subject is now heard as anything more than a background.

Similarly in WTC II.9, 'diminished' versions of the subject begin at bar 26 soprano, last crotchet (some of them also inverted), but soon disappear into the contrapuntal flow. So little does Bach care about the inverted-diminished entry of 37, last crotchet, tenor, that he transposes the first two notes down an octave to make it playable. Tovey's recommendation, in the Associated Board Edition that these two notes should be put back in their 'correct' place shows a Beethovenian rather than a Bachian attitude to thematic development.

(g) rhythmic permutation. This is a fairly old device: in the various sections of the early ricercars and canzonas a different rhythmic version of the theme might be used in each section. Perhaps one of the most interesting well-known uses is in the *Grosse Fuge* of Beethoven, where the device of *Unterbrechung* (Latin *interruptio*), which Beethoven learned from his teacher Albrechtsberger,[47] is employed. Strictly speaking, this device—the breaking up of the theme's rhythm into disjointed notes off the beat—is not used 'in the fugue', since it appears already in the initial entries, the 'straight' version of the theme having first been heard in the introductory (non-fugal) bars. The device appears in the 'false start' at bar 26, but the listener has no way of recognising it here, since nothing occurs on the strong beats—a typical late Beethoven ambiguity.[48] Only when the 'proper' start to the fugue is made does the countersubject help the listener to detect the true accentuation of the subject. Beethoven has another rhythmic permutation in store at bar 139, where the notes of the subject are brought close together and displaced by a quaver, and yet another at 233 where the subject acquires a jaunty 6/8 rhythm.

(h) filling in of the leaps in the subject. Not a common device, and one that naturally tends to obscure the theme. Many players and listeners must miss (as the present writer would have done had he not read Tovey's notes) the stretto on the subject thus varied in WTC II.9, bars 23–7. The entries are: soprano 23 beat 1, alto 23 beat 2, bass 25 beat 1, and tenor 25 beat 2.

47. This interesting fact, which calls in doubt Beethoven's supposed scorn of his teacher, was first revealed by Warren Kirkendale, *Fuge und Fugato in der Kammermusik des Rokoko und der Klassik*, p. 298.

48. Compare the off-beat grunts on low woodwind which introduce the 'Alla Marcia' in the last movement of the Ninth Symphony. Nothing can tell the listener that these are off the beat until the tune arrives.

(i) alterations to the beginning and/or end of the subject to fit into the flow of the counterpoint: curtailment of the subject. As was mentioned under stretto, the opening of the subject is usually remembered by the listener better than the latter part. A number of fugues discontinue the latter part of the subject as they proceed, and only the listener can decide at what point this process can reasonably cause the piece to cease to be a fugue in the true sense. Two cases where true fugal nature may reasonably be said not to be lost are Handel's 'Amen' chorus in *Messiah* (mentioned under stretto) and the last movement of Haydn's String Quartet in F minor, op. 20, no. 5. In both these the opening of the theme is its most characteristic phrase—this is especially true of the Haydn with its diminished seventh leap. (If the opening of the subject were an inconspicuous formula and a later characteristic part were dropped during the fugue, the opposite argument would apply.) Similarly only the listener can really distinguish an incomplete entry from episodic development of the first phrase of the subject (see Chapter 3).

Alteration of the beginning of the subject is on the whole more likely to obscure the whole entry. It is, however, feasible even with short subjects, provided that the main features of the theme are left intact.

Example: WTC I.11, bar 65 soprano; WTC I.4, bar 48 soprano: so characteristic is the diminished fourth leap in this short theme that Bach can alter the end (bar 51) as well, and yet the entry is still heard as such.

(j) free melodic alteration of the theme's intervals (not explicable by tonal answer principles or change of tone and semitone steps). This varies very much from composer to composer. In the earlier Baroque it is, as might be expected, rather rare, the old rule about the preservation of the theme being a powerful influence even as late as early Bach.

Example: Bach Brandenburg Concerto no. 4 in G, last movement (concerto fugue), bars 67 and 207, bass: opening fourth altered to octave in both cases. Handel: *Messiah*, no. 28 'He trusted in God': bars 44, bass, and 53, soprano, replace the high note by a repetition of the previous note. The original would have been a shriek in the sopranos at 53, but the change in the bass also suggests that this was anyway intended as a genuine melodic alteration.

(7) *Key-variety of entries*. In Chapter 2 the question of the melodic tonality of the fugue-subject was mentioned. In the present section it should be made clear that we are concerned with the melodic tonality of entries, not with the harmonic tonality of the total mass of parts. 'Key' thus means 'melodic tonality' unless specifically stated otherwise.

Key variety of entries was a surprisingly late addition to the resources of fugue. Even up to Buxtehude it is little used. When found before Buxtehude it seems usually to be restricted to the employment of the position a fourth above (fifth below) the subject or fifth above (fourth below), whichever was *not* the position of the original answer: in many cases this would in fact be what we would call a 'subdominant key entry', the dominant position, as we have seen, becoming more and more frequent in the original answer. Even in Buxtehude's best-known organ Präludium—that in G minor (Hansen 9)—there are two fugues on different subjects: during the whole course of these only one entry departs from the original subject–answer scale-position, and that, to the horror of the examiners, is the *last* entry of the second fugue, which is in C minor, the subdominant!

Clearly the reason for the reluctance to use the other keys was the old rule preserving the sanctity of the subject's tone and semitone steps. Within the directly related keys—those normally employed in the 'classical' period of fugue—only dominant and subdominant keep the same mode as the tonic: the other keys involve a change from major to minor or vice versa, thus considerably—more considerably perhaps than textbooks make clear—changing the tone-semitone relationships.

Significantly perhaps the Buxtehude fugue which shows the nearest approach to a key 'scheme' of entries has a chromatic scale figure subject. It is the second fugue of the A minor Präludium (Hansen 4) which is on a chromatic variation of the diatonic subject of the first fugue. At bar 83 (of the whole piece) the subject[49] enters in the relative major C in the soprano and is promptly answered by the alto: the tenor and bass (pedal) follow suit so that a complete 'exposition' occurs in this key. A further answer occurs at 91 (soprano) and a cadence in C at 93–4 is followed by free homophonic material (resource 13, below—free, that is, unless any rising fourth or fifth is said to be the first two notes of the subject! Four entries follow in close succession—C answer (98), C subject (100), A minor answer (100, last note) (these two in genuine stretto) and A minor answer again (102 last note). A cadence in A leads to a toccata ending (resource 15 below) with Buxtehude's favourite plagal cadence.

In the second fugue of the G major Präludium (Hansen 8) a single relative minor entry occurs at bar 98 (soprano). The fugue begins at bar 57 and runs into a toccata ending at 140: this shows where this single entry comes in relation to the whole, much of which is taken up with episodic or false entry treatment of the gigue rhythm. A very long episode follows the entry in question, almost as if it were to be the

49. Taking this fugue to be a resumption of the first one the form of the theme here is a subject-form; the initial entry of this second fugue is an answer. If the second fugue be taken on its own, then of course bar 83 is an answer-form.

last; Buxtehude does, however, introduce a further tonic entry at 126, as if he had been reminded of 'the rules' at the last moment.

In the G minor Präludium (Hansen 22) the second fugue, beginning at bar 58, shows a relative major entry at 88, pedal. Two attempts to answer this (90 tenor, 92 pedal) prove to be only false entries and there are no further full entries in the piece, though so many false ones occur that the rather neutral theme tends to disappear. The first fugue of this piece, incidentally, has one 'middle' entry—significantly the last one, at 47 pedal: a tonal answer from F to C minor (tonal answer variation, resource 6(a)).

These entries and some other more tentative ones show the gradually increasing interest in entry key-variety. Buxtehude's whole treatment—the relegation of most of the entries concerned to the second fugue, where matters tend anyway to be freer, and the use of false entries—suggests that the old rule of 'original subject and answer positions only' still held sway, and one feels almost that the composer is a little ashamed of trying to break away from it. In the organ fugues of Lübeck (1656–1740) the same attitude seems to prevail: in the C major (Peters, 6) the second fugue attempts one relative entry at bar 71. The C minor (Peters 5), which only has one fugue (though from the odd ending on the dominant it would seem to be incomplete—there are no other symptoms of the Phrygian mode) shows a single relative entry at bar 61 (there are 84 bars in all). In all the cases mentioned it will be noted that there is no attempt at a 'balanced' form as far as the entries are concerned: usually the key-variety tends to feature near the end of the fugue, and this is what in fact it does in many cases in Bach.

Bach begins by keeping the old rule. He then seems to go to the other extreme in one or two not-so-early examples such as the D major organ BWV 532 with its entries in E major and C♯ minor. By his maturity, however, he was, for the most part, keeping to the directly related keys, with some excursions just beyond these in the case of fugues written in a minor tonic key (e.g. WTC II.8, bars 27–9, soprano: C♯ minor from D♯ minor): the minor scale is, as we saw in Chapter 2, very chromatically inclined, and this probably explains the difference, which is borne out also in Bach's non-fugal work. Entries still further afield in mature fugues either involve 'preparatory' chromaticism (see resource 17, below) (G major organ BWV 541, bars 66–9, pedal: note tonal answer variation also) or a minor-key subject so unalterable that its entry in what would normally be a related major key turns that key into a minor one (cantata 46 first chorus, bar 47 of the fugue, bass: first note freely altered from F to A: key F *minor* from D minor): but key, it cannot be too often stressed, is only a *possibility* with Bach, as with most Baroque fugal writers. There are still mature fugues such as WTC I.6, I.14 and II.6 with virtually no entry key-contrast—certainly no changed-mode entries. When key is used, as was mentioned at the outset of this chapter, there is often no systematic key scheme in evidence. WTC I.7 has been seen to be a reasonable ternary form, but Bach's clearest 'key-forms' are paradoxically rondos, of which the great G minor organ BWV 542 is a beautifully clear example and WTC II.10 and II.20 two others.[50] It is strange that neither Riemann nor Prout tumbled to the possibility of a 'key rondo': Prout actually analyses the G minor[51] and it remains a mystery how he could include the tonic entry of bar 65, prepared by a climactic device, in the 'middle section'.

Handel seems to follow what appears to be the tendency of the late Baroque in using key-contrast of entries, but again with what the ternary enthusiasts must find a deplorable lack of system. The two strictest fugues in *Messiah* are typical: in no. 25 'And with His stripes' the entries after the exposition are tonic-dominant (answer form), subdominant, tonic, VII (E♭), relative major, tonic, answer, answer: in no. 28 'He trusted in God' they are VII (false stretto), relative major (false stretto), subdominant (incomplete), dominant, tonic, tonic. In a sort of a way no. 28 keeps the ternary scheme, but the use of the dominant before the tonic in the 'final section' does not make the form very convincing. Handel also ventures somewhat further afield with a minor-key fugue: the G minor keyboard fugue which became 'They loathed to drink of the river' in 'Israel in Egypt' has an F minor stretto at bars 33–8.

In this period, *when* key is used systematically the tendency is for the relative and keys on the sharp side to be used nearer the opening and keys on the flat side near the end. This is in keeping with a tendency in

50. In the G minor the sections are:
1–32 Tonic and dominant entries.
32–37 Modulating episode.
37–57 Entries in relative, dominant, and relative of dominant (F major) and associated episodes.
57–65 Episode, employing intense counterpoint (61–2) and dominant pedal (resources 11 and 14 below).
68–72 Episode tending towards subdominant—modulation completed at 72.
72–82 Entries in subdominant and its relative, E♭, and associated episode.
82–93 Episode at first discursive, but ending on the dominant.
93 (last note)–end: Entries in tonic and associated episodes and coda. It will be observed that some dominant entries are heard in close association with the tonic while others (those in the section 37–57) are equally not so associated. This dual function of the dominant entry was never made clear in academic teaching of the key-scheme.

51. *Fugal Analysis*, pp. 38–51.

all strongly tonal music and can be seen also in concerti grossi. The subdominant has become almost a cliché for a feeling of conclusion and repose (the village organist's final tonic pedal always contained subdominant digression) and the three Bach 'rondos' mentioned above all reserve flatter keys for the 'C' of the ABACA scheme. But again those who look for a scheme such as this where key is clearly *unsystematically* used will be disappointed.

As would be expected, the range of keys used for entries gradually expands as the history of fugue progresses. We find Mozart, for instance, in the Fugue in C minor for two pianos K.426 introducing false stretti in D♭ and E♭ minor (bars 44–9), Beethoven using G♭ and D♭ in the 'meno mosso e moderato' bars 167–75 of the *Grosse Fuge*, and Brahms introducing inverted entries of the subject in D♭ major and G♭ major from B♭ major (the same relationships, as it happens, as in the Beethoven example) in the fugue concluding the Variations on a Theme of Handel (bars 33–7).

The furthest distance in keys and the most abrupt introduction of the remoter regions appears in the 24 fugues of Shostakovitch, who seems to favour a middle section of remote entries contrasting strongly and abruptly with directly related keys on either side, the subject being more or less diatonic: No. 6 in B minor, bars 66–95—entries G minor, D minor, C minor; No. 7 in A major, bars 43–61—entries F major, B♭ major, C minor (incomplete); No. 10 in C♯ minor, bars 85–128—two pairs in subject–answer relationship (D minor answered by A minor and C minor answered by G minor).

The remotest distance of all is probably B♭ minor (genuine, not an enharmonic notation for A♯) from F♯ minor tonic in no. 8, bar 33 bass: but this has a chromatic subject which makes the use of remote regions less surprising. The first three examples have diatonic subjects, and these fugues certainly exemplify a strong ternary form by key. It cannot be said, however, that such abrupt key-ternaries are in any way typical of fugue generally, whether classical or modern. The abrupt use of remote keys is really a dramatic feature somewhat alien to a contrapuntal type of music, and such switches of key as occur, for instance, at bars 60–2 of the A major fugue (a return from E♭ to A by enharmonic circle) seem more sonata-like than fugue-like. Paradoxically the first two 'middle' entries in virtually all the Shostakovitch fugues—before the excursions into remote regions start—are a relative (major or minor) one and its answer. This procedure is of course taken from Bach (e.g. WTC I.16), who, however, uses it only when he feels so inclined. The 'ternary' key form just spoken of in Shostakovitch is thus not the official academic one, since some of the 'middle' entries are much closer to the tonic than others: when very remote regions are used the nearer entries, by comparison, seem to belong to the 'A' rather than the 'B' of the ternary key-scheme. Here again, as in so many other respects, the conventional terminology is inadequate.

Shostakovitch also sometimes writes genuine key-rondo fugues, as for instance the G major no. 3; here B♭ and E♭ entries feature in the first substantial departure from the tonic (44–51), after which there is a definite tonic return at 61. The next departure features F major (75) and B♭ major (79), variety being obtained here by the use of stretto. This fugue, incidentally, is an exception to the general rule—the first 'middle' entry is in A minor (22), E minor, the relative, appearing as answer to A minor at 26. In other cases the rondo form is more apparent than real because, again, some entries are closer to the tonic than others: in actual fact nos. 6, 7 and 10 mentioned above are technically rondos, since after the tonic return Shostakovitch introduces a subdominant entry and in no. 6 also an entry in II♭ (C major). In no. 5 in D the converse occurs—the first departure is to near keys (the inevitable relative and its answer) after which there is a tonic return at 52. Suddenly at 75 a B♭ entry occurs, answered at 82, and there is a varied entry in E♭ at 92. At 98, equally suddenly, the tonic returns. Yet another departure, but again only to nearer keys, occurs later at 117 with the stretto using the C answer form of the theme.

The more typical moderns seem to prefer chromaticism of subject to remoteness of key of entry. In the first movement of Bartók's *Music for Strings, Percussion and Celeste*, described by Dr Edmund Rubbra in his book *Counterpoint* in the present series, the tonic is A and the subject has an A melodic tonality; from the outset, the entries proceed by fifths outwardly from A:

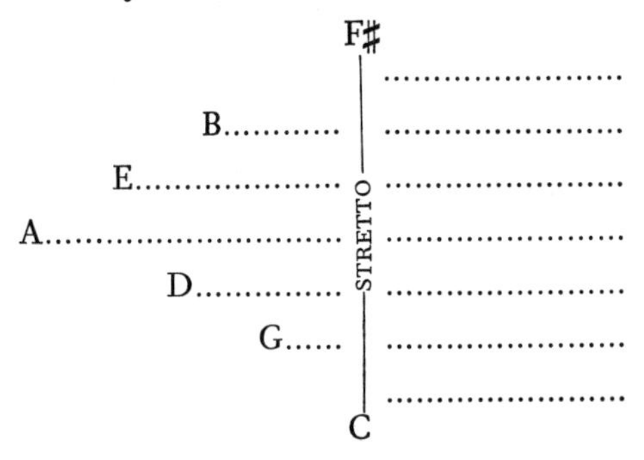

This is really only an expansion of the idea seen, for instance, in the incidental fugue 'Have thunders and lightnings their fury forgotten?' in Bach's *St Matthew Passion*. After some development and varied entries Bartók introduces an entry in E♭, his favourite tritone relationship (compare the Fifth Quartet B♭–E♮ and the Concerto for Orchestra F–B). This proceeds to a climax in E♭ at bar 56. The way back is through inverted entries in G (partial stretto) at 68, last note, D at 72 last note, and the tonic A at 77 last note, the last being combined with a slightly varied direct version. Thus although the remote key of E♭ is employed it is used only at the remotest point from both beginning and end, the other entries being in a pattern of perfect fifths.

Similarly Hindemith, in many of the fugues of LT, has a fairly 'conservative' key range of entries used with tonal but mildly chromatic subjects. In the fugue no. 6 in E♭, for instance, we have B♭ (17) (the answer was in A♭ in order to give tonic in answer to dominant), C♭ freely inverted (21), B♭♭ (written A) freely inverted (24), D♭ freely inverted (28), concluding with direct entries in C♭ (written B) (36) and the tonic (43). Only B♭♭ here exceeds the classical range. In the following fugue in A♭ the entries after the exposition are C (23), F (29), D♭ (42) and F (46), the fugue ending on a chord of C, A♭ however being confirmed in the first chord of the following 'intermedium'.

Generally speaking, then, it can be said that modern fugue has tended to come back to a more 'classical' view of entry key-contrast, chromaticism being relegated to the design of the subject itself rather than employed to introduce a more diatonic subject in vastly remote keys. Similarly in music generally the unity of the twelve-tone system has replaced the rapid and remote modulations of the late romantic period. The modern period also shares with 'classical' fugue the idea of the importance of preserving the theme, the difference being that it is now preserved by the free use of chromatic notes rather than by restricted positions of entry within a diatonic scale. Another 'classical' idea that has returned is that of the prevalent importance of the melodic tonality of the subject: more than ever does entry key-contrast depend upon this rather than upon a 'harmonisation' of the subject.

Before leaving this resource mention may be made of a device to which the Germans give the rather forbidding term *Modulierende Durchführung*. This is a kind of exposition during the course of the fugue in which all or most of the parts in turn deliver the subject, each in a different melodic tonality. A good example, involving four out of the five parts, is seen in WTC I.22, bars 25–34, the entries being D♭, soprano I (varied) (25), E♭ minor answer, soprano II (27), tonic, tenor (29) and E♭ minor, bass 32. The term 'modulating exposition' may perhaps be used in English as long as the rather superficial relationship to the true sense of 'exposition' is understood.

(8) *Harmonic tonalities and modulation.* Academic fugue missed one of its most fascinating fields of study when it prescribed only one kind

of tonality for fugue—the modulatory episode leading to the entry 'in' such and such a key, the further episode leading 'back into the tonic for a tonic entry', etc. The present section cannot do more than touch on the subtle problem of exactly how harmonic and melodic tonalities relate and how one melodic tonality may relate to another. It is hoped that the few instances given will encourage the reader to find others both in fugue and other contrapuntal work.

Example 47 shows two examples from Froberger of simple subjects of definite melodic tonality stated without any unusual dissonance

Ex 47(a) Froberger, Ricercar IX (DTÖ Jahrgang X/2, Band 21): subject
(b) ibid., bars 32–6
(c) Froberger, Ricercar XI (DTÖ Jahrgang X/2, Band 21): subject
(d) ibid., bars 70–5

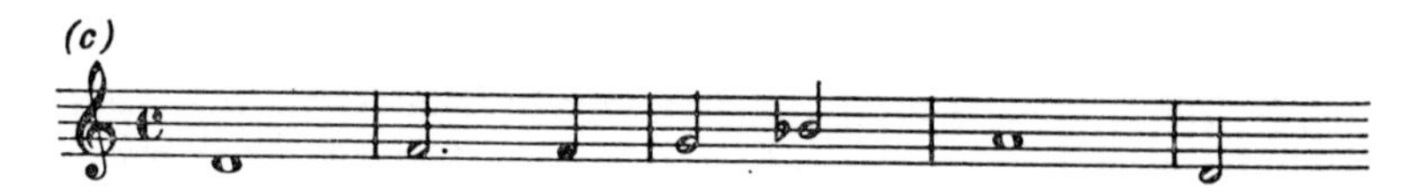

against a chord progression which is harmonically, and conventionally speaking, in another key. Buxtehude's A minor Präludium (Hansen 5) shows at bars 47–9, in the first fugue, a good example of a subject entry in G melodic tonality entering over a definite C major cadence, the harmonic tonality arriving at G only at the very end. The D major Präludium (Hansen 11) similarly shows F♯ melodic tonality against A–C♯mi–A harmonic (bars 49–51). Three cases in Bach show (by coincidence) E major melodic against largely C♯ minor harmonic tonality: WTC I.23, bars 24–6; WTC II.18, bars 111–15; WTC II.23, bars 53–6.

In I.23 it is true that the E melodic tonality is weakened by the sharpening of B to B♯, the leading note of the harmonic key. The II.18 instance is interesting as showing the combination of main and subsidiary subject of a double fugue *both* in the E melodic tonality! Here eventually the pull of E is too strong and the harmonic tonality gives in to it, but only at the last two notes.

Mozart's fugue 'Pignus futurae' from the Litany in B♭ (K.125) quoted by Prout (*Fugal Analysis*, pp. 190–200) suggests that composers of the classic period were not unaware of these possibilities. The entry in G–D melodic tonality (it is a 'modulating' subject) at bars 44–53 and its D–G answer at 53–62 both show strong harmonic tendencies to the subdominant of the first key—C minor at 44–7 and G minor even more definitely at 53–8.

Another feature unrecognised by academic fugue is the completely independent modulation—independent in the sense of being unrelated to a subject entry. Buxtehude shows this in the G minor Präludium (Hansen 24) second fugue, where at bars 125–7 a cadence occurs, complete with 'preparatory' chromatic chord (a strangely jazzy sound, especially in the context) in B♭, the relative major. The preceding entry was in the dominant and the following one is in the tonic, its D–B♭ descent 'harmonised' as a cadence in E♭ (128–9). A Bach case many pianists and harpsichordists must know is WCT I.3, where after the definite tonic entry of bars 26–8 an equally definitive move is made away from the tonic at 29–30. By repeating bars 12–14, which led to D♯ minor (II), Bach, starting now from the tonic instead of the dominant, arrives at G♯ minor (an indirectly related key) from which the purpose of bars 31–5 is to get back to the tonic. Yet because no entry occurs in G♯ minor an academic analysis would tend not to recognise this modulation, which is both tonally and (since it repeats earlier material) structurally important. Another well-known fugue, the six-part ricercar of the *Musical Offering*, has even more emphatic independent modulations to E♭ (38–9) and A♭ (81–3, note preparatory chromaticism): the very feeble false entry in A♭ can hardly be said to invalidate the use of the word 'independent' of this modulation. The other great late fugal work, *The Art of Fugue*, also makes important use of this procedure.

Let it be said in passing, however, that Bach is perfectly prepared also to allow a harmonic modulation to lead to an entry in the same key. In the so-called 'Dorian' organ fugue BWV 538 *every* entry or stretto from bar 101 (the F major stretto) onwards is prepared by a fat cadence in the appropriate key. However, you can't win with academic fugue—Kitson, in *The Elements of Fugal Construction* (ch. V, p. 57), says 'The Episode should not clench the modulation to the new key before the entry of the S[ubject] in the new key'. Bach must again have 'confused the issue'.

It will be seen that important harmonic modulations, either independent of entries, clashing with an entry's melodic tonality, or sometimes agreeing with it, are an important basis for describing form in certain ricercar-type fugues, and in some others where much involved stretto is used.

After Bach it seems that independent modulations are more rarely found, and in most modern fugue, of course, harmonic tonality is anyway a very much weaker factor, if indeed a factor at all.

(9) *Structural recapitulation*. The holding together of a design by the more or less exact recapitulation of material is well known through its use in the classic sonata: all the 'forms' familiar from textbooks—sonata form, rondo form, minuet and trio—depend upon it. However, apart from the element of recapitulation present in any entry of the subject (more marked when one or more countersubjects are regularly employed), its use in fugue is, for various reasons, restricted to certain composers—chiefly J. S. Bach, and, under his influence, Hindemith and Shostakovitch. Bach lived at the time when fugue was being influenced both by the dance-suite and the concerto, and moreover when sonata form was itself evolving. He, so to speak, caught the device of recapitulation while fugal style was such as to be able to adopt it appropriately: after him, while sonata form and its allied forms came to depend more and more upon it, fugue took other paths and became obsessed with device, complexity and exciting climaxes, and apart from one or two exceptional uses and the aforementioned modern imitations it seems to have died out.

Probably the earliest traces of 'binary' recapitulations are found in the dance movements of Froberger, in some of which a recognisable cadence heard in the dominant or relative key at the end of the first 'half' is recapitulated in the tonic at the end of the movement. In the French Suites of Bach the recognisable passage may go back well before the cadence: in the Partitas (suites with longer movements) it is evident considerably before the cadence. In many of the (single movement) keyboard sonatas of Domenico Scarlatti a fully-fledged 'second subject', continuation and cadence theme can be identified and the 'exposition-recapitulation' idea now dominates the structure of the whole movement (although, as a matter of passing interest, the recapitulation of the *first* subject is still fairly rare). This 'binary' form influenced fugue probably by way of the fugal gigues which had by this time become conventional finales to the suite. The basic 'binary' form is seen in WTC I.14 (half-way cadence at bar 20), I.23 (bar 17–18) and II. 23 (bars 26–7). In each case the 'binary' idea is emphasised by the occurrence of a new device after the cadence (inversion in I.14 and I.23, new countersubject in II.23). In II.21 (mentioned above in connection with Morris's remarks) there is a recognisable passage before the cadence as well (cf. 29–32 with 90–end; note here also 'preparatory' harmonies). A well-known vocal fugue, that concluding the eight-part motet 'Sing ye to the Lord', also shows the procedure, marked by the characteristic cadence on 'Hal-le-lu-jah' (bars 46–50, 109–end). One Hindemith fugue, LT 12 in F♯, provides a comparable case, bars 14 (last note) to the cadence at 18 in C♯ being exactly recapitulated in the fugue's last four bars. Bach's influence is patently obvious here.

From another direction the evolution by Bach of the organised episode (Chapter 3) also led towards recapitulation as a formal device. The more recognisable and characteristic an episode is the more point there will be in repeating it at some later stage of the fugue, perhaps with interchange of the parts and/or a change of key. An important event in the 'great' G minor organ fugue of Bach (BWV 542) is the return of the episode which originally led to the relative major for the 'B' of the key-rondo scheme; it now appears in the tonic key, thus showing in a different way an element of 'binary' structure (cf. bars 33–7 and 106½–10). Similarly near the end of WTC I.24 there is a return of the episode on a non-thematic sequential fugue which occurred twice near the beginning (bars 17–21, 26–30: cf. 65½–9).

Hindemith's uses of the recapitulated episode are seen in LT no. 7 in A♭ (soprano of bars 14–22 recapitulated in subdominant relationship at 33–41, bass) and no. 9 in B♭ (12–15 recapitulated without interchange of parts at 42–5 a third higher, and at the very end a sixth higher).

Shostakovitch also uses—one might say over-uses—the idea of the episode recapitulation; the vast majority of his episodes are based on the answer-codetta, the procedure being the same in all the fugues. As observed, the rather undifferentiated nature of the codetta in most cases deprives the device of the significance it has in Bach and Hindemith.

A step further towards the idea of strict recapitulation occurs when a recapitulation involves not only an episode but also, say, an entry or entries on either side of it as well. In WTC I.3 bars 1–12 (the exposition, first episode and an entry in the dominant) reappear at 42–53. Similarly in WTC I.12 bars 13–22, consisting of entry (tonic)—episode—entry (dominant) are recapitulated at 47–56. In both these cases an adjustment is made in the episode to bring the succeeding entry into the tonic so that here, too, we can see a 'binary' element, comparable with the changes made in the so-called 'bridge passage' in sonata form, to bring the second subject recapitulation into the tonic. In Morris's other 'binary' example, I.6, bars 9–21 first beat correspond with 30–end: the correspondence is quite strict between 17–20 and 39–43 first beat—the essential binary cadence and its lead-in—but by comparing the uppermost voice of 30–35 with the bass of 9–14 we can see a further correspondence. 15–16 are however more freely treated, being represented by three bars; 36–38. 43–44 is an added coda.

A step still further in the direction of strictness is seen in WTC II.13, where bars 12–36 consist of episode (new material)—entry (tonic)—episode (development of end of subject)—entry (dominant): this whole passage is recapitulated at 44–68 in subdominant relationship to its original and with interchange of parts and other small alterations. The entries of course are now subdominant followed by tonic, so that yet another link with sonata form (not the textbook variety) is seen—the idea of a subdominant recapitulation, as, to take the best-known case, in the first movement of Mozart's Piano Sonata in C, K. 545.

So we approach the completely strict fugue, a type curiously ignored by academic teaching, which ought by rights to have delighted in the good discipline it would afford the student. The best-known case is the two-part WTC I.10. Bars 20–38 recapitulate bars 1–19, the recapitulation starting again in the subdominant, A minor, and interchanging the parts. Bar 19 is in consecutive octaves, a conspicuous device akin to that of homophony (resource 13, below), the purpose of which is to point the listener's attention to the beginning of the recapitulation. A very crafty alteration, typical of Bach, in bar 29 ensures that 30 arrives not in C, the equivalent of G at bar 11, but in D minor, a tone higher. Thus instead of arriving at D minor at 38, the equivalent of A minor at 19, we duly arrive at E minor, a tone higher, which happens to be the tonic key. The consecutive octaves are duly recapitulated and lead to a short coda consisting of an extension of the subject so designed as to end with a tonic cadence instead of the original dominant one.

Bach's 'concerto fugues' also make much use of more or less strict recapitulation. Space does not permit discussion of these, since the system of recapitulation is often very complex. An obvious—and simple—example is the 'Wedge' organ fugue in E minor BWV 548 (cf. bar 173–end with bars 1–59). Other cases are mainly in the overture fugues in orchestral suites and in the sonatas for violin and obbligato harpsichord.

There are two cases where Hindemith follows Bach in this respect. It has already been noted that no. 3 in F is an almost completely strict fugue, the recapitulation being, however, unrecognisable since it is in retrograde motion (the end to bar 31 repeats bars 1–30 backward: the only free notes are the three in the middle of 30 and the parts added near the end to keep three-part writing). LT no. 10 in D♭ is also almost completely strict, bars 18–end being an inversion of 1–18 first beat except for the replacement of 17 by two bars, 34–5, giving a direct entry of the subject to finish up with. In that 17–18 are a (modern) cadence on A♭, the dominant, the figure shows another case of a 'binary' structure.

(10) *Instrumental timbre*. This resource applies, of course, almost entirely to fugues for ensembles, particularly choral fugue accompanied by instruments. Variety is obtained by the contrast not only between vocal and instrumental tone, but between one instrument and another, and also between voices doubled by instruments and voices without instrumental doubling. A climax can be obtained by the use of a distinctive instrument (e.g. the trumpet).

Example: Bach's choral fugues show the greatest variety in this respect. Both 'Et in terra pax' and 'Pleni sunt coeli' in the Mass in B minor show the contrasts mentioned: in each case voices are first heard without instrumental doubling, subsequently with it. 'Et in terra' is the simpler design in this respect, the entries from 120(the beginning of the fugue)–137 being without doubling and all subsequent ones with it. The trumpets are sparsely used, at climax points. 'Pleni sunt coeli' is much freer in its use of timbre, but contains interesting features such as a bass entry doubled at the third by trumpet I (131–7), and a stretto between soprano I and trumpet I (147–53).

(11) *The Pedal*. A pedal is a long held note in one (occasionally more than one) of the parts against which the others continue to weave contrapuntal lines. In the 'normal' case the long note is in the bass, the name obviously originating from the habit of organists of extemporising on the manuals while the foot remains conveniently stationary. In an 'inverted pedal' the long note occurs in an upper part.

The most commonly known pedals are those occurring on dominant or tonic notes. Given appropriate circumstances (this is important) the pedal on the dominant will act as a prolonged V of a V–I cadence and will thus have the effect of keeping the listener waiting for the expected I. Similarly—and again, given the right circumstances—a tonic pedal can give an effect of repose, of dying away after the expectation caused by the V has been resolved. This use of the pedal tends to feature in academic fugue and in fugues of the classic and romantic periods. Typically 'exciting' dominant pedals are the twenty bars leading into the 'Poco piu Allegro' of the 'Cum sancto Spiritu' fugue of Beethoven's *Missa Solemnis* (bars 440–59 of the Gloria section) and bars 76–93 of the final fugue of Brahms's Variations on a Theme of Handel. The latter is interesting as showing a gradual growth in the pedal effect: in 76 the low F is barely perceptible as a pedal at all; by 81 it is obvious, though not yet very strong; 82–6 (the F octaves in the treble) shows a very strong pedal, but inverted; in 87–93 the F octaves are transferred to the bass, giving the maximum effect of expectation. Typically, Brahms diverts the expected cadence and the true V–I is not heard until 103–4. The use of the two pedals in turn is conveniently seen in Mendelssohn's organ fugue in G (Peters II): the dominant one occurs at bars 43–8. It leads to a prominent pedal entry of the subject homophonically accompanied (resource 13, below) and some further development of the latter part of the subject with rests (resource 16, below) and the tonic pedal follows at 57–61, more or less free stretti occurring above it. There is still a V–I cadence to come—a tonic pedal does not have to have the last word.

As has been said, this use of the pedal is really a classic-romantic device, associated with the desire at all costs to make the fugue exciting. In the Baroque, when fugue was a more normal means of expression, pedals are usually a more casual business. Dominant and tonic pedals can, and do, fulfil the preparatory/repose functions, but they tend to be less frantic affairs than in later music. Handel's 'Amen' chorus of *Messiah*—the culmination of the whole three-hour (or more?) oratorio—has a dominant pedal of 2½ bars plus a crotchet (bars 76½–9) and a tonic 'pedal'—hardly long enough to deserve the name—of 1½ bars (80–1). Yet it is a rare listener who complains of the 'Amen' chorus being a 'let-down'! Bach's most classic-type dominant pedal is that of the C minor organ fugue BWV 546, bars 127–36, but it is static rather than exciting, and has been curiously criticised as being too Beethovenish for Bach! More typical of the Baroque is probably such an example as WTC I.1, last 7 bars, which firmly but without excitement clinches the whole fugal design.

Both in the Baroque and sometimes in later composers imitating the Baroque 'incidental' pedals are introduced which are not of a climactic nature at all. In WTC II.11, for instance, the tonic pedal of bars 61 to 65 turns out to be intended for a move to the subdominant, with the subdominant entry following it at 66. Schumann, in no. 5 of 'Six fugues on the name B-A-C-H', op. 60, quoted by Prout, also shows incidentally introduced pedals, which puzzled Prout, with his classic-romantic outlook on the device.[52] The long tonic pedal of bars 76–101 has only a short dominant one (74–5) to introduce it, and although the effect of gradually increasing repose and forthcoming conclusion is present further dominant preparation is necessary fully to clinch the tonic key: hence the further dominant pedal of 104–10 and the final (quite different and slightly decorated) tonic pedal of 114 to the end. So far from being 'irregular' Schumann is here, although original, far nearer to the spirit of Baroque fugue than most other classic and romantic composers.

The remainder of the resources can be dealt with more briefly since most of them are of an obvious nature and they are largely designed to assist in producing a climax—often, though not necessarily always, the final climax.

(12) *Use of quicker (more rarely, slower) movement.* Since fugue is essentially a continuous style without sudden changes in the type of movement, the use of faster movement will have an intensifying effect causing the listener to expect an important event.

Example: near end of fugue—Mozart, Fugue in C minor for two pianos, K.426, bars 106–15; preceding event in middle of fugue—Bach, *The Art of Fugue* no. 8, bars 90–2, introducing first appearance in this fugue of the main theme of the work (see also 119–21, introducing prominent tonic entry of 'local' subject and countersubject).[53]

The use of slower movement, which achieves climax by ponderousness rather than excitement, seems much rarer—but see Schumann 'Six Fugues on the Name B-A-C-H' op. 60, no. 2, notably 122–8 and (with harmonic colour, resource 17 below, and also rests, resource 16 below) 143–62. In a much milder way Bach uses this resource in WTC I.4, bars 94–end—cessation of quaver movement which has been present since bar 36.

(13) *Use of homophony instead of counterpoint.* This again depends for its effect on a sudden change in the prevailing movement and texture.

52. *Fugal Analysis*, pp. 98–106. §106 runs 'A very curious and most irregular point about this fugue is the treatment of the dominant and tonic pedals. Of these there are no fewer than five . . .'.

53. Knowing Bach's methods in this work, bars 119–21 are probably intended to raise the listener's expectation of the combination of the main theme with the 'local' themes: this, however, does not arrive until bar 148, and then not in the tonic!

In fugues in an otherwise strict number of parts the use of chords often involves the addition of 'free' parts to the existing ones.

Examples: against an entry of the subject—Mendelssohn, organ fugue in C minor (Peters I), 8 bars before the end (see also last bar of preceding episode); D minor organ fugue BWV 538 ('Dorian') last 4 bars (on dominant pedal, resource 11).

(14) *Use of thick or intense counterpoint, especially thirds and sixths.* This device is especially effective on the harpsichord, where the 'busy' effect is more noticeable than on the piano, organ, or in ensemble work —although the device is by no means absent from these genres. It may take the form of added parts, if the fugue is in a definite number of parts (WTC II.17, last 2 bars) or it may simply consist in more intense movement in the already existing parts (WTC I.12, 3 bars from the end). Very commonly intensification is obtained by the use of consecutive thirds and/or sixths (or their compounds). The use of thirds and sixths has been seen to have a connection with invertible counterpoint at special intervals (see resource 5, above), and as such it appears in WTC II.16, where there is a gradual intensifying of the entries up to the climactic one of bars 59–63.[54]

Examples: In an entry—WTC II.22, last 6 bars (stretto of direct and inverted subject); free—Bach 'great' G minor organ fugue BWV 542, bars 60–4; note especially the consecutive first inversion chords (thirds and sixths together) of 61–3 first beat. The passage prepares not the final climax but the second 'A' of the ABACA entry key-scheme (see above, resource 7).

(15) *Toccata-ending and written-out cadenza.* The early Baroque toccata, which gave rise to the 'toccata'-type subject (Chapter 2), consisted of alternating toccata and fugal sections, the pattern commonly being 'toccata–fugue–toccata–fugue–toccata'. By the late Baroque the pattern 'toccata–fugue'—a single alternation—had evolved, both sections being, of course, much longer. But the return of the toccata style at the end still survived in a number of examples as a form of coda to the fugue.

54. Cecil Gray, in *The Forty-eight Preludes and Fugues of J. S. Bach*, p. 123, pokes fun at the analysis of this passage in terms of invertible counterpoint: '. . . Bach wanted to write a passage in thirds for its rich harmonic effect and he did so. Voilà tout.' Quite apart from the fact that it is not all pairs of themes that will go in thirds together, such a view ignores the fact that for thirds (or sixths) to be introduced either suddenly or, as here, gradually into a piece which has hitherto exemplified four-part linear counterpoint is a quite different affair from their use in one which has shown a mainly chordal texture. There is more 'voilà tout' about, say, Beethoven's use of thirds and sixths in the Piano Sonata, op. 22, first movement, bars 30–5.

Example: In pre-Bach work the device is usually an integral part of the composite toccata, and as such can be seen as late as Buxtehude (the G minor. Hansen 24) already mentioned in other connections as a typical example). The rarer separate fugues of Buxtehude also show its use, as in the C major gigue fugue (Hansen 3) only, however, in a very small dose here (last bar but one).

In Bach, or rather Bach (?),[55] the obvious case is the well-known D minor organ BWV 565, last 17 bars. A more mature (and authentic!) instance is the G minor organ BWV 535, last 8 bars. Bar 5½ to 4 from the end of this example is technically cadenza (reasonably defined as the prolongation by decoration of an inconclusive chord leading to a cadence): bars 5 to 1 from the end of the well-known A minor organ BWV 543 are similarly cadenza. An optional cadenza—to which, however, a solution is given and appears in all the texts—is indicated in the fugue in D minor BWV 948, which is almost certainly not by Bach. The insertion of cadenzas, or for that matter any kind of decoration, into authentic mature Bach is a very dubious business: it would, however, perhaps not be entirely unthinkable to insert a 6/4 cadenza in the penultimate half-bar of the great E♭ organ fugue BWV 552.

(16) *Conspicuous use of rests. Pause.* This is a favourite device with Handel (not only in fugue), and it is barely necessary to quote the three fugues in *Messiah* which use it: the Overture fugue, 4 bars from the end, no. 28 'He trusted in God', 3 from the end, and 'Amen' 4 from the end. Only the 'Amen' rest is marked as a pause: in no. 28 the rest and following chords are directed 'Adagio' and the Overture has no marking. In fact many conductors treat these two rests, perhaps not incorrectly, as pauses.

The device is less readily associated with Bach, but there are a number of cases, e.g. G major organ fugue BWV 541, bar 71, where the pause occurs on a chromatic chord (resource 17, immediately below) followed by a short rest, introducing the first occurrences of stretto. See also WTC II.10, bar 83 (preceded by cadenza) and II.16, bars 73–4 and 78–9 (75 proved to be a 'false end'). Conspicuous rests without pause occur near the end of the 'concerto-fugue' concluding Brandenburg Concerto no. 4, bars 229–3. Homophony (resource 13, above) is often associated with rests.

(17) *Use of harmonic colour.* The use of chromatic harmonies to prepare an important cadence, theme entry, recapitulation or other special event is a common feature of Baroque music and indeed it has an important influence upon later styles. Such 'preparatory chromaticism' is

55. See below, p. 160.

especially common in the major key, where it often takes the form of borrowings from, or an actual excursion into, the minor of the same key. In fugue its use can sometimes affect an entry of the subject, as has already been seen, either in making one or more notes chromatically inflected (above, resource 6(b)) or in causing a whole entry to appear in the minor of a normally major key. Its use preparing independent modulations has also been mentioned (resource 8). Instances of conspicuous use near the very end seem not very frequent before Bach: Buxtehude, for instance, seems to rely frequently on an elaborately decorated plagal cadence (see D major (Hansen 2) bars 95–end, F♯ minor (Hansen 13) 111–end, G minor (Hansen 24) 142–end), which *is* harmonic colour in a mild way. In the G major (Hansen 7) however we do find II major and I minor c in the last three bars. The most impressive Bach instance to both ear and eye (the B♭♭'s are plentiful!) is bars 44–6 of WTC II.17 (note also rests and pause resource 16). The chord mainly responsible for this 'purple patch' is II♭b, the so-called 'neapolitan sixth', which Bach also uses in the prelude, bar 74. (The fugue was originally a Fughetta in F ending at bar 25—see below p. 174.) A romantic period use has already been seen in the Schumann fugue mentioned in the immediately preceding section, and even a good modern one occurs 8–5 bars from the end of Shostakovitch 24, no. 6 in B minor.

(18) *Use of a very prominent sequence or scale figure.* Curiously enough this device is almost always a descent, not an ascent.

Examples: Bach WTC II.5, bars 38–40, bass; Beethoven, fugue concluding the 'Hammerklavier' sonata, bars 342–50, upper parts; Hindemith LT no. 5 in E, bars 11 to 5 from the end, upper parts.

It is curious how in academic fugue everything that is important seems to have to happen in subject entries. Key, as we have seen, is entirely related to entries, and climax is obtained mainly by stretto, the biggest climax being the final entry (or stretto), and so forth. In the following, the last three resources to be mentioned here, an effect of climax is obtained in episode by means analogous to those used in entries, a possibility that seems never to have occurred to the theorists.

(19) *Episodic stretto.* By this is meant stretto either of an independent episodic theme or of an obviously episodic development of an exposition theme (to be distinguished from 'false stretto', already discussed, in which the opening of the subject was used in such a way as to resemble real stretto).

Examples: Bach A minor clavier fugue BWV 904, bars 71–2 (stretto of independent theme): WTC II.18, bars 128–32 (development of second bar of subject).

(20) *Use of an unusually high entry of an episodic theme.* This is a rare device, but sopranos who have struggled with Bach's Mass in B minor will know it. It occurs at bar 51 of the second 'Kyrie'. The figure makes its first appearance at bars 5 (second half) to 6. It grows and grows in prominence, and the chromatic (hence difficult to sing, quite apart from the pitch!) version at 51 beginning on high A is really the climax of the whole movement. (The passage 51–3 also exemplifies episodic stretto.) Ironically—from an academic standpoint—the 'real' stretto of 54–7 is simply a consolidation of the design after the climax is past—necessary, but not the high point of the movement.

(21) *Ending the whole fugue with a statement of a prominent thematic figure (not in an entry).* This naturally tends to occur in fugues with organised episodes which can give a particular figure from the exposition considerable prominence. In such cases the ending of the whole piece with a conspicuous statement of the figure concerned is extraordinarily effective.

Examples: Bach WTC I.14, last 1½ bars, tenor (figure from countersubject) and WTC I.23, last 1½ bars, tenor (episodic figure, see second half of bar 9 bass, etc.); Hindemith LT4 in A, second part, last bar, soprano (inversion of opening of subject); LT6 in E♭, last 1½ bars, bass (opening of subject).

Some account now follows of the various ways in which the resources just described have been used by composers in the construction of complete fugues. The distinction between incidental and complete fugue has already been discussed. In the early Baroque, when fugue as we now understand the term emerged, it is not always possible to tell from the title whether a true complete fugue or something much vaguer is to hand. When Gibbons calls a piece 'Fantazia', for instance, we shall probably find a piece written on motet principles, i.e. a series of incidental fugues one after the other. The 'Fantazia of Four Parts' in Schirmer's *Early Keyboard Music* (p. 46) is a good example of this type, five 'points' being 'exposed' in turn, together with a certain amount of homophonic and toccata material. Similarly Andrea Gabrieli's 'Ricercare del 12° tono' (HAM I, no. 136), which is, confusingly enough, not a ricercar but a canzona, also shows insufficient thematic unity for it to be considered a complete fugue—despite the repeat of the first 14 bars by way of conclusion. Even Purcell's fantazias, dating near the end of the seventeenth century, exemplify incidental rather than complete fugue with the possible exception of the first 58 bars of the four-part Fantazia no. 9.

As was seen in Chapter 2, the idea of separate themes in turn was replaced by that of a single theme, variants of which would be treated in turn. When this method is used we have what can reasonably be called a complete fugue. It is true that today we tend to think of a fugue as a single continuous composition, but there is no reason why a sectional composition should not be included in the definition provided always that the essential quality of thematic unity is present. Beethoven's *Grosse Fuge*, after all, is sectional, as is Hindemith's LT4 in A, to mention only two post-Baroque examples.

The fugues of Sweelinck (1562–1621) are probably the first which show a true fugal form. Here is an analysis of 'Ricercar del Nono Duono' (Peters, vol. II, no. 3):

bars 1–51 'Exposition' in the general sense (technically exposition plus a number of 'additional' entries). There are one or two independent entries of the rather neutral countersubject, first heard at bars 5–7, soprano.

bars 52–62 Combination of subject with chromatic countersubject.

bars 63–74 Mild key contrast: entries in what we should call E minor (the former answer having been subdominant) leading to prominent tonic cadence.

bars 74–90 Stretto on a freely varied version of the theme with syncopated rhythm leading to diverted cadence in D, against which there enters (tenor)

bars 90–108 decorated version of the subject, in the soprano, with (amongst other things) the leap of a sixth filled in with semiquavers (resource 6(h), above); new countersubject in alto. Some 'free' entries of this countersubject. Cadence in tonic again.

bars 108–29 A new subsidiary subject is 'exposed' against which the main subject proceeds to enter in augmentation at 115, soprano (resources 5 and 6(e)). There is some overlapping and false stretto.

bars 130–195 Subject in double augmentation, first against quaver movement, then against various other figures. The entries, which may not be immediately perceptible to the eye, are:

soprano	132–143	subject
alto	146–156	answer
tenor	159–170	subject
bass	183–195	answer

bars 195–206 Subject in diminution (resource 6(f)) with new countersubject.

bars 206–214 Normal subject with new countersubject in semiquavers.
bars 214–220 Subject in diminution with dotted-rhythm accompaniment.
bars 221–236 New version of subject in triplet rhythm: at 226–7 the position used is that of G major—but the subject is so freely varied here that there is little effect of an 'entry in a major key'.
bars 236–239 Subject in diminution with new countersubject in mixed rhythm.
bars 239–242 Subject varied in repeated semiquavers.
bars 242–244 Normal subject with yet another countersubject.
bars 244–247 Semiquaver arpeggios against subject.
bars 247–250 Free version of subject with demisemiquaver decoration.
bars 250–256 Conspicuous sequence (resource 18) leading to prominent cadence in C.
bars 256–264 Echo effects on double diminution, leading to
bars 264–279 Normal subject with new countersubject in minims. Some free entries of the countersubject:
bars 280–293 Reiterations of the figure A–E–G–A, presumably a free reference to the subject. This is then reiterated in subdominant position (D–A–C–D).
bars 293–end Toccata ending (resource 15): elaborated plagal cadence in the tonic A.

This analysis has been made in detail in order to show the many factors which have to be taken into account in dealing with fugal forms. The form revealed is clearly very much a form by device; key is shown to be of importance at the cadences, but apart from the three 'E minor' entries, there is hardly a shred of entry key-variety. To the listener used to Bach and Handel it may seem that so many resources of a thematic nature are used one after the other that it is not easy to detect any sense of overall form. Similarly the cadences are not sufficiently varied to arouse the listener's expectation of a final climax at any particular point. Nevertheless the double-augmented entries hold together the middle part of the fugue and there is a definite build-up in the last twenty bars, with the reiteration of the short figure and the toccata ending. The trouble with earlier fugues such as this is that we tend to judge them by comparison with Bach and are not content to take them on their own terms. We should in fact do better to reverse the process and allow the methods of the earlier composers to throw light, as they undoubtedly will, on those of Bach. It is true that Bach is a greater composer than Sweelinck, but not *because* his prominent cadences are all on different chords and he uses, when he so wishes, key variety of entries.[56]

Another good example of Sweelinck's technique is given in GMB no. 158, the subject here being the chromatic scale figure described in Chapter 2. The main events here are:

bar 25	Key variety of entries: the subject is given beginning on E instead of D—a kind of 'answer to the answer', in fact.
bar 29	Stretto.
bars 36–7	Tonic cadence.
bar 37	Augmented subject with new countersubject.
bar 71	Doubly-augmented subject with (73) semiquaver 'accompanimental' part.
bars 85–6	Diverted dominant cadence.
bar 116	Direct subject treated in sequences. Entries here begin on C and B♭, but the chromaticism is ironed out so that there are no A♭s.
bar 134	Even faster movement in 'accompanimental' part.
bar 138	Very prominent stretto. Further key variety—a true entry beginning on G.
bar 151	Diminution of subject. Dominant and tonic pedals, and toccata ending.

The increased entry key-variety in this fugue is probably due to the chromatic scale subject, which increases the number of foreign notes anyway present and which also lacks specific major or minor characteristics (cf. above, p. 125). Another interesting point is the difference between the more casually introduced stretto at 29 and the very prominent later stretto, where everything except the theme itself suddenly ceases, at 138. Yet of the two the second one is less close in time-interval! Again, excitement near the end increases, not here by reiteration of part of the subject, but by diminution, as well as the well-known resources of pedals and the toccata-ending.

The effect of a very different chromatic subject, but a basically similar way of constructing a fugue, can be seen in Frescobaldi (1583–1643). The subject of *Ricercare Cromatico post il Credo* from *Fiori Musicali* (Peters, no. 31) was mentioned in Chapter 2. The fugue is a much simpler affair than either of the Sweelink examples, although it has

56. The old attitude to the early Baroque as existing purely to 'pave the way for Bach' is admirably seen in Bairstow's *The Evolution of Musical Form*, ch. IV, pp. 60–3. The comparison of the evolution of fugue with the development of the internal combustion engine (p. 60, middle) is significant of the attitude shown.

perhaps to modern ears a more effective ending. There are three sections:

1–19 Exposition and four 'extra' entries, slight overlap between last two. Tonic cadence, pause.

19–41 Subject combined, rather freely, with two new countersubjects. Note answer beginning E instead of D at 24 last note (and later). Tonic cadence again, this time coincident with a soprano entry beginning on B♮ instead of A (tonal answer variation, resource 6(a) above); pause.

41 Augmented subject combined with scalic figure. A final climax is built up by close entries (resource 3) at 59 and 62, overlap at 65, actual three-part stretto at 65–9 with some freedom at the end of the entries, and tonic pedal. (The third stretto entry is normal, not augmented.) The harmonies that result from this final collection of entries are remarkable:

66 (2nd half)	D major 6/3
67 (1st „)	F major root
67 (2nd „)	A major 6/4
	C♯ minor 6/3
68 (1st „)	D major root
	B♭ major 6/3, etc.

When one considers that C♯ minor 6/3–D major is the *final cadence* of the fugue, one can see how strongly theme influences harmony in contrapuntal music; in effect, here, harmonic colour (resource 17) is added to the other climactic devices. It would be amusing to confront a student with this set of chords, without actually showing him any of the part-progressions, and ask him to guess the composer (Vaughan Williams, perhaps?).

In many fugues of the early Baroque, 'form' is little more than the sectional structure itself. This is true of many of the fugues (ricercars, fantasias, canzonas and capriccios—the composer uses all four titles) of Froberger (1616–1667), a composer whose work Bach is known to have studied. Ricercar 9, for instance, one of the few pieces available outside the big editions[57] (Peters, *Alte Meister des Orgelspiels* part I, p. 102), divides into three sections, bars 1–68 on the subject in its original form, 69–111 on a rhythmically changed form (triple time) and 118–end on the augmented subject (with also a change of note values so that all the notes are now equal in length) combined with a countersubject which is sometimes heard in tenths (bar 143), i.e. it is

57. DTÖ Jahrgang X/2 Band 21.

'invertible at the tenth' (resource 5). The final section is prepared by a short link at 112–17, and 190–1 might be called 'harmonic colour' of a very mild kind, but apart from this the interest within each section relies purely on position and time-interval contrast (resources 1 and 2) and the counterpoint itself. (The piece is in the Phrygian mode—hence the 'dominant' feeling of the final chord to a listener used only to major and minor keys.) Occasionally Froberger uses 'preparatory' harmonies (resource 17) before the end of a section (see the following ricercar, 10,[58] bars 36–7: we should say 'G minor harmonies preparing G major cadence'). Toccata endings are also used ending both individual sections and/or the whole piece (Capriccio 14,[59] bars 77–82,9 9–end). Capriccio 11[60] is in fact a single section fugue of the type that became general in the late Baroque and is familiar to us today. The resources, apart from position and time-interval contrast, are simply a false stretto (four entries) at bars 26–8 and a toccata ending. (Stretto is, of course, itself only an extreme use of time-interval contrast.) It is these early single section fugues in which any definite 'form' is most difficult to detect.

With Buxtehude (1637–1707) it has been seen that the beginnings of key variety of entries begin to be perceptible. Nonetheless most of Buxtehude's fugues are still in the sectional forms, deriving in his case from the toccata. It was observed above that, for instance in the G minor Präludium (Hansen 2), the only entry in a key other than those of the original subject and answer was the final one of the second fugue, in the subdominant. It is clear, however, from the design as a whole that this entry is really symptomatic of a move towards the subdominant as part of a much extended plagal cadence with which the fugue is to end. The 'form' here really remains the form of the whole, and apart from the independent B♭ cadence in the second fugue (see above, resource 8) there is little in either fugue, considered in isolation, of a formal nature. Even in the A minor (Hansen 4) second fugue, the 'best' key scheme in Buxtehude, the very late use of the so-called 'middle' entries is again related to the fact that a toccata ending is to follow which confirms the tonic A minor, which, as far as entries are concerned, has only returned hurriedly in the last four bars of the fugue.

Buxtehude also wrote the occasional single-section fugue, the best known of which is the C major Gigue (Hansen 3), almost certainly the model for Bach's famous 'Gigue' fugue in G. The answer of this fugue was discussed in Chapter 2. The fugue itself is an interesting example of a fairly substantial length sustained on few resources. The subject is

58. DTÖ Jahrgang X/2 Band 21.
59. ibid.
60. ibid.

of course long, and the 'proper' exposition takes up to bar 24. Buxtehude now starts again with the soprano, but at the position higher than the original initial entry: the entries follow again in descending order, each entry now repeating earlier positions but with a different relation to the other parts (thus the initial entry position appears again at bar 31, but is now accompanied by an upper part). A very slight variation in the second bar of the theme appears in some of these entries. At bar 50 the original initial entry position is used yet again, but now as the uppermost part of a fairly homophonic accompaniment (resource 2). At last an episode occurs with the extension of the subject at 55 (is 55 the 'end of the exposition'?) and some free key-variety is introduced. A definite final section effect is produced by a kind of chordal pedal at 69–75, the tonic triad being ruthlessly retained against a rising scale in the bass (really a mixture of resources 17 and 11) and there is a very short toccata ending (one bar).

Before approaching the infinitely varied fugal forms of Bach another example of a pre-Bach single-section fugue with few resources may be considered—the fugue in E major from the collection *Ariadne Musica* by Johann Kaspar Ferdinand Fischer (?1660–?1738) HAM II, ex. 247. In this fugue there are thirteen entries of the theme, some slightly varied. Position and time-interval contrast are again the essential basis of the piece: and there is an actual stretto at bars 13–19 (soprano to bass). Germinal elements of form are the episode of 19–23, where a descending scale figure is heard (significantly this idea overlaps the entry of 24), the high climax (resource 1) at 32–6, and the prolonging by miniature pedals of the final II–V–I bass progression. The fugue is of exceptional interest, not only as being a perfect example of the ricercar type with few resources, but also in that Bach's WTC II.9, in the same key, on the same subject, and in a similar collection, is clearly a vast expansion of it (see below).

Suddenly with Bach, the problem of dealing with fugal form reverses itself—the trouble is not to find formal elements, but to find space to deal with the manifold forms which appear. The present chapter cannot, of course, attempt even a brief survey of the complete fugal output of this composer whose name is still virtually synonymous with fugue and yet whose procedures have been so often misunderstood. It is proposed, therefore, to look not at the standard examples (WTC I.2 is the great favourite for an introduction to Bach's technique, I.1 being, for good reasons, beyond the understanding of the conventional theorist!) but at some of the more 'difficult', and, it is hoped, interesting forms.

Bach's characteristic, even in youth, was to write at length. It is not presumptuous to say that, for instance, the two extremely lengthy fugues the (second version even lengthier than the first) which the young composer wrote on a theme from an Albinoni trio sonata (BWV 951 and 951a) are failures, in that they try to apply the old rule regarding key of entry—with the exception of a single incomplete relative major entry and its answer, even these much reduced in conspicuousness in the later version—to a design longer than it will stand without other resources such as stretto, inversion, etc. It is interesting, though, to observe that even here Bach's methods of extending the fugue into its later version include a rudimentary form of recapitulation (resource 9) and a new pedal and chromatic passage (resources 11 and 17). In the *Fuga all'imitazione della cornetta di postiglione* concluding the *Capriccio on the departure of a beloved brother* (note how the word 'capriccio' has now ceased to mean a type of fugue: the piece is a kind of pictorial sonata, probably modelled on similar works of Kuhnau) the length is more reasonable, and we find yet again a single entry in a new key (D minor) occurring near the end.

To turn now to better-known examples, one of the most infuriating fugues to analyse is the early mature F minor organ BWV 534. This piece has actually been criticised for its lack of structure. Here is what happens:

bars 1–27	Exposition and continuation, ending with prominent cadence in the dominant.
bars 27–42	Quaver movement now appears, and the number of parts is reduced to three to mark a new section. The two 'missing' parts re-enter with the theme at 31 and 38; note stretto, soprano to lowest manual voice. At 40 the dominant cadence is quickly diverted back to the tonic.
bars 42–63	Again parts are reduced, to two this time and new quaver counterpoints (incidental) appear. The pedals are silent. At 60 a prominent descending sequence (resource 18) introduces
bars 64–96	re-entry of pedals, very prominent, with the subject in the tonic and all five parts in thick chords to give a climax effect. Will this be the end of the fugue? A cadenza-like pedal passage leads to a relative major entry at 73, and already the feeling of climax is beginning to wane. After another dominant cadence at 88–9 parts are again thinned out—clearly this is not going to be a final climax.
bars 96–119	Yet another start is made in the tonic, pedals being silent with incidental counterpoints of suspended

crotchets, different from those heard before. (Too many returns to the tonic? How many such returns are there in a Beethoven rondo—the last movement of the Eighth Symphony, let us say?) The prominent sequence of 113–16, with intensifying quaver movement (resource 12) at 117–19 suggests that something is to happen.

bars 120–end The pedals re-enter with the theme in the dominant closely followed (resource 3) by a further dominant entry at 123. One would here, being examination-minded, expect two or three tonic entries, the final one probably delivered by the pedals. Actually, however, bars 123–6 is the last entry of the fugue—not even in an outer voice! The final clinching of the design comes by reiteration of the incidental quaver figure at 126, which eventually turns into an unaccompanied cadenza at 134–5. Perhaps not by coincidence the final 6/4–5/3 cadence is prepared by the diminished seventh chord on iv♯, the note which figures so prominently in the subject.

The above analysis attempts to describe *what the listener hears* rather than the relation between what Bach does and what is prescribed in a textbook. It will be observed that definite form emerges, but one which bears no relationship to a ternary design whether by key or anything else. Indeed if any 'stock' form is to be named it would be the rondo, though again not in the strict key sense, as described in resource 7, but rather in the sense that from time to time the subject does seem to make a 'fresh start' in the tonic. In this way Bukofzer's 'continuous expansion' idea seems to come nearer to expressing what happens, except that the 'expansions' are expansions in the general sense, not in the sense of episodes developing exposition material. It is hoped that this kind of analysis makes sense of a design which happens to be one of the worst from the point of view of almost any standard method. The Fischer fugue mentioned above, for instance, has the advantage, in one way, that there is no entry key-variety at all; it is a short piece, having a continuous and consistent texture, and no notable effects. Someone brought up on the conventional idea of fugue could well describe it simply as an 'extended fugal exposition'. Similarly the Bach 'Albinoni' fugues, although long, can be regarded as an exposition extended so long as to be boring. But the F minor organ cannot be got rid of so easily. Clearly it has form and equally clearly some parts of it are exciting while others express relaxation. As regards key, Bach uses the relative major, thus dangling a carrot before the key-analysers, who soon find out that he uses it without system. Those who seek device, again, find one stretto in an impossibly 'wrong' place. Not even the final entry, as we have seen, has the grace to obey a rule which seems reasonable enough. Analysis has to learn not only what to include but also what to leave out. Neither key of entry nor stretto are important in this fugue: this is not a decision made by the theorist analysing it, but something which the composer tells the listener by the way in which the design unfolds.

A fugue possibly earlier than the F minor and nearer to the ricercar spirit is the very beautiful WTC I.8—beautiful despite the tendency of the young Bach to go on too long. Here again key or any other conventional analysis is hopeless. What is needed above all is to sort out the important events. Analysis by device, such as emerged from the Sweelinck examples above, and as given by Tovey in his notes to the fugue in the Associated Board Edition, will not really do, since Bach mixes key and other resources with device:

bars 1–19 Opening 'exposition', in general sense, ending with modulation to the dominant.

bar 19 First stretto (direct subject) in the dominant key (contrast the original answer with a genuine dominant entry, as here). The key soon moves away from the dominant, and is in fact rather indefinite for some bars.

A stretto of the normal subject with a rhythmically varied version is introduced (24–7, upper parts), not very conspicuously. Cadence in the relative major introduces

bars 30–44 inversion of the subject, beginning in the relative major, but further entries move away.

bars 44–61 Stretto of the inverted subject: but the important factors are the conspicuous return to definite tonic tonality impressed on the listener by the very low entry (resource 1). Here the design becomes very intense. A three-part stretto appears at 52: the stretto is false, but this is the first time three parts have been involved in stretto, and the listener does not worry about the 'falseness'. After a conspicuous descending scale (resource 18) at 60–1 there follows

bars 62–67 fully augmented entry, bass, in the subdominant. This of itself forms a climax. Against it two normal entries, one direct, one inverted, occur; but it is the augmentation that attracts the listener's attention.

bars 67–77 Relaxation—despite another augmented entry: this one has not the importance of being the first, it is in the middle voice and in the relative major after the opening note (tonal answer variation, resource 6(a)). There follows one further direct entry, 72–5, much varied and very chromatically accompanied, presumably as an approach to the final part of the fugue (resource 17).

bars 77–end The design is finally clinched by a high augmented entry, against which the normal and the rhythmically altered subject is heard in various ways (the former twice). The beautiful Phrygian end to this has already been noted. After this a scarcely less beautiful falling melodic phrase has a kind of 'postlude' effect. A chromatic ascent (resource 18 again) marks the final conclusion.

In this design the fascination of the interplay of device with key is fully evident. It is perhaps this which must make Bach's fugues the despair of a rigid analyst. Everything is important—melodic tonality, harmonic tonality (the three vital cadences of 19 and 29–30), stretto, augmentation—but the form in the true sense can only be assessed by balancing the effect of all these together and judging which at any time is most conspicuous to the ordinary listener.

Another good example in a fairly early fugue of the interplay of stretto and inversion with other resources, but with a 'canzona' type subject, is WTC I.20. Here again we find puzzled theorists: Tovey, for instance, analysing mainly by device, finds the fugue 'not without redundancies'. The 'device' analysis is simple, viz.:

bars 1–14 Exposition, four entries.

bars 15–27 Inverted subject in all four parts in turn: note, in passing, how 'badly' the subject inverts and the unusual position of the fourth inverted entry, using the octave B–B in A minor. (For the normal inversion system see above resource 6(c).)

bars 27–46 Four stretti on the direct subject.

bars 48–61 Three stretti on the inverted subject.

bars 64–70 One direct and one inverted stretto, this time using the 'twelfth inversion' relationship (see resource 5).

bars 73–76 Additional inverted stretto, normal position (presumably one of Tovey's 'redundancies').
bars 76–78 An attempt at an inverted/direct stretto at one bar's interval, but it proves to be 'false' and leads to
bars 78–end a series of false stretti stressing the opening figure of the subject.

There are many more details even in the above which should be considered in a detailed analysis, but on listening to the fugue it becomes clear that this inversion-stretto pattern is only a part of the actual effect of the music. Again without going into the full details, it may be said that the main events are:

bar 16: The first inverted entry inflects its F with a ♯, and its cadence, which should be on E (see resource 6(c), above), is changed (as are all the other inverted entry cadences). This presages the first move away from the tonic.

bar 24: Bach's choice of an 'odd' position for the last inverted entry of these four seems to have been designed to effect a tonic return: this happens at 27 (cadence) and a definitely tonic section, with dominant in its 'answer' function, lasts until 40 beat 1. This could have been the final section of the fugue.

bar 40: A definite relaxation is evident in the episode (the longest one of the fugue!) 40–3. A second discursive section follows, visiting a number of keys. At 56 a conspicuous ascent in the bass (resource 18) introduces a tonic return, but this is less conspicuous than the previous one. A dominant pedal at 60–2 is clearly preparing something bigger and better: it could lead to a final climax, but is promptly diverted to the subdominant (cadence at 64).

bar 64: By discontinuing other voices and preceding each entry by a rest in the part concerned Bach here gives the stretti climax value. But even this is not to be the end. Typically, Bach contrives yet another relaxation, in the key of F, not so far visited. This is Tovey's 'redundant' stretto. Note the non-climactic pedal on vii at 76 (see p. 137 above). At last the real ending is near. With a fine disregard for rules that had not then been invented the final climax contains almost every resource but the one it ought to contain—there is no complete final stretto in the tonic, or in any key for that matter. The resources are harmonic colour: the 'neapolitan sixth' of 79 second half, the diminished seventh on iv♯ 81 second half and the 'supertonic chromatic seventh' 82 beat 3 (resource 17), pause 80 (resource 16), rests and homophonic chords 79–82 (resources 13 and 16), false stretto everywhere (resource 4), additional voices 80 onwards (resource 14), tonic pedal 83–end (resource 11), ending with conspicuous figure, last bar (resource 21) in thirds (resource 14) using inversion and direct subject together (resource 6(c)), last bar. Admittedly this is not Bach's greatest fugue: it may be said that its 'middle' does not fully sustain the interest, but again the 'redundant' stretto is not the *reason* for this. It may be that Bach is still writing at greater length than the material will stand, though even this perhaps is a dangerous criticism. As always with Bach the ending is a great success.

To turn now to a few mature fugues, those most awkward from the conventional analysis point of view are probably those with little key interest. WTC I.6 has already been noted to show a large element of binary form, accounting for 25 out of the 44 bars of the fugue (see resource 9 above). There is really little else here—inversion is not used schematically, there is no key variety of entries and no variety of fixed harmonic tonality except for the definite dominant end to the first 'half' (bars 17–20). The final cadence (42–3 corresponding to 20–1) is prolonged by a brief tonic pedal with the opening of the subject stated, as in I.20, with its inversion in thirds (resources 6(c) and 21). The very beautiful I.14, with a chromatic (not modulatory, surely!) subject also shows an element of binary form: here inversion does not appear until after the 'half-way' cadence. The codetta is, as often in Bach (Chapter 2, above) responsible for some of the main episodes: episode 1, bars 11–15, digresses to the dominant, subdominant, and relative major in turn, the last digression leading direct to an additional tonic entry;[61] episode 2 (18–20) leads to the dominant for the 'half-way' cadence; and episode 4 (28) is an exact repeat of the codetta an octave higher. The inverted entries (20–3, middle voice and 32–5, bass) are classically 'correct' (see resource 6(c) above): the first runs from v down to i and back, while the second, introducing the only new melodic tonality in the fugue, runs from i down to iv below. The last episode, 5 (35–7), introduces added thirds (resource 14) and is remarkable for 'false relations' and its coincidental prophesying of a passage by Granados.[62] The final entry is over a tonic pedal with a characteristic 'dissonant 6/3' chord on its third note. In this fugue, form is again a mixture of contract between direct and inverted subject (here significant, as it is not in I.6), episodic recapitulation (including, of course, the answer-codetta as 'germ') and the overall binary structure, the conclusion being marked by comparatively mild but appropriate resources.

An early 'ricercar'-type fugue, I.8, has been studied. It may be appropriate now to compare this example with what is perhaps Bach's

61. This entry is not exposition: see Chapter 2, p. 31, note 11.

62. Goyescas: 'Quejas ó la Maja y el Ruiseñor.' The resemblance is best seen 25 bars from the end.

greatest essay in this style, WTC II.9. This is on the same subject as the Fischer fugue discussed above. This would be a matter of little consequence—Froberger uses the same theme, to name but one—were it not for the fact that the rather rare key of E major is shared by both fugues, and Fischer's fugue is also one of a series in (nearly) all the keys. Add to this other evidence from WTC that Bach knew Fischer's *Ariadne Musica* and it is clear that Bach modelled II.9 on the earlier work. The expositions of both correspond in ascending order of entries: both Fischer and Bach achieve final climax by a very high entry (Fischer, bars 32–6; Bach, bars 37–9); in both the last entry is a dominant bass one (Fischer 39–43: Bach 40–1); and we may even compare Fischer's descending soprano of 36–42 with Bach's at 38–9 and possibly that at 41–2 also (resource 18).

II.9 is again a fascinating exercise in mixing of resources. At bar 9 the exposition and its continuation finish on the dominant. To the chagrin of the examiners Bach now proceeds to introduce his 'best' stretto—four parts 'stretto maestrale' at the closest possible time-interval, and in the tonic at that! Clearly this student has little idea of how to conserve his resources. After this there is a relaxation and a move away from the tonic, and a cadence is formed in the relative minor (15–16). A new stretto combines the subject in a rather complex way with a chromatic countersubject. The key moves both melodically and subsequently harmonically to II (F♯ minor). Clearly we are now in for a much longer fugue than Fischer's. At 23–6 the subject is varied by filling in of its leaps (resource 6(h)). The keys are melodically F♯/C♯ and G♯/D♯. More important than this is the fact that the subject in diminution arrives in stretto at 27–8 and a dominant harmonic cadence arouses expectation of a return to the tonic key. (How typical of Bach to introduce diminution *before* a conspicuous tonic return!) A fairly definite return seems to be being made by the alto entry of the normal subject at 30, and the piling up of 'diminished' entries increases excitement. But Bach has still more in store, for the key moves harmonically to G♯ minor (III) with a cadence with chromatic preparatory chord. Modulation to III with Bach in a major tonic nearly always presages a tonic return, and there is now a 'stretto maestrale' in the tonic but with the more exciting diminished theme as well as the normal one (so Bach had something in store after all!). The biggest climax however is the high entry of 37–9, Bach here paying his tribute both to Fischer and to the oldest resource of fugue, position-contrast (resource 1). A conspicuous sequence and rests (resources 18 and 16) also feature near the end, whose resemblance to 'Rule Britannia' perhaps obscures the fact that it is a relaxation after a climax, not a boisterous new theme.

A fugue very well known but rarely analysed in WTC I.1, a design on ricercar principles though the subject is more a canzona-like type than those just examined. Here again Bach brings his closest stretto immediately after the exposition. A repeat of this with the antecedent in answer position brings the consequent on to the D position—the first element of entry key-contrast in the fugue. It is interesting that the ends of both antecedent and consequent (B and F♯ respectively) occur when harmonically the key is on the way to A minor, to which with the assistance of an E entry in the A minor scale (resource 6(b)) modulation is effected at bars 13–14. Against the A minor chord itself Bach restarts tonic stretti, and a total of six entries in original subject/answer relationship follows. This new tonic section is thus far more impressive than the exposition and its following stretti. The next move away is to D minor, with 'tierce de picardie' cadence, against which entries on A and E appear in stretto—yet another clash of melodic and harmonic tonalities. The rest of the fugue is really an elaborated II–V–I cadence in the tonic. A new, less close, stretto at lower sixth brings its consequent on to the strange position of B (resource 6(b) again) but the dominant pedal now prepares the final cadence and the tonic pedal ensues with its feeling of relaxation. Faster movement (resource 12) marks the end of this fugue—despite the stretti a less exciting, more formal, and also much slighter design than I.8 or II.9.

Many of the other keyboard fugues of Bach have been mentioned when discussing the resource concerned—the rondo key-schemes, for instance, were mentioned under resource 7 above. The supposedly 'normal' ternary key-schemes such as I.7 will need little explanation to anyone who knows them: as has been said, the interesting thing about these is their comparative rarity and the lop-sided 'forms' which may arise from key analysis alone. Any good analysis of I.12, for instance, must take into account not only the recurrence of episodes but the fact that, as was seen under resource 9, bars 47–56 first beat are a recapitulation of 13–22 first beat and introduce a strong 'binary' element into the form.

Fugues which introduce new themes, whether second (and/or third) subjects or new countersubjects are fairly easily analysed in thematic terms, but even in clear-cut cases many other factors have to be taken into account to give a true picture of the music. A purely thematic analysis of the great B minor organ fugue BWV 544, for instance, would arrive simply at a ternary scheme (subject+first countersubject (or by itself) 1–28: subject+second countersubject (again sometimes by itself) 28–58: subject+third and also first countersubject 59–end). This is correct but takes no account, for instance, of the entry key-variety in the first section (entries in E minor, D major, A major); of the fact that a very definite harmonic modulation to the dominant occurs before the introduction of countersubject 2(22–7); of the whole musical sense of the middle section, which is designed to keep the listener waiting for something—he does not yet know what; nor of the fact that 59 is not only the addition of the third countersubject but also a most conspicuous return to the tonic, the only prominent tonic return in the whole fugue (even here Bach characteristically has the pedals in reserve—they enter at 61 in the answer to the 59 entry: the entry of the conspicuous third countersubject both in the tonic and in the pedals is saved for the last entry at 85). The last section—'section' here still assuming the thematic analysis, which it is now clear is only part of the story—is itself full of interest: there is, to mention only one feature, the interruption caused by the sudden use of C♯ minor for the entry of 68, soprano, just when the tonic key has been well and truly restored.

To conclude this obviously inadequate account of Bach's forms, which is really only intended to suggest the kind of way in which a true analysis might be arrived at, one choral fugue is discussed. Many of the choral fugues are of the 'incidental' variety consisting of exposition and little more, these often being introduced into movements based on the ritornello principle. 'Cum sancto Spiritu' in the Mass in B minor is a well-known example, the introductory ritornello which obviously originally began the movement having been cut out when Bach adapted this piece—its source is not known—into the Mass. Even the gigantic first 'Kyrie' of the same work is similarly constructed, although here the ritornello is based on the same theme as the fugue. The ritornello, bars 5–29 (numbers include the four bars of introduction), recurs in the dominant at 48–72 and in the tonic at 102–end, in both cases with voice-parts added. The 'incidental' fugues—the term is admittedly inappropriate in cases of such great length!—are 30–47 and (after a brief instrumental interlude including a curious A major entry of the theme with its chromaticism ironed out) 81–101. 'Et in terra pax' in this work is a complete fugue, but is built up on the 'round fugue' (*Permutationsfuge*) principle mentioned in Chapter 2. There are two episodes, 137 second half to 143 and 160–70 (numbering from the beginning of the 'Gloria'). The rest of the fugue consists of two sets of voice entries, the first, as often without doubling, from 120 last note to 137 (note the second soprano entry in E minor, with the first countersubject in the bass making 'odd' harmony at 136 first note) and the second, where the voices are doubled by instruments (resource 10), from 143 (soprano) to 160 (the bass entry at 133 last note is in the subdominant). Two further entries conclude the fugue. 'Form' in 'round fugues' is largely dominated by the entries themselves, and we have seen that in Cantata 21 Bach wrote a complete fugue consisting of nothing else—no key-variety even, although again instrumental timbre (resource 10) was a source of contrast. The 'Et in terra' fugue adds two entries showing key-variety and the two episodes to these resources: timbre has also been seen to be important in the two trumpet entries of 157–60 and the last three bars.

It is the second 'Kyrie' of the Mass in B minor that has been chosen for slightly more detailed study here, since this is both a complete fugue and one not reliant on 'round' principles, having instead yet another of the highly individual forms which make Bach's fugues the despair of theorists who like neat categories. The subject is of the quasi-ricercar type, very chromatic at the opening (cf. Chapter 2, p. 44). The answer-codetta, already mentioned for its subdominant touch (Chapter 2, p. 84) is also responsible for episodes 1 and 2 (14–18 and 21–4). The alto entry of 18 appears during the course of the contrapuntal flow and even the harmonic progressions give no hint of a break. (In passing we may note the first three chords of 22, which involve the enharmonic treatment of the diminished seventh chord—a rarity in fugue—causing an abrupt switch from intended E minor to C♯ minor. The impression is almost that Bach had cut something out here, although this is unlikely, since his later adaptations of works are always longer than their originals.) Entries so far still adhere to the old rule of 'original two positions only', and those of 25 (bass) and 29 (tenor) are still marked by no break of any kind, episode 3 (27–9) being purely prolongation of the counterpoint. In spirit, so far, what we have heard is exposition.

At 31 we see the beginning of the episodic development which is to provide the climax described in resource 20, above. The listener will not have noticed this figure yet, but it was there at 5 second half, and 7 (continuo), more noticeably at 11 (bass), then at 13 second half and 15 (tenor) and 22 second half (tenor). Episode 4 (31–5) for the first time introduces the figure in imitation, thus making it quite obvious to the listener, and the first cadence of the fugue is now made in the subdominant B minor. Coincident with the cadence Bach introduces stretto: significantly neither of its entries are in B minor, but the tonic and dominant F♯ and C♯. Parts are reduced to only three, alto, tenor and continuo, and the stretto is an almost bi-tonal one, the F♯ and C♯ minor scales being heard simultaneously, although the C♯ entry does make slight concessions to F♯ minor by introducing E♯ and later D♮. After a purely prolonging episode (38–40) the stretto is repeated in soprano and bass in B minor/F♯ minor, restoring all the four voices again. Episode 6 begins the build-up of the episodic figure again; as we have seen in other fugues, this is the sort of passage which might lead to a final climax—two stretti and two episodic 'developments' (in a loose sense—these are not strict episodes) being sufficient to suggest a forthcoming conclusion, and in 46 first half the music is firmly in the tonic. Suddenly Bach switches to the dominant, and in this key makes the second important cadence of the fugue at 48. In view of the prominence of this cadence it is now unlikely that the fugue will end just yet. What follows is, of all things, a near exact (apart from the additional voices) recapitulation of the original answer-codetta, whose purpose was, of course, to restore the tonic after the dominant answer (Chapter 2, p. 84): but instead of leading to an entry it now leads to the climax—the high A of the sopranos beginning the episodic figure again and the other voices following in imitation (resource 20). Surely no other fugue can show a phrase so transformed in importance as this one, as between its first unnoticed appearance in bar 5 and the present climax! After this, consolidation, rather than further excitement, is what is needed, and this is the function of the final stretto (bass, tonic, 54–7: soprano, dominant, 55–7) and the last two bars.

The points that emerge here are: (a) the length of the opening section in which nothing happens outside the potentialities of the first section of one of the older ricercars. Until the second note of bar 32 this could have been going to be a simple 'exposition'-type fugue, such as Fischer's E major mentioned above, or countless others of pre-Bach days. (Nor, of course, would this necessarily have been 'wrong', though it would not have been Bach.) (b) the unimportance, yet again, of entry key variety. Bach does not care to present this subject, with its early use of ii♭, in the major. (c) the vital part played by the two cadences, neither of which relates to the key of any entry near them. (d) the holding together of the design by the use of the answer-codetta in episodes 1 and 2 and its later recapitulation. (e) the achievement by episodic means of the final climax of a fugue which contains a perfectly good stretto (a final insult to the conventional examiners, this! And yet many of them must have heard, and perhaps even conducted, their university choirs singing this very work!).

Before leaving Bach two matters may be briefly mentioned. First, *The Art of Fugue*. This work is spoken of in hushed terms, and has even been compared by some to the late quartets of Beethoven—a kind of final testament of a great composer. Whatever is to be said about Beethoven's late quartets—and it might reasonably be pointed out that Beethoven did not know he was going to die at the not very advanced age of fifty-seven, and much in these works is obviously experimental (as, at an earlier period, are the sonatas op. 26 and 27)—Bach's *The Art of Fugue* is certainly nothing more than a very fine technical exercise:

to the Baroque period the idea of bequeathing a last great work to Posterity would surely have seemed very odd. What is relevant here is that, despite Tovey's view, the *The Art of Fugue* is a complete work whose individual numbers make sense only as parts of the whole. It demonstrates, in fact, the ultimate potentialities of a single theme, realised in a series of fugues none of which is typical of the rest of Bach's fugal output for the very good reason that in no other fugues was this the aim. The musical evidence for this is overwhelming: mainly it lies in the fact that in the fugues where another theme or themes appear at the outset and the main theme of the work enters later to combine with them, the main theme dominates over the others because of its more complete melodic characteristics—just the very point which was made in Chapter 2 in distinguishing between subject and countersubject or subsidiary subject. It is true that some of the other themes—that of Contrapunctus VIII for instance—could have stood on their own, but as soon as the main theme enters the local subject sounds subsidiary by comparison. Quite the opposite position was seen to apply to the normal double and triple fugue, where the second and third subjects (where present) never usurped the function of main theme. The subject of Contrapunctus X is in fact rather vague for a fugue-subject anyway (note the, for Bach, rare opening on the leading-note) and had it been left to its own devices the result would hardly be a true fugue. Further evidence pointing in the same direction can be found in, for instance, the subject of Contrapunctus III: within Bach's style the strange Æolian mode effect of this theme, with a third note C♮ where obviously a C♯ seems to be needed, is explicable only when it is considered as an answer-form of the main theme, which the listener will have heard in the first two fugues. Similarly the second subject of Contrapunctus XI (bar 27, tenor) is a very 'poor' theme intelligible only as the inversion of the subject of Contrapunctus VIII, which the listener will already have heard. In short, then, the *The Art of Fugue* is neither a 'great work' in the romantic sense nor is it Bach's demonstration of how fugues ought to be written: it is a special *tour de force*, quite outside the main stream of Baroque fugue, and as such must regrettably be left out of detailed consideration in the present short survey of fugal forms.

Second, authenticity. The present book is again not the place for a scholastic discussion on the ways in which Bach's authorship of a work may be either established or called into question. It is sufficient to say that many works by other composers have been wrongly attributed to Bach, and stylistic doubts in the minds of scholars have in several cases (Cantatas 15, 160 and 189, for instance) been confirmed by what is regarded as 'proper' (i.e. extra-musical) evidence. In fugue one of the neatest ternary key designs—the so-called 'fughetta' BWV 900—is on stylistic evidence almost certainly not by Bach, and on similar evidence (notably the vague treatment of the subject in the exposition) the 'Little Preludes and Fugues' for organ BWV 553–560 are even more certainly unauthentic. Perhaps it is time that one or two other fugues were added to the 'doubtful' category. Is *the* organ Toccata and Fugue in D minor BWV 565 (actually entitled Toccata) really Bach? No other final minor plagal cadence in Bach closes on the *minor* tonic chord—in such contexts the chord is always major. There are no other completely unaccompanied pedal entries in Bach (see bars 109–11) and the inner and upper trills against the strange C minor entries of 86–90 are most un-Bach-like. Of course all early works show characteristics which disappear in maturity—the question is here whether we can find anything in other early fugues which could reasonably parallel the features just mentioned. These remarks do not constitute an essay on the authenticity of BWV 565: they are merely thrown out in the hope of interesting the reader in the kind of evidence which has to be taken into account in deciding questions of this kind. We all know this fugue so well that it is only when we come to listen to it dispassionately that we suddenly realise that it really does not sound very much like J. S. Bach.

Whatever may happen to fugue in the modern period it seems difficult to believe that there can ever again be a composer of fugues as great as Bach. But these things are, in the end, unpredictable. After all Bach himself arrived 'too late'; up to shortly before his day the concept of a fugue was still basically what it had always been—that of a homogeneous contrapuntal piece with entries in two fixed positions, both basically tonic, contrasted with other parts which were free to modulate. Now, degenerate developments such as entries in new keys, concerto episodes, exact recapitulations and thematic development were coming in from outside to disrupt the old scheme of things. That the greatest genius of fugue should not only arrive on the scene at such a time, but should actually use the new resources, and successfully at that, must surely have seemed beyond belief to anyone living in 1700.

Handel's fugues are well known for being 'freer' than those of Bach. In point of fact most of the fugues are either choral or French overture fugues from operas or oratorios: there is no real equivalent of Bach's large output of 'pure' fugues. Rather than Handel being 'free', it was anyway Bach who was 'strict' in his mature fugues compared with the general fugal tradition of his day. The '7 Pieces and 6 Fugues' of Handel (Augener no. 5096) do show Handel writing 'pure' keyboard fugue, although these fugues may well be adapted from orchestral works. A fair example is the G major fugue (no. II). Here stretto is unlikely to be a decisive factor since it appears as early as bars 22–3 (bass/soprano) and again at 26 (alto/soprano). Only the last of these entries is a true one, and indeed the fugue is full of false entries. More important is the move away from the tonic at 30, leading to a B minor entry without its opening notes and employing at first the E minor scale (resource 6(b)) at 34, bass. There is a momentary tonic return at 44–5 (note how the tonal answer opening on G coincides with a D major harmonic cadence). Reduction of parts to two at 48 introduces an episode freely treating the end of the subject accompanied by the relevant portion of the countersubject (the combination originally seen at bars 8–9). A small climax is made by the return of four parts at 57 and some use of consecutive tenths (resource 14). There is a conspicuous false stretto, one entry only complete, at 62, but in the relative minor. Still further development in tenths seems to predict an important entry, but Handel has typically by now introduced so many false entries that a special device will be necessary to convince the listener of a 'big event'. This eventually arrives at 84 with a stretto of direct with inverted subject (soprano 84, bass 85), the latter using a low position (resource 1). At 91 the flat-side key of D minor (dominant minor) appears, another sign of an approaching final climax. There are still more false entries to come (note the sixths at 100–3) and a further use of the direct/inverted stretto, now in B minor, at 104 (soprano/bass). The final entry is in fact not in stretto (110 soprano) and the final climax devices are dominant pedal (resource 11) and a conspicuous scale descent (resource 18) accompanied above by the subject's original octave-leap figure carried through two octaves (4–3 bars from the end).

This fugue is in some ways akin to Bach's F minor organ, except that key-variety is a little more systematic (the definite flat-side visit at 91) and although there are many unimportant entries and even stretti there is one important one, the direct/inverted one at 84.

The 'Amen' fugue in *Messiah* can, despite the masses of false stretto, be analysed in terms almost entirely of key, with some use of instrumental colour (resource 10). This latter appears chiefly near the opening, with the contrast, not unlike some things in the 'concerto-fugue', between voices with continuo only, two violin parts alone, and tutti. After bar 45 the course of the fugue is almost entirely a matter of key, with a small amount of thematic contrast provided by the countersubject figure (53–6, soprano, for instance). The key scheme, which, since only part of the subject is heard after bar 42, is really based on conventional harmonic tonalities, is thus:

1–56 tonic and dominant;
57–62 relative minor and F♯ minor (sharp side);
63–67 tonic, then subdominant (flat side);
68–74 build-up in tonic, leading to
75–end climax entry with trumpets and drums (the point of this is completely lost in Mozart's edition and its successors, which allow the trumpets and drums to sound continually during the passage 57–74). Short dominant pedal, pause, and final cadence.

The preoccupation with device in many post-Baroque fugues is well seen in Mozart's C minor Fugue for two pianos, K.426. The form here is, unlike WTC I.20, for instance, more dependent on the use of stretto than upon key, which latter is used unsystematically. The fugue does indeed begin as if key were to be its basis: after the 'extra' entry of 14, bass, Mozart proceeds in sonata-like manner to the dominant of E♭, the relative major, and introduces an E♭ entry over the dominant pedal—the pedal which would in sonata form introduce the second subject. (Thus even in the classic period we find ourselves still no nearer to the academic idea that an episode does the modulating and an entry follows firmly in the new key!) Any idea that key is to be systematic is, however, promptly destroyed at this point, and the likeness to sonata form—possibly a matter of unconscious habit with Mozart—henceforth disappears: entries follow in F minor (22), G minor (25), A♭ (30), and B♭ minor (32), forming a 'modulating exposition' (see resource 7, p. 130) and there is then a prompt return to the tonic with the first stretto at 35–8, which is a two-part one of the inverted subject; this is given an answering stretto in the dominant at 39–42. A similar stretto of the direct version, but 'false', follows in D♭ at 44 and in E♭ minor/A♭ minor (using E♭ minor scale in both parts) at 47. These dark keys could be very significant in a different kind of fugue, but Mozart has introduced so many keys already, including B♭ minor, the equivalent of D♭ and next darkest to E♭ minor, that these further ones have only a 'development' effect, and it is no surprise when the tonic promptly returns at 51 with a two-part stretto of the direct and inverted subject (tonic/dominant). Mozart now steps up the stretto by increasing the number of parts involved. A three-part stretto (direct–inverted–direct) in the subdominant begins at 57, and some further false entries lead to intense free development of the last figure of the subject. There is a very prominent cadence on the dominant at 71–2, 72 is an obvious link, and at 73—yet again in the tonic—we have the direct and inverted subject stated together (see resource 6(c)). This is a big climax but Mozart has more in store. At 82 last note a four-part stretto (two inverted, two direct, entries) is conspicuously introduced, each entry preceded by a rest in the part concerned. This is wholly in the dominant. 88–9 are an episodic intensification—a 'stretto' of a three-quaver figure from the subject (resource 19). At 91 another four-part stretto begins in the tonic, continuing in the subdominant. 100–2 are a further episodic intensification, the diminished seventh inverted figure of the subject being combined with a virtually new figure in the upper parts. Yet another four-part stretto, wholly of the direct subject, follows at 103 (tonic/subdominant/vii♮/tonic). Mozart has thus introduced three consecutive four-part stretti, all within reach of the tonic key, and two episodic intensifications! After this *tour de force*, which the well-brought-up student probably thinks has no right to come off, continuous semi-quaver rhythm is introduced (resource 12) and the two pianos fall into octaves in the right hand at 112, then into complete unison at 116. The stretto with which the fugue ends is nothing new—it is in fact the one of bars 84–7: the climax lies in the fact of the two instruments being in unison. Added parts, homophony and rests mark the final cadence.

Although one could analyse this fugue as a key rondo this would probably be a poor representation of the way it strikes the listener. There are so many returns to the tonic that it is doubtful whether the listener really notices them after the first one or two. Paradoxically, for a composer living in the period when key contrast had, in sonata form, established itself as a dominating factor in the construction of long movements, Mozart's fugue is more faithfully described in the same terms as the Sweelinck example with which this section of the chapter began—as essentially a form by device with little key interest. It is not too far-fetched to read into this fact a reflection of the new view of fugue as essentially a *tour de force* in an archaic idiom.

A vote on which was the most difficult of Beethoven's fugues to analyse would almost certainly show a majority for the *Grosse Fuge*, op. 133. A first hearing of this, whether by itself or in the context of the String Quartet in B♭, op. 130, is certainly a rather confusing experience for the listener. The piece seems to 'go on' interminably; the more Bach fugues the hearer knows, and the more arduously he has 'done' fugue in examinations, the less understandable must seem Beethoven's vastly different treatment of fugal form. There is little doubt, however, that the piece is somewhat more readily understandable as finale to op. 130 than it is as a separate fugue. It is true that the opening on G and subsequent statements of the subject in various keys are the sort of thing that Beethoven might anyway have done in his last period (we have already mentioned the opening of the Ninth Symphony on A), the listener having to know in advance that the key is B♭. When the fugue follows the rest of the quartet, however, the G links up not only with the mediant of E♭, key of the preceding Cavatina, but also with the G major of the movement before that ('alla danza tedesca'). Again, the great length of the fugue and the reluctance to end are much more logical when the ending is that not only of the movement but of the whole work.

As has been hinted, the less the listener knows about fugue the more easily he will come to terms with this huge movement. The first thing to realise is that the change to 6/8 'allegro molto e con brio' at bar 233 is intended to sound like the beginning of a final section. The ordinary listener noting the sudden lifting of the dark colours of the preceding section, the light-hearted rhythms and the absence of the intense counterpoint of the first section of the fugue proper (30 onwards), would probably take it this way instinctively. Those who know that the piece is going on for another 500 bars or so are at a disadvantage here.

So far then the design is an A–B–A both by sectional structure, key (overall) and speed of movement. The changes in the kinds of movement in the first section were mentioned under resource 2, above. With previous analyses in mind this first section can perhaps be 'taken as read', it being sufficient to point out the important tonic returns, each marked by a different kind of movement in the 'accompanying' parts, and by a different variation of the subject at 111 and 139. The section ends not with a normal cadence but with a sudden interruption on the chord VI♭, a great favourite (both note and chord) for dramatic interruptions in this period. The interrupting chord then becomes a key, and the slow G♭ section which follows stems from bars 17–25. It, too, needs little explanation: its emotional difference from the preceding is obvious, and since the subject is still constantly heard (now in even crotchet rhythm) the passage is not an interpolation but an integral part of the fugue. Four bars of 6/4 chord of B♭ (minor, then brightening to major at the last moment) lead back to the main tonic and the 'finale'—as it appears to be.

What follows is a series of interruptions of expected processes. The interruptions themselves suggest new developments, and then there is the need to restore the *status quo*. In this way the last movement of the Eighth Symphony is prolonged, and the same, carried to a much further extent, happens here. The first of the interruptions is the A♭ at 272. Again the interrupting note becomes a key, and there is a new exposition with the subject in steady long notes and a fragment of the 'finale' rhythm as countersubject. Each entry here has a trill on its last note (cf. bar 10) and this trill becomes itself a matter for free development. Eventually an actual enharmonic circle on the flat side occurs from 326 onwards, the keys being A♭, D♭ (328–9), G♭ (330–1), C♭

(332–3—the notation in sharps is meaningless), F♭ (334–5), B♭♭ (336–7), E♭♭ (338–9), A♭♭ (340–1) and D♭♭ (342–3). When the next key arrives at 344–5 it will probably be recognised by pitch as F the dominant (this is what is meant by an enharmonic circle). Yet another version of the opening of the subject is now seen at 350–4, viola. The keys here are those more or less closely related to A♭. Beethoven rather daringly uses G♭ again at 371–7, but we are now sufficiently far from the original G♭ section for there to be no risk of tautology. The passage which follows is perhaps the most incredible of all as a feat of composition. For Beethoven obviously intends the B♭ minor scale from 378–405 to be a preparation for a tonic return (see resource 17; notice the way the G♭ bass of 371–8 falls to F, the dominant, at 378–80: cf. C♭–B♭ before the last movement of the 'Emperor' Concerto—a highly dramatic use of the same procedure). In the end this is diverted to E♭ minor (406–13)—but not before it has given this 'preparatory' effect. Now another new version of part of the subject, the portion originally B♮–A♭–G–B♮–C, appears, rhythmically very much changed, in E♭ major. This starts off another new development and eventually there is a Brahms-like interrupted cadence back again in A♭ at 451–3—'interrupted' in that the A♭ which arrives is a single bass note, starting off still more development of the beginning of the subject, only 'straight' this time. From 477 onwards an actual dominant pedal on the dominant of A♭ makes an even more determined effort to set up this key. Suddenly A♭ arrives (by a typical late Beethoven 6/4 to 5/3 progression of the tonic chord) and, of all things, the slow section reappears, firmly in A♭—just as much an 'interruption' as the earlier single note! At last at 510 a conventional cadenza formula appears (different from the Brahms-like cadence). (The trill which follows is normally on ii with a V chord, but by another typical late Beethovenism it is given on the bass note v.) The close in A♭ never arrives. A series of deeply mysterious chords, and we are back at the 'finale' in B♭.

Judged purely as an interruption the passage from 272 to the present juncture seems almost incredible. Any composer could of course have devised 250 or so bars, with plenty of variety, in a key other than the tonic. In almost any other composer this would have simply shifted the key to A♭ and the succeeding tonic B♭ would have sounded weak and unsatisfactory. Here the key of A♭ is pushed to the very brink of overbalancing the key-scheme of the whole work—but by a miracle it never does. The main reason is almost certainly the insertion of the aforementioned preparatory passage for B♭ at 379–405. Yet this, which is really an interruption of an interruption, is itself interrupted by E♭ minor–major, so that in fact a series of interruptions within interruptions has occurred. No one but Beethoven could have introduced so many such interruptions without becoming boring or even (as indeed some cases in lesser Beethoven come near to being) unintentionally funny.

533 must surely be the beginning of the 'final finale'? Broadly speaking it is—but there is still quite a lot to happen. The original interruption of 269 is now replaced by a much more 'final'-sounding passage beginning at 565 and going on for some bars. The 'real' finale must obviously be of greater weight than the previous 'false' one. Suddenly at 609 the plan subject is heard very high with dissonant harmonies (notice particularly how the two B♮s are treated, making what in a student's exercise would be marked 'poor' harmony). A strange interrupted cadence makes as if to visit A minor (a key completely absent from any previous interruptions). This is brushed aside and the first conclusive (literally) sign of the end appears in the cadential chords of 629–36 leading to a further build-up in the 6/8 rhythm which eventually quietens down to end on a pause on a 7/4 chord. Without resolving this on to the expected 6/4 which might have introduced a cadenza, Beethoven now employs a device unique in fugue but familiar to us all from the opening of the last movement of the Ninth Symphony: he recalls the openings, first of the fugue proper (30–2) and then of the slow section with semiquavers (22–5). This stroke of genius has the effect of binding the whole together in a way—dare one say?—utterly superior to that of the Ninth itself. There is here no incursion of operatic recitative without words, the proper understanding of which depends on previous musical knowledge. The two openings are simply stated in turn, and since both are obviously incomplete their 'rejection' for the final conclusion of the piece is obvious to the listener in a purely musical manner. They are swept aside for the straight subject in full unison, now freed from Albrechtsberger's *Unterbrechun* (resource 6(g)) and all the other devices with which it has been treated. Yet even now Beethoven cannot resist one further interruption—on, of all chords, IV (688–9), the oldest of all the chords used for this purpose, one which features in interrupted cadences in Palestrina and is traditionally forbidden in harmony exercises. After this the way to the final bar is set by the return of the original countersubject at 716.

What strikes one about this enormous fugue is not its departure from fugal traditions but its dependence upon them. Despite the period when it was written there is no trace whatever of the 'ternary key' idea, the organised development episode, or the stretti which were rapidly becoming fixed features of academic design. Whether he knew it or not Beethoven is here in the direct descent from Sweelinck—indeed if fugal history were to be neat and tidy it should begin with Sweelinck and end with the *Grosse Fuge* in which the older composer's methods are expanded to the very limits, miraculously without breaking the bounds of logical unity.

As a representative of romantic-period fugue there can surely be no better example than Mendelssohn's fugue in E minor from Six Preludes and Fugues, op. 35. This piece sums up the whole attitude to fugue as seen through the eyes of a later preiod whose natural method of composition was increasingly removed from the 'classical' fugal style. Significantly the subject itself is a Baroque-like theme—the almost complete absence of romantic style fugue-subjects was mentioned earlier—and indeed the first 30 bars or so could easily be mistaken by the non-expert for a Baroque fugue. At bar 29 the direction 'un poco accelerando e sempre crescendo' appears, and from here on the fugue gets faster and more exciting until eventually all counterpoint ceases and a kind of cadenza in octaves leads to a triumphant chorale in the tonic major. After this there is a romantic 'sunset-glow' conclusion in which the fugue-subject is heard now at peace in the major key. In retrospect the minor fugue is seen as an at first severe, and subsequently increasingly stormy, minor preparation for the major chorale, which triumphs over the severity and stormy nature of the fugue: 'preparatory chromaticism', it could be said, carried to its logical conclusion.

It is interesting that even here many of the resources which produce the fugal form are still those which we have observed in earlier writers. Space does not permit a full analysis, but the main features may be mentioned:

bars 23–24 Modulation to G major (relative) independent of any entries (resource 8) followed by relaxation.

bar 29 *Accelerando* begins.

bar 34 Faster movement (semiquavers), independently of the *accelerando*, especially in the bass (resource 12).

bar 39 Return to original movement. Interrupted cadence in the dominant (B minor) at 40–1 leading to first appearance of inverted subject (41 alto).

bar 58 Return of semiquaver movement after a half-cadence on the dominant.

bar 73 Return of direct subject in the tonic.

bar 77 From here on, gradual disintegration of counterpoint into decorative accompaniment.

bar 83 Dominant pedal (resource 11) prepared by chromatic descent in the bass (resources 17 and 18).

bar 91 Final entry with chords and rests (resources 13 and 16) leading to cadenza, chorale and conclusion as already mentioned. (The concluding tonic major entry, ten bars from the end, derives from the relative major entry of 17–19, soprano, thus introducing an element of binary form into the whole design.)

Perhaps no composer since Bach has captured the late Baroque method of prolonging a fugue as Mendelssohn has here (Beethoven's methods in the *Grosse Fuge* were more dramatic, and depended more upon sudden interrupted cadences and differing treatments of the subject). In the present fugue the anticipation of the end is very strong right from the half-cadence at 58. Certainly any of the tonic entries at 73, 77, 86 could have been the final one, and the way Mendelssohn prolongs the excitement without over-use of any device is a mark of a truly great composer. Particularly noteworthy is the fact that after the 'piano' marking at 55 there is no relaxation at all—Mendelssohn is thus depriving himself of one of the most useful ways of delaying the final climax, that of a 'false' relaxation which proves only to be the preparation for a further build-up.

Both fugue and chorale are of course Baroque types, and even here the fugue and the chorale, each considered in isolation, are not impossibly far from the Baroque in style. But the idea of the major chorale triumphing over the severe and stormy minor fugue is in spirit as far removed from the Baroque use of these genres as it is possible to be. Bach's Mass in B minor, it is true, depicts triumph over terror in the setting of 'Et expecto resurrectionem mortuorum', but he does not employ fugue or chorale here—and even this, it must be recalled, is not only a most exceptional procedure for the period but is also very late on in the Baroque (this part of the Mass is now dated a little before 1750). What Mendelssohn has done here is not only to produce a highly original use of fugue: he has also epitomised once and for all the way in which not only the romantic period but many of us even today regard fugue—as a severely academic, serious, yet exciting type of music, expressive somehow of conflict and difficulty which need ultimately to be resolved.

The 'exciting' view of fugue predominates throughout the romantic period, and it is only with the moderns that the more formal Baroque type of treatment returns. Two excellent late romantic 'exciting' fugues form the last movements of sets of variations—Brahms' Variations and Fugue on a Theme of Handel, op. 24, and Reger's Variations and Fugue on a Theme of Bach, op. 81. In the former work the fine example of dominant pedal has already been mentioned (resource 11, above). Another notable feature, typical of the composer, is the preoccupation with flat keys, notably the tonic minor and its relations, which appear as early as bar 25. The way back from the romantic-sounding inverted entry in D♭ (relative of tonic minor) is by enharmonic circle (37 is C♭, 38 F♭, 39–40 B♭♭ minor, the tonic being recognised by pitch at 41). As if this were not enough Brahms promptly starts a further enharmonic circle, this time much shorter (42–3 C♭ minor, 44 A♭♭–D♭♭ major, 45 F major recognised by pitch). From here on gloomy augmented entries and developments of them keep the music round about the tonic minor until after a long passage of waiting (66 onwards) the major returns at 75, the entry employing direct and (free) inversion together in thirds and sixths (resources 6(c) and 14). 76 onwards begins the pedal already discussed.

Reger's is a true double fugue on a chromatic main subject (Example 20(b) above) which is rather freely treated as to interval even in the first answer. Inversion is used in the entry of bars 30–34 soprano but is not to be a main feature of the fugue. The romantic, sonata-form influenced attitude to the 'middle' entries is interesting. There is a very definite cadence in D major, the relative, marked 'poco a poco rit', and the entry in D is directed 'espress e ben marcato (una corda)' *ppp*. This entry transposes the latter part of the theme up a tone from 44 on; its answer at 51 last beat soprano is more strict (note the openings B♭–A and E♭–D respectively, preserving the characteristic semitone by chromaticism—see resource 17). After a further 'middle' entry at 56 bass the tonic reappears in the entry of 61 soprano. Once again we find the listener being deceived into predicting the final climax before time: the faster movement (resource 12) at 69 onwards, the low bass entry in octaves at 73 and the dominant pedal at 77–8 all suggest the end of the fugue, but they are in fact only the end of the first (thematic) section. The second subject follows the tonic cadence of 79, in the soprano, and its exposition occupies the next ten bars. This theme is itself in faster movement, and Reger allows it to build up its own separate climax, with intense counterpoint (resource 14) at 93–4 and a very prominent bass entry at 99. The expected combination arrives at 105 last beat and is answered at 110, last beat. From here to the end the writing is a pianistic *tour de force* carrying resource 14 to its ultimate extreme. A stretto is introduced, almost as if the composer had remembered suddenly that every fugue must have a stretto, at 116 and again, with a clever use of false entry, at 121: the impression given here is of a three-part stretto with the second subject accompanying the first entry, but in fact neither second subject nor the second entry of the stretto (upper part of left hand, 122) are complete. Beneath the complexities of the last five bars are hidden the conventional dominant and tonic pedals, the former prepared by diminished seventh chords and a 'neapolitan sixth' (C major) in bar 125 (resource 17). The fugue is interesting as showing a mixture of the conventional 'examination' key scheme with thematic combination—the ternary key form applies to the first part of the fugue (thematically speaking) only, after which the interest centres largely in the thematic combination and in the stretto of the main subject.

Several modern fugues have already been discussed under the resource which largely governed their forms. Hindemith's LT 3 in F was seen to be a strict design, bars 30–end being an exact reversal of bars 1–30 (resource 6(d), above). The D♭ fugue LT 10 is similarly strict, bars 18–end in this case being an inversion of 1–18, except that Hindemith inserts an additional direct entry by way of conclusion (last three bars). In this case, unlike LT 3, the scheme is perceptible to the listener. A binary scheme, not strict, was also observed in LT 12 in F♯, bars 14 last note–18 in the dominant reappearing in the tonic to conclude the fugue. LT 1 in C is a fairly simple double fugue, the second subject appearing as early as bar 11 and the combination at 35. The Hindemith fugues are on the whole simple designs with use of entry key variety and some use of inversion and stretto, but with no very complex or subtle forms. It must be remembered that unlike WTC, LT was intended for consecutive performance of the whole work, and each fugue thus belongs to its context, the form of the whole work being the dominating factor. As an individual form the fugue in A no. 4 is probably the most interesting, since it makes a partial return to the early Baroque idea of a sectional fugue. The three sections here are, however, not based on variants of one subject but are the three thematic sections of a double fugue. The idea of variants of one theme does affect the design in that the second subject, which appears in the 'slow, grazioso' section, is rhythmically changed when it combines with the first subject at the 'tempo primo'. The ambiguity of the opening tonality has already been mentioned: probably with this in mind Hindemith gives a prominent intermittent A pedal lasting from bar 8 (last beat) to 12, and leading to an inverted A entry, very low (resource 1). The first fugue is very much concerned with subject entries, but there is a short episode treating the second phrase of the subject in sequence at 15–17. This fugue has its own climax—direct and inverted subject together (resource 6(c)) at 24–5—and then ends on the dominant, thus also introducing a binary element into the overall form. The second subject, as it first appears, is utterly different in rhythm and speed from the first. Its exposition is given in a melodic tonality of C♯ minor, and the short episodes of 35–6 and 41–4, emphasise the disjointed rhythms, and also the less intense nature, of this section. The combination appears immediately on resumption of the 'tempo primo' at 45: the first subject follows the original exposition, the entries being C–A, E–C♯, C–A; the second subject's tonality is that a tone below the opening tonality of the first, viz. B♭ minor, D minor for the first two entries, but at the third entry the second subject takes the 'inversion at the twelfth' position (resource 5) and thus appears in F minor instead of B♭ minor (its first note is altered from C to G). This section is, appropriately, far more intense than the first one, entries following almost consecutively (resource 3) until at 60 they begin to overlap in stretto: G–B♭ inversion 60–1, bass; D♭–B♭ direct 61–2, soprano; and A♭–C♭ inversion 62–3 middle part. (The entries are described in two tonalities in view of the nature of the subject.) A conspicuous bar of octaves (resources 18 and 13) introduces again the direct and inverted first subject together at 69 (B♭–D, B♭–G) and, to avoid repeating the climax of the first part too exactly, this device is immediately repeated with very high and very low entries (resource 1) at 71–2 (G–B♭, C–A♭ chromatically altered from A, resource 6(b)). The last four bars make quite sure of A as a tonality, although they contain no strict entry. The fugue ends with resource 21—the first four notes of the inverted subject, at first in octaves (resource 13) but ending on a firm triad of A major.

It has been said that tradition is not something on which an artist falls back as an easy way out of his problems, but rather something which he strives to acquire. If this is true Hindemith can certainly be said to have 'acquired tradition' rather than just accepting it: he is a composerof his day and in his own modern idiom he has brought alive the tradition of the Baroque fugue. The difference in the degree of complexity of design between the A fugue just discussed and the simple ternary form by key of entry (supplemented by the use of inversion) of the following fugue, no. 5 in E, shows Hindemith to be fully alive to the enormously varied possibilities of fugal form.

With Shostakovitch, on the other hand, the feeling cannot be resisted that he has accepted tradition rather than acquiring it. Most people would seize upon his diatonic subjects as a reason for justifying this remark, but in fact these are the most original and most widely varied feature of the collection of fugues, and such variety as there is between fugues is largely due to the different characteristics of the various subjects. Formally the designs are almost entirely similar, being key ternaries or rondos (see above, resource 7) with episodes based upon the answer-codetta, with some use of inversion or stretto, and occasionally augmentation (no. 15 in D♭ major) and diminution (no. 13 in F♯ major). Another feature shared again by almost all the fugues was seen to be the use of a relative (major or minor) entry and its answer as the first two 'middle' entries of the key-scheme. The impression of all this is of a composer who knows Bach's fugues well but is not himself a natural fugue writer. One feels that very original material has been poured into a set mould. Originality of *design* appears only occasionally: two cases are certainly the first fugue in C major, in which Shostakovitch takes a typically romantic view of the key as a 'plain' one devoid of colour and keeps its pure scale throughout, entries occurring, as has been seen (resource 6(b), above), in every one of the seven possible positions but without the use of any foreign note. The D♭ fugue no. 15 is also original—again, not for the obvious reason: the chromatic subject itself is nothing special in relation to modern fugue generally, but there is a kind of conflict between chromaticism and diatonicism which gives the fugue a character of its own. This is reflected for instance in the homophonic accompanimental chords which suddenly interrupt at bars 116–17 on part of the tonic chord, and even more markedly in what is virtually a new resource—the use of prominent V–I tonic, and in one case subdominant, cadences punctuating the last part of the fugue (125–6 tonic, 133–4 tonic, 138–9 tonic, 143–4 subdominant, 161–2 tonic, 166–7 tonic, 171–2 tonic, and again at 173–4, 175–6 and finally twice in 179–81). As has been remarked, the subject is not atonal, since it has a melodic tonality, and it is thus not reasonable to interpret the fugue as a conflict between tonality and atonality in which 'tonality wins the day', as is suggested in Irwin Freundlich's introduction.[63] None the less the idea of a contrast between a melodic tonality of the modern type and the old-fashioned harmonic cadence is a very original and effective one. Another of the fugues which departs from Shostakovitch's normal plan is the E minor no. 4, which is a true double fugue (resource 5(c), above). There is however none of the subtlety of Bach's thematic combinations: the phrasing of the second subject is the same as that of the first and the combination is thus in a sense 'given away' in advance.

If one had to choose the 'greatest modern (complete) fugue' it would probably be the opening movement of Bartók's *Music for Strings, Percussion and Celeste* on which one's choice would ultimately fall. This has already been described above under resource 7, since it is basically a design based on the key of the entries. One might add to what was said above the notable use of timbre (resource 10), especially the use of percussion to mark the lead-up to the E♭ climax of bar 56 and the wonderfully mysterious celeste part which accompanies the direct/inverted subject combination at 78–81: and also the coda (82–end), which, after fragments of both direct and inverted subjects have been heard, sums up the whole design by stating the subject's second phrase in direct and inverted forms together (resources 6(c) and 21), each moving from A to E♭ and back, E♭ being the ultimate point to which the opening entries led in their journey further and further from

63. Introduction to the 24; edition of Leeds Music Corporation, New York.

A. Here then is another case of a composer 'acquiring tradition'—in this case the ternary key idea—and employing it with complete originality and effectiveness. It is rather comforting at last to find a fugue in which the ternary key form, which has been responsible for so much misleading analysis and so much bad fugal teaching, really does justice to what happens; and yet how ironical that this should be a modern fugue, and how different Bartók's treatment of the form is from anything ever written in the examination-room!

It is hoped that no one will take this chapter to be an 'account of fugal forms from Sweelinck to the present day'. All that has been attempted here is to show in a kind of 'sample survey' of fugue the kind of way in which a more faithful analysis of form than the conventional ones might be achieved. If nothing else, it may at least have suggested that in many fugues there are formal principles at work, and that fugue is very, very much more than just a texture.

A final point worth making is that generally speaking fugal forms are not 'sensitive' in the sense that the slightest alteration in, say, the opening section would entail far-reaching changes of design in the whole. Such sensitivity is a feature of the classic sonata style, but it has only very limited application to fugue. It would be unthinkable to add or subtract a single bar to the first movement of Beethoven's *Eroica*; but Bach added twenty-seven bars to his Fughetta in F major BWV 901 to make the fugue WTC II.17, with negligible alteration to the original. However, the study of Bach's adaptations of earlier works, even in fugue alone, is a matter for a complete book—and it would be much larger than the present one. The most apt conclusion for this chapter is to remind ourselves that ultimately the best fugues are those which are the greatest music; and greatness can never be revealed (or disproved) by analysis.

5

'EXAMINATION' FUGUE VERSUS 'LIVE' FUGUE

'There is probably no branch of musical composition in which theory is more widely, one might almost say hopelessly, at variance with practice than in that which forms the subject of the present volume.'

These are the first words of Prout's *Fugue*, from which we quoted, at the end of Chapter 1, a rather similar passage. Certainly the history of writings about fugue seems continually to show on the one hand theorists like Kitson accusing Bach of 'confusing the issue' and on the other hand emotional attacks on the pedants undertaken by would-be protagonists of live fugue. Live fugue, in such attacks, is almost always linked with the name of Bach. ('Bach's fugues are the finest in existence... whatever Bach does systematically, and not merely exceptionally, is the correct thing for the student to do' affirms Prout later in the same Preface.[64]) Bach is regarded, by the defenders of live practice, as a kind of fugal Beethoven who freed the form from the shackles with which the theorists had bound it. Not only Prout, but more recently George Oldroyd, in a book called *The Technique and Spirit of Fugue*, spends a whole chapter[65] comparing (or purporting to compare) Fux and Bach's attitude to fugue. This writer also devotes a huge music example (five whole pages of music type)[66] to a complete model fugue by the early nineteenth-century theorist Cherubini, simply to show what a poor affair it is by comparison with Bach.

The moral of all this, as it is usually drawn today, is simple: the Kitsons are wrong and we should teach all music by reference to the great composers—fugue according to Bach, the more sectional forms according to Haydn, Mozart and Beethoven, and so forth. In this way

64. *Fugue*, p. iv.
65. pp. 9–12.
66. ibid., pp. 33–7.

the student will learn not a concocted academic style but a live idiom in which great music has been written. This sounds fine, until we imagine a few specific cases. A student, for instance, is given the first four bars of Beethoven's Pastoral Symphony (melody only): he is asked to harmonise it and continue, to make 24 bars in all. This particular student put a single tied note under the first three bars and his sixteenth to twenty-fourth bars are all as near as no matter identical. Would he pass? The student was, of course, Beethoven. In relation to the 512 bars of Beethoven's first movement the procedures he used in the first 24 are absolutely right. But what of the examination student, whose three-hour paper has to include two other kinds of question? He has no time to indicate how his 512 bars would go; it will be said, indeed, that no student could conceive such a stretch anyway until he was well past the examination stage. But many students might well, if they were to produce a result like Beethoven's, have had at least some vague idea in their minds about how this would sound at the beginning of a long movement, and even possibly a rudimentary thought about some later use of the material. The examiner, however, sees only the 24 bars; he will mark the first three bars 'harmonically unadventurous' and bars 16–24 'tautologous', if not something even ruder. It seems, then, that the student must write 24 bars complete—to make sense as it stands. He may do this, but he will not then be writing in the style of Beethoven: there are no Beethoven pieces 24 bars long—not at any rate in the style indicated by the given four bars.

Here is—put admittedly in rather extreme form—the difficulty with teaching in live styles. Apart from the simplest miniatures (German dances and the like) live styles deal mainly in long movements or successions of movements, and students have insufficient time, and in the early stages at any rate probably insufficient ability, to produce long pieces. The Bach chorale is one of the few examples of live music which is short enough for the student to produce a complete example in examination time, and for this reason it is one of the best types of examination question. Even so, it is not quite perfect: for instance the first chord of Bach's four-part harmonisation of 'Aus tiefer Noth' is a 'dominant seventh' third inversion (E major with D in the bass). The student might reasonably deduce that 'a chorale may begin on a discord': but in fact in Cantata 38, of which this chorale is the conclusion, the D is prepared by the final chord of the preceding movement, which ends in D minor, the 'dominant seventh' thus effecting a close connection between the two movements. Even the chorale, therefore, is not quite immune from considerations involving a longer time-scale.

Fugue is in this respect midway between the chorale and the long symphonic movement. A reasonable complete fugue can be written by a good student in three hours. Moreover, as was seen in the last chapter, fugal forms are not sensitive in the sense that what is done in bar 3 has a direct effect on what is done in bar 100. But for a student to write in the style of Bach is not a simple matter, simply because, as has been seen, the possibilities are so vast—and yet, of course, there are also many possibilities that are excluded (Shostakovitch-type entries in very remote keys for instance). Students are on the whole happiest with strict rather than free forms; when there is no 'given part' or specifically prescribed procedure they tend to become lost. It is for this reason that even teachers such as Oldroyd, who purport to be violently anti-examination-fugue and pro-Bach, have had, when it comes down to it, to set to and prescribe a form for the student which amounts, in Oldroyd's case, to nothing other than that old friend, the ternary scheme by key of entries and stretto.[67]

Here, then, is one reason for the existence of the 'examination fugue' and similar academic exercises which depart from the practice of live music. In the case of fugue there is also another, namely the unfamiliarity of the live fugal idiom to the average student who is 'doing' fugue. Today there is of course much greater familiarity with Baroque music and, as we have seen, modern composers have returned to something much more like the Baroque attitude to fugue as a normal type of composition rather than a highly academic *tour de force*. When writers such as Kitson were producing their textbooks, however, the sonata-form harmony-orientated attitude still dominated, if not the music actually being written, at least the music with which the average student would be likely to be familiar. There was the need, therefore, not only to make fugue feasible in examinations but to make it more understandable to the average student in an age to which the 'classical' fugal style had become basically foreign. This, at heart, is the reason for the 'ternary form' idea and many others such as the 'implied harmony of the subject' and so forth—all points which will be briefly examined below.

A further stage in the relationship between academic and live practice is reached when rules originally designed for the student become mistaken for fundamental rules of music to which the great masters 'yielded their loving obedience', to quote a famous remark of the theorist Rockstro.[68] It is easy to see how this can come about. The rule against consecutive fifths and octaves, for instance, is obeyed, in

67. op cit., ch. I 'The Lay-out of a Fugue, absorbing the chief devices used by Bach'.

68. Quoted by Morris, *Contrapuntal Technique in the Sixteenth Century*, p. 1.

contrapuntal music at any rate, over a wide and very well-known period of musical history. In the case of a simple rule of this type academic practice represents (albeit in exaggerated form) not a fundamental law, but at least a principle obeyed by many composers. To ask a student to obey this rule is very different from saying to him 'in fugue you can do anything Bach does'. But it is only a stage from obeying the 'fifths and octaves' rule to obeying the 'ternary form rule' of fugal construction. The student may not, and the pupil still at school almost certainly will not, know that of the two rules one is a faithful reflection of at least a substantial corpus of live musical practice whereas the other is reflected in a mere handful of works.

Yet a further stage in all this is reached when Bach (whose name in this discussion continues to stand for 'live fugal practice') gets criticised by theorists for not obeying the rules. This is at the root of Kitson's famous 'confusing the issue' remark (whose precise implications are discussed below under 'Answer'). As Chapter 1 suggested, however, far more can be learnt about Bach's answer-procedure from this remark of Kitson's than from the confused arguings of the violently pro-Bach Oldroyd.[69] Kitson at least is consistent, and by his criticism of Bach we can learn exactly where a typical late nineteenth-century point of view diverges from that of the Baroque. A more unfortunate attitude to the 'rules versus Bach' is that still taken by many teachers today, who say to their pupils 'Ah yes—Bach can do that, but you're not Bach'. This gives the young pupil little encouragement to study the works of great masters and to model his own upon them. Most pupils are all too well aware that they are 'not Bach' but they probably cannot see why they should not try to be. Akin to this point of view is the already mentioned idea of Bach as a great revolutionary, throwing the old scholastic rules to the winds. This has already been seen to be false in a number of contexts above, for example the question of strict order of exposition entries. Yet again, there is the idea of the 'examination fugue' as a kind of 'norm' from which real fugues depart in various ways but to which they are all sufficiently allied for the 'norm' to be a useful thing for the student to learn. It might be true, and perhaps is partially true of sonata form (though the wrong 'norm' is there taught); but it is certainly untrue of almost everything taught in academic fugue. Finally, perhaps the most depressing of all the rationalisations of academic practice—though fortunately perhaps it is less common today—is that of absolute discipline. The student must submit himself to the academic rules simply because it is good for him —it is a training which will stand him in good stead in his later musical life. Here the confusion has arisen between discipline and training in,

69. op. cit., ch. V.

say, athletics and that in an art such as music. Physical fitness may be induced by exercises and disciplines which have no point apart from this aim, but there seems to be no evidence whatever that the D.Mus. students of Oxford who in 1904 had to write eight parts note-against-note strict counterpoint[70] were either better composers or interpreters for this 'discipline', or that they and their equivalents had any better understanding of music because of it. Like the other ideas just discussed, this one also arises from a failure to see why 'examination' procedures and the like came into existence in the first place. Unfortunately it is the writer's experience that in greater or less degree all the fallacies mentioned here are still in evidence in the world of music-teaching today.

In general it is the nineteenth-century writers who are responsible for the 'examination' attitude to fugue as we have known it for many years and as, alas, it still appears to predominate in many academic circles even today. Before looking at the main divergencies between this attitude and live practice, and attempting to see how they came about, it will be helpful to discuss briefly the work of Johann Joseph Fux, the earliest of the famous fugal theorists, and a figure still derided, by those who have not read him, as a kind of archetype of all that is dull and bad in fugal teaching—the original dry-as-dust theorist, in fact. At his door are laid almost all the lifeless old rules against which the great composers have since been busy rebelling. Fortunately, Fux's fugal theory is now more readily accessible in Alfred Mann's *The Study of the Fugue*, where it can be read in English instead of the original Latin. Page references in the following few excerpts are to Dr Mann's book. It should be mentioned that Fux's treatise takes the classical form of a dialogue between his teacher Aloysius—i.e. Palestrina—and himself, Josephus, as the pupil.

First of all Fux makes it abundantly clear that the elementary fugal study is only a gateway to more advanced, freer methods of composition:

p. 89: '. . . you will perhaps hear some people ridicule and criticise these subjects [those of the elementary fugue] as being too simple and unimaginative. . . . But we are concerned here not with the finesse of invention, but rather with the true nature of the modes of the diatonic system—a system that has narrow limits indeed. Greater opportunity to let our thoughts run free and capture more interesting themes will arise when we admit the use of the mixed system [i.e. free use of accidentals in the themes themselves].'

Even at this early stage one may perhaps wonder if these can really

70. Kitson, *The Art of Counterpoint*, p. 211.

be the words of the dry old pedant of fugal teaching. Let us see what else can be learnt from the treatise:

p. 80: 'A fugue arises when a succession of notes in one part is taken over in another part, with due regard for the mode, and especially for the position of whole and half-tone steps.'

This is of course none other than Rule 1 of answer-procedure as already discussed above in Chapter 2. Here, in Fux of all people, is the solution to all the problem answers such as WTC I.18 and I.23 which have been baffling theorists since, and producing such absurd explanations as 'implied modulations to the dominant' and so forth (see below).

p. 83: It is interesting that although Fux does demand a stretto near the end of the fugue (not, however, cumulative stretti) he does also demand two intermediate cadences on V and III, not connected with entries of the theme, thus foreshadowing the idea of important independent modulations occurring at certain points in the fugue (Chapter 4 above, resource 8).

p. 84: '*Josephus:* I see in this fugue sharps and flats are used, notwithstanding the rule that they should not be employed in the diatonic system.

Aloysius: Those rules are to be understood for the themes, where only natural half-tone steps are to be used, without sharps or flats, so that the nature and characteristics of the modes may be realized. It is different in the free continuation of the composition where the use of sharps and flats is not only allowed but even needed. . . .'

Here we have in strict form the rule obeyed to a large extent by nearly all writers of fugues before about 1700 (see Chapter 4). The distinction between the melodic tonality and diatonic nature of the theme and the passing digressions and chromaticisms of the other parts is made quite clear. This is, of course, the complete antithesis of the ternary form by key of entries.

pp. 88–9: The fugue in the mode of A shows the only case of tonal (i.e. altered) answer in these simple fugues. It is interesting that Fux regards the alteration in terms of Rule 1 ('The effect of *fa* on the second note could not have been expressed otherwise'. *Fa–mi* is always a semitone) not, as a later theorist would regard it, as a tonal alteration to give tonic in answer to dominant.

The passage also refers to the practice of using the unaltered ('real') answer later in the fugue (cf. Chapter 2, p. 87, above). '[This] device will not detract from the quality of the composition. On the contrary, it contributes to it if it occurs in the middle of the fugue, because the formation of the subject becomes more nearly consistent through such an adjustment. It is different in the beginning of a fugue, where the character of the mode and the requirement of choosing the proper tone for the entrance of the subject . . . must be observed strictly.'

p. 91: '*Josephus:* Which of the two preceding parts should the third part [in a three-part fugal exposition] follow [=correspond to], in so far as the interval on which the entrance occurs is concerned?

Aloysius: As a rule, it should follow the one in which the subject first appeared. This will ensure greater variety. . . . Yet, if the arrangement of the parts seems to suggest another interval, you may follow your own judgment and make the necessary adjustment to the rule.'

So much for Bach in WTC I.1 (see Chapter 2) defying the rules! And the student, it will be noted, is actually allowed to use his own judgement!

pp. 92–3: Here Fux encourages the use of various cadences against subject entries. In Example 57 a firm cadence in C occurs as the subject enters on D. This is the clash of melodic and harmonic tonalities mentioned in Chapter 4 (resource 8).

pp. 95–6: The same point again: in bar 12 of the fugue in D the subject enters on D against an A cadence in the bass. 'This entrance occurs on a strong dissonance, which helps to point out the presence of the theme.' (The G♯ here has, in our conventional theory, to be accounted chromatic—a 'supertonic chromatic seventh with omitted root', no less—since it does not lead to a chord of A.)

p. 101: In bar 21 of the three-part fugue in A the theme (answer form) fills in the leap of a third with the note B (see Chapter 4, resource 6(h). This does not appear to be mentioned by the teacher.

p. 105: 'Do not be surprised that [in four-part fugue] the four parts rarely appear together. . . . We should not force a part where there is insufficient space [and] it is not required in four-part writing that there always be complete four-part chords. It is perfectly adequate if just three parts move while the fourth rests in order to resume the subject later.'

The tendency towards three-part writing in large numbers of fugues, especially those for keyboard, has already been noted in Chapters 2 and 3. It is a common fault of students to (a) try to write too much of the fugue in four parts and (b) to fail to allow proper spacing of the parts so that notes which on paper are supposed to be in two separate parts sound either like one part or are just a muddle. But how many textbooks point this out?

These passages have been quoted because in each one of them Fux mentions features and procedures which occur regularly in live fugue and *not one of which finds any place in the conventional fugue textbooks*. The aim is less to defend Fux as to show that fugal teaching once had very considerable connection with what went on in real life—and this moreover despite the author's confessed aim of teaching the beginner in a very restricted system. Clearly the rot set in after Fux, and exactly how this came about is a matter for a full history of fugal theory. (Cherubini is probably the chief culprit, certainly as regards fugal form.) The remainder of this chapter is concerned with the conventional examination fugue in more recent times: its chief misunderstandings of fugal practice are here briefly listed and discussed:

The Subject

The common case of the unaccompanied initial entry was never understood by these theorists. Their concept of music was entirely harmonic: in the absence of any harmony (except in subjects with arpeggiated harmonies) they spoke of 'implied' harmony—the set of harmonies they would expect to accompany the subject. The whole rationale of the subject's behaviour and particularly the evolving of a correct answer would depend on these 'implied harmonies'. Even Prout could not shake himself free of this doctrine—and indeed there is still one examining board which at any rate until very recently was still criticising students for 'failing to discern the harmonic background of the subject'. The whole idea of anything 'implied' in music is of course complete nonsense. The ear hears what it hears, and if no harmony is present, no harmony is present, and that is that. It is significant that in the 'classical' period of fugue, as we have seen, composers designed their subjects so that the initial entry made perfect sense on its own, both tonally and melodically. 'Implied harmony', like 'implied 6/4 chords' and even 'implied consecutive fifths and octaves' with which examiners used to (do they still?) taunt their poor students, should be seen to be the nonsense that it is. It is of course true that on seeing or hearing a fugue subject a listener (a) knowing who the composer is and (b) having a good knowledge of his style may be able to *predict* harmonies which will later accompany it: but prediction is no part of the true naïve listener's reaction to music. And how often is even this prediction right? To mention one case alone, there is an 'implied modulation to B♭' in the subject of Bach's 'great' G minor organ fugue BWV 542. How often in the fugue does Bach so harmonise it?

One example of an academic subject with a misleading melodic tonality has already been quoted (Example 19 above). There are, alas, plenty more.[71]

71. eg.:—Oldroyd, op. cit., p. 215 (intended key G, actual key C with final dominant cadence: this in a book which purports to be based on Bach!); Gédalge, *Traité de la Fugue*, part I, pp. 357–371, no. 40 (tonality ambiguous—A♭ or F minor?); ibid., no. 128 (intended tonality almost certainly F, as there is a C♮ but no C♯: actual tonality D minor ending on vii♮); ibid., no. 209 (intended tonality obviously C with cadence in G, actual tonality G—there is no C in the whole theme!).

The Answer

It would take several large books to deal in full with the misunderstandings here. The 'answer' was always the catch question (if one can so put it) of the 'examination' fugue, and many a student must have spent a worried half-hour out of the three hours puzzling out the 'correct' solution:

(a) for reasons mentioned in Chapter 2 the answer was thought of as normally 'in the dominant key'. But if the subject modulated from tonic to dominant the answer began in the dominant and modulated back to the tonic. In real life the purpose of the answer has been seen to be to confirm the tonic key and scale already established by the subject, while still preserving the theme's tone-semitone relationship. The idea of a contrast of two harmonic tonalities (the harmonies 'implied', of course) rather than one melodic tonality comes of course from the 'sonata form' outlook upon fugue.

(b) the dominant key/tonic key alternation was supposed to concern all the parts (usually two) involved in the answer, the essentially harmonic outlook seizing thankfully upon anything remotely resembling real chords. We have seen that in fact the answer rules apply literally to the answer, not to any part or parts accompanying it.

(c) although the opening of the answer was invariably 'in the dominant key', for some reason which was never made clear, but was evidently accepted by generation after generation of docile students, the dominant note when it appears near the opening of the subject must in many cases be answered by a tonic note, with consequent alteration to the theme where necessary. (This is, of course, Rule 2 as explained in Chapter 2, but it makes sense only when the answer is regarded as *tonic* in tonality!) The decision as to whether this should be done or not depended, needless to say, upon the 'implied' harmonies. If the dominant in the subject was long and prominent enough to 'imply dominant harmony' then it must be answered by tonic ('implying' tonic harmony): but if it was only a short note—say in close association with the tonic in a fairly quick i–v progression—then the 'tonal alteration' was not appropriate, and the dominant would be answered by the dominant of the dominant. It was here that Bach 'confused the issue'. Kitson words the above principle slightly differently,[72] saying that it is all a question of the 6/4 chord (he means the 'arpeggio 6/4'): the short dominant note would make a good arpeggio 6/4 whereas the long note needs its own harmony. In WTC I.2, I.17 and II.21 Bach makes the tonal alteration although the i–v in the subject is an arpeggi-

72. *The Elements of Fugal Construction*, pp. 18–19.

ation of tonic 'harmony' in quavers. It was of II.21 that Kitson used the famous phrase. As a matter of fact Bach 'confused the issue' much more in WTC II.15, where an initial semiquaver v, part of an actual arpeggiated full tonic chord, is none the less answered by i with tonal alteration, spoiling the nice arpeggiated chord. The maintenance of a melodic tonality of the tonic is of course the true explanation of all these answers, the initial note (as in II.15) having more importance than notes near the opening.

(d) the alterations for Rule 1 in WTC I.18, I.19 and I.23 caused endless bother. I.18 was a 'modulating' subject and thus the early switch to 'subdominant' position was supposed to have something to do with the 'modulation'. With the other two we get explanations like 'So strongly is the leading note felt as the third of the dominant that it is not seldom answered by the third of the tonic, even when there is no modulation' (Prout)[73] and 'Bach took the unusual view that the notes [vii–i–ii–v in I.23] were in F♯ and thus arrived at the tonal answer' (Bairstow).[74] All these far-fetched explanations could have been thrown away if only the inventors of them had read the much-despised Fux.

(e) the real bane of fugue examinations was the 'modulating' subject (that ending on the dominant with digression). The whole difficulty lay in deciding where the modulation was supposed to occur. Prout's section on this,[75] which need not be gone into in full, is a fair example of the confusion—note especially the continual occurrence of the word 'implied'. Prout's golden rule is to 'regard the modulation as being made at the earliest possible point',[76] and this reaches the height of absurdity when in WTC I.18 the leading note of a *minor* key is taken as the beginning of a dominant modulation—this being the one note which, in the conventional 'scale' view of tonality, to which Prout of course would subscribe, is absolutely decisive for the tonic key! In live fugue the answers to these subjects—not a very common type outside the examination-room—normally obey Rule 2 at the beginning and end and make the best of it in the middle, both rules and the character of the theme all being weighed up together.

(f) finally, the 'subdominant' answer. This, originally a common type in the days of short subjects with no prominent cadence, became, as we have seen, rarer as more and more subjects ended on a tonic cadence with a strong progression leading up to it. By the time such writers as Prout and Kitson were writing, the 'subdominant' answer

73. *Fugue*, §133.
74. *Counterpoint and Harmony*, p. 318.
75. *Fugue*, §§114–32.
76. ibid., §121.

was regarded as a rarity. Prout[77] claims, probably with justification as far as post-Fuxian theory is concerned, to be the first to recognise it as a possibility. His explanations of it are, of course, based on harmony—'dominant harmony is answered by tonic harmony'. Yet in his example 76(b), the well-known D minor toccata, there are as many tonic 'harmonies' (arpeggiated) as dominant ones. He also, as would be expected, speaks of these answers as 'in the subdominant key' whereas even on a 'scale' view of tonality his Example 71(b) ends in the tonic and 76(a) never enters the subdominant. Kitson[78] regards the subdominant answer as only applicable to 'modulating' subjects with unalterable melodic lines, and even suggests a *completely* subdominant answer to Bach's WTC I.24! Prout, clearly, is nearer the mark. Had he only seen that it was the dominant *note* that tends to cause subdominant answers, he would have been nearer still. But Rule 1, the other important factor in causing many of these answers, finds, it need hardly be said, no mention at all.

The Countersubject

The examination tradition is that the fugue should normally have a regular countersubject. Presumably the idea here was to test the student's ability at writing invertible counterpoint, which, if there were no countersubject, would remain untested throughout the fugue. It has been seen that in real life the countersubject is a purely voluntary matter, and when it does occur it may be a very rudimentary kind of theme. The countersubject with a definite melodic character of its own is partly the product of vocal fugue, but the 'examination' fugue almost certainly inherited it from Bach, particularly WTC and some of the better-known organ fugues. Here yet again is the paradox that a resource used by Bach in a number of cases is first misunderstood and them made compulsory for all cases.

The misunderstandings surrounding the countersubject are two. First, of course, there is the question of harmonic background and definite key. The combination of subject and countersubject is regarded entirely harmonically. In *Studies in Fugue*[79] Kitson devotes considerable space to 'the harmonic considerations affecting the combination of Subject and Countersubject'. Considerable complications arise with regard to the various 'implied harmonies' involved and what happens to them in the inversion of the combination. All this is, of course, irrelevant, since as we have seen the relationship between the two themes, in Bach especially, is essentially contrapuntal: the harmonies

77. ibid., §§71–80.
78. *The Elements of Fugal Construction*, pp. 21–2.
79. pp. 9–14.

which arise when more parts are added are the servants and not the masters of the contrapuntal combination, 'poor' harmony being often justified by linear considerations. To do him justice Kitson's point about the treatment of the fifth from the root[80] does draw attention, in nineteenth-century harmonic terms, to the problem of conspicuous sixths between the two themes when this interval occurs to the lowest part (the B minor Mass example on p. 157 above). But what with Kitson is a difficulty is in fact simply a characteristic—there is nothing 'wrong' with it.

The second misunderstanding concerns the view of the countersubject as a theme of equal melodic character and importance to the subject, sharply contrasting with it. Many academic countersubjects—this one of Oldroyd's is a good example—seem to be composed not only with a rather slow speed in mind but also as if only a couple of occurrences of the combination were ever to occur (see Example 48).

Ex48 Oldroyd, *The Technique and Spirit of Fugue*, p. 41

The two themes here sound very attractive together—once: but given eight or nine entries—quite a likely number in a reasonable-length fugue—the last bars of the countersubject would drive the listener mad. It must always be remembered that a regular countersubject is what its name implies: it must stand up to repeated hearings without interrupting the flow of the counterpoint or—and this is equally vital—usurping the function of the subject as the one main theme of the fugue. As in other matters the faults in academic countersubjects seem to arise from a desire to make things harder for the student. They may also be unconsciously connected with the strong first subject/second subject contrast in sonata form. All that a countersubject needs, for a subject of average length, is a single melodic feature such as a long note (Chapter 2) to identify it and contrast it with the subject. The motto for the student ought to be 'Don't make it too interesting!'.

One further matter may be mentioned, of which academic fugue

80. ibid., p. 10.

makes very heavy weather—the adaptation of a countersubject to the subject form of the theme when it has first appeared against an altered ('tonal') answer form, particularly in the case of the dreaded 'modulating' subject. The difficulty here is due to the idea that at a fixed point the subject 'goes from tonic key to dominant key' and since the countersubject must always be in the same key as the answer (or subject) it too must 'modulate' with its companion theme. Even Kitson[81] admits that 'it cannot be said that there is a hard and fast rule about it', and, as has been seen, in fact an alteration is made, often inconspicuously, at the most convenient point: if it is not the same point as that where subject (answer) alters, the changed relationship between the themes does not matter provided that no fundamental rule of the relevant style is broken.

The Exposition

Here the academic rules in their natural desire to make a specific section of the 'exposition' (compare the meaning of the term in sonata form) have failed to account for the continuous, essentially non-sectional, nature of fugue and for the fact that such requirements as clear initial tonality become gradually, not suddenly, less necessary as the fugue gets under way. Most of the points here have already been mentioned, but it may be as well to sum them up under the present head:

(a) academic practice allows a 'modulatory' codetta between initial entry and first answer, and does not normally specify a position of octave for the latter. In live fugal practice the 'modulatory' codetta is rare, any codetta at all normally very short, and the two entries are usually at the closest pitch position possible;

(b) having not been strict enough, academic practice becomes too strict, and demands that the third entry be of the subject: in fact a further entry of the answer is quite permissible, as indeed also is slight variation of the theme, whether subject or answer;

(c) assuming that the fourth entry is of the answer, academic rules normally require it be identical with the first answer. But by now the tonality of the fugue is clear, and a different form, e.g. a 'real' answer with more marked dominant (or subdominant) tonality than the first answer, may well be appropriate, signifying the beginning of a move away from the tonic.

(d) academically all exposition entries are entries of a new part. Each part must enter in the exposition and must follow the strict subject–answer sequence. In real life the strict number of entries is usually three (just as three-part writing is the mainstay of fugue). After three entries

81. *The Elements of Fugal Construction*, p. 38.

either: (1) a fourth, fifth, etc. may occur without adding to the number of parts present (WTC I.19); (2) the entry of a further part may be delayed until after an episode (WTC I.12), or still later (II.2); (3) the entry of a further part may break the subject–answer sequence completely, being in a key other than tonic, dominant or subdominant (Mass in B minor, 'Et in terra pax', fifth entry).

Yet again we find academic practice based on what Bach does in well-known cases. Most of the WTC fugues are 'regular', since it was Bach who gradually became more and more rigid, in this particular procedure, than his predecessors. (There is only one really blatant case of (1), only three of (2) and none of (3).)

One further academic rule—that an exposition entry should always occur in an outermost part—is probably due to a failure to understand that on the Baroque instruments (Baroque organ, harpsichord and clavichord) an inner part can be quite clearly perceived provided that the disposition of other parts and the type of movement used is suitable. On the piano, of course, the necessary entry can be 'brought out' by the player, and in ensembles timbre and the location of the player will help to make it clear.

Episode

Much of the divergence between academic and live practice here has already been dealt with in Chapter 3. It was made clear that only one of the many possible types of 'episode' was adopted by the 'examination' fugue—the 'development' type. The 'examination' fugue took this, needless to say, from Bach, whose creation it was, but who uses it only in a limited number of fugues, nearly all of them in WTC. As always, sonata form gives us the clue to the adoption of a procedure by academic teaching: the 'development' episode is the nearest thing in fugue to the development section of a sonata movement—or, to be more precise, what Beethoven made of the development section and what is in the teaching of sonata form always assumed to be its purpose: the splitting up of the themes into fragments and the making of new sentences with these fragments. It has been seen that the treatment of themes by Bach in the relevant fugues is only superficially similar to Beethoven's development, since with Bach the thematic fragments do not obtrude themselves and are often dominated by 'free' parts.

One further matter in which almost complete misrepresentation has occurred is that of the episode as a modulatory device. From the fact that entries are conceived as being in definite keys, the 'middle' entries being in those other than tonic and dominant, it seemed to the theorists to follow that the episode must be the means of getting from one key to another. The fugue is, say, in C minor: the exposition finishes in C or G minor and it is then necessary to 'get to E♭' for the first 'middle' entry. The whole idea of tonality implicit here has anyway been seen to be inapplicable to fugue, but quite apart from this the idea that an episode is necessary in order to 'get to E♭' from C minor is patently absurd: E♭ is the third of the C minor scale and an entry could follow in this key without any break, and only the tiniest of links would be necessary to lead to an entry in any of the other directly related keys—those normally used in 'classical' and academic fugue. Moreover, as has been seen, the subject itself can, with the aid of 'tonal answer variation' (Chapter 4, resource 6(a)) produce modulation itself when this is required. What the typical 'development' episode produces is in fact not one big modulation but a series of incidental ones, or digressions as they are better called. Since WTC I.2 is often used as a kind of model in this matter it may be as well to recall what really happens in episode 1. The exposition ends in C minor at the first note of bar 9: the second half of bar 9 digresses to F minor, bar 10 similarly visits B♭ major and E♭ major. On the second quaver of bar 11 what proves to be an E♭ entry begins in the soprano—but not only has E♭ received no more stress than F minor and B♭, but against the opening of the entry the sequence in the lower parts continues its own sweet way and digresses to A♭! Obviously, although this episode is an agreeable and desirable form of contrast to the exposition, any idea that it 'effects a modulation to E♭' is nonsense—indeed as we have seen Bach uses the same material later at bars 22–4 without any possible modulatory context—this passage connects a tonic entry with (ultimately) another tonic entry! In both WTC II.13 and II.17 the first middle entry occurs immediately after a tonic entry with not the slightest break (bar 40 and bar 24 respectively); yet in both these cases substantial episodes had already occurred—in the case of II.13 two out of the four main episodes of the fugue—between entries in tonic and dominant. Of course an episode *can* be used for modulatory purposes, as in the already quoted bars 32–6 of the 'great' G minor organ fugue BWV 542: but even then it is not the sequential procedure which effects the modulation, but the inflection or otherwise of the appropriate notes which suggests (or digresses to) the new key (try playing F♯ instead of F♮ in bar 35 of the last-mentioned passage) plus the confirmatory cadence (bars 36–7); this is the one absolute essential for modulation, but significantly it is outside the sequential scheme!

The Complete Fugue

On this topic enough has been said in Chapter 4 to make clear the enormous divergence between 'examination' and live fugue. Since before Bach's day the signs of a ternary key scheme have been seen to be neither frequent nor conspicuous it must be assumed that the old story has once more repeated itself: a procedure used by Bach in a few well-known cases has, because of its superficial—in this case *very* superficial—resemblance to sonata form been adopted by academic teaching and made a general principle. It must be said here that the excuses for the theorists who were responsible are in this case really pretty feeble. Even a study of WTC alone, in complete ignorance of all other fugue whatever, would be enough to convince an intelligent first-year student that as an overall 'form' for fugue the ternary scheme was useless; and, as has also been pointed out, in many cases—again quite well-known ones in WTC—where it does appear, on paper, to apply, it produces such a badly proportioned form that someone should have begun to look again at the whole idea. One can only surmise that theorists were so preoccupied with comparatively superficial exposition matters such as the answer that they had little time for the design of the fugue as a whole. It seems particularly sad that Prout of all people should have fallen for this piece of deception without a murmur.

This chapter has of course only touched the surface of the relationship of academic to live fugue. It has attempted only to enumerate the main points in which the conventional 'examination' fugue as still taught in many places today fails to do justice to live practice. It is to be hoped that it has helped to show that the theorists who prescribed fugal procedures for students were not necessarily the dry-as-dust pedants they have for so long been considered. Many of them—even Prout—were, it is true, lacking in the intellectual stature which is necessary in any teacher of an advanced academic subject. Kitson should have seen that if Bach appeared to do the wrong thing this must reflect a change of attitude, perfectly explicable, as between the Baroque and the late nineteenth-century outlook. Prout should have seen that if the deciding factor for defining the middle section of a fugue is that the theme-entries are in keys other than tonic and dominant, then the statement 'we sometimes . . . meet with a middle entry in the tonic'[82] is logically unacceptable. Oldroyd, the would-be protagonist of Bach, should have taken more trouble to see that some of his examples did not contradict Bach's practice and should at least have pondered on the logic of recommending Bach's methods and then laying down an overall scheme for the complete design which can represent only a tiny fraction of the possibilities actually found in Bach. If there is to be a set form for examinations is there not something to be said for adopting Kitson's and telling the student that this is not related to live fugue at all?

82. *Fugue*, §302.

This last point—honesty in dealing with the student—seems to the present writer the most important thing for the teacher of fugue, or any other subject in musical theory, to cultivate. Any rule given to the student must be related to its applicability or otherwise to live music. There are no fundamental rules of music at all. All one can say is 'this is what Bach does', 'this is what Bach does rarely' (perhaps, say, only in early works), 'this is a purely academic rule, but it may be a stepping-stone to something else', and so forth. Not that the present writer recommends teaching of fugue according to a purely academic formula: his own recommendations, for what they are worth, are that for the average third-year student half of a three-hour counterpoint paper should consist of a question in which the student is asked to write a four-part fugal exposition, an episode and one further entry, the subject being given. The style should be that of a Bach fugue of what we have called the 'canzona' type—that with a fairly long rhythmically varied subject. The student should be told that this is the beginning only of a longer piece and the end of what he writes should make this clear by 'directs'. No regular countersubject should be demanded, but if the student wishes to write one he should be warned that whereas a good countersubject will make his task in the third to fifth entries easier, a bad one will spoil four out of the five entries. Any alterations in the answer beyond obvious initial ones for Rule 2 should be given. The type of episode should be left to the student's discretion, as also the key and position of the 'extra' entry. Needless to say all this would be supported by study of real Bach fugues of this type, as well as study, although not at this stage actual imitation, of the other types—ricercar, toccata, concerto fugue, etc.

For the more advanced student—in some universities a fourth-year B.Mus.—the writing of a complete fugue in Bach style is recommended. This is, of course, a complex study and should if at all possible embrace all the mature styles of the composer. For the examination there should be a choice of two or three subjects, the student recognising from each the kind of fugue appropriate to it.

Either of these levels of study can also embrace a modern-style fugue. This may be set as an alternative to the Bach, but is perhaps better as an additional question if sufficient time, for both teaching and examinations, can be found. Hindemith and Bartók are here probably better models than Shostakovitch, the use of a chromatic but (melodically) tonal subject being nearer to the spirit of modern music generally than the introduction of a diatonic subject in remote keys. As has been seen, there is much in common between Bach and modern fugue and the two studies can reasonably proceed side by side. In the modern study the student must, of course, to a large extent be left free in what he does, which means that given half a chance he will choose a Bach question.

This book ended its first chapter with a quotation from Prout's *Fugue*. It is perhaps appropriate that it should also conclude with an excerpt from that author's two final paragraphs:[83]

> Beyond these general hints, it is not possible for us to go. The farther we advance . . . the more we are compelled to leave the student to his own resources. . . . As soon as the teacher approaches the higher branches of composition, his relations to his pupil become to some extent modified. From a pedagogue, whose word is 'You must', or 'You must not', he now becomes an adviser who can only generally indicate the direction which the student's work should take, by setting before him the best models, and showing him how to imitate them. . . .
>
> One word in conclusion. Many of the rules laid down in this volume differ materially from those given in most other treatises on fugue. The reason of this is that this work . . . is founded, not upon any other theoretical works whatever, but solely upon the practice of the great masters themselves. Not one rule is given which is not enforced by the example of distinguished composers. Where theory and the practice of Bach, Handel or Mozart come into collision, theory must give way; and the student who writes fugues according to the directions given in this book may at all events comfort himself that if he is wrong, he is in exceedingly good company.

The present book has not, of course, aimed to 'give directions' as to the writing of fugues; Prout's aim here was too complex for either himself or indeed any writer unless he restricts himself to the style of one composer or at best a limited period. All that has been attempted here is to give some account of fugue as it has actually been written, and to clear up as far as possible some of the muddles which have arisen from divergence between teaching and live practice. In the present age, as has been said, we are in a much better position to appreciate fugue than were the contemporaries of Prout. Much modern music helps us, either directly or indirectly, towards a better understanding of fugue as a method of composition, and we are no longer hampered by a desire to relate everything to the outlook of sonata form. The present book may in a small way contribute to that better understanding. It must always be remembered, however, that for the enjoyment of fugue, as of any other kind of music, the best thing is to forget all words written about it and simply to listen.

83. *Fugue*, from §449–50.

BIBLIOGRAPHY

BAIRSTOW, Edward C., *The Evolution of Musical Form*, OUP, London, 1943

BUKOFZER, Manfred F., *Music in the Baroque Era*, Dent, 1948

BUYS, Hans Brandts, *Het Wohltemperirte Clavier van Johann Sebastian Bach*, van Loghum Slaterus, Arnhem, 1955

GÉDALGE, André *Traité de la Fugue*, Enoch et Cie., 1901

GRAY, Cecil, *The Forty-Eight Preludes and Fugues of J. S. Bach*, OUP, London, 1938

KELLER, Hermann, *Die Orgelwerke Bachs*, Peters, Leipzig, 1948

KELLER, Hermann, *Die Klavierwerke Bachs*, Peters, Leipzig, 1950

KIRKENDALE, Warren, *Fuge und Fugato in der Kammermusik des Rokoko und der Klassik*, Schneider, Tutzing, 1966

KITSON, C. H., *The Art of Counterpoint*, OUP, London, 1907

KITSON, C. H., *The Elements of Fugal Construction*, OUP, 1929

KITSON, C. H., *Studies in Fugue*, OUP, London, 1909

MANN, Alfred, *The Study of Fugue*, Faber and Faber, 1960

MORRIS, R. O., *Contrapuntal Technique in the Sixteenth Century*, OUP, London, 1922

MORRIS, R. O., *The Structure of Music*, OUP, London, 1935

NEUMANN, Werner, *J. S. Bachs Chorfuge*, Breitkopf und Härtel, Leipzig, 1953

OLDROYD, George, *The Technique and Spirit of Fugue*, OUP, London, 1948

PROUT, Ebenezer, *Fugue*, Augener, 1891

PROUT, Ebenezer, *Fugal Analysis*, Augener, 1892

RUBBRA, Edmund, *Counterpoint*, Hutchinson University Library, 1960

TOVEY, Donald Francis, *Essays and Lectures on Music*, OUP, London, 1949

TOVEY, Donald Francis, Notes to: 'Forty-Eight Preludes and Fugues by J. S. Bach' and 'Beethoven Pianoforte Sonatas', Associated Board of the Royal Schools of Music, London, 1924 and 1931

EDITIONS OF MUSIC REFERRED TO IN THE TEXT

Palestrina: Le Opere Complete di Giovanni Pierluigi da Palestrina, Edizione Scalera, Rome
Sweelinck: Ausgewählte Werke, Band II: Werke für Orgel (Ed. Hellman), Peters, no. 4645b
Frescobaldi: Ausgewählte Orgelwerke, Fiori Musicali (Ed. Hermann Keller), Peters, no. 4514
Denkmäler der Tonkunst in Österreich, Breitkopf und Härtel, Wiesbaden, 1959
Denkmäler der Tonkunst in Bayern, Akademische Druck und Verlagsanstalt, Graz
Alte Meister des Orgelspiels, Neue Folge/Teil I, II (Ed. Straube), Peters, no. 4301a and 4301b
Spielbuch für die Kleinorgel/Band I, II (Ed. Wolfgang Auler), Peters, no. 4527a and 4527b
Early Keyboard Music: A collection of Pieces written for the Virginal, Spinet, Harpsichord, and Clavichord, vol. II (Ed. Louis Oesterle), G. Schirmer, New York, 1904
Historical Anthology of Music (Eds. Archibald T. Davison and Willi Apel), vol. I, OUP, London, 1947, vol. II, OUP, London, 1950
Geschichte der Musik in Beispielen (Ed. Arnold Schering), Breitkopf und Härtel, Leipzig, 1931
Buxtehude: Sämtliche Orgelwerke herausgegeben von Josef Hedar, vol. II, Wilhelm Hansen Edition no. 3922, J. W. Chester Ltd, London
Bartók: String Quartet no. 5 (min. score), Universal Edition, Alfred A. Kalmus Ltd
Bartók: Music for Strings, Percussion and Celeste (min. score), Boosey and Hawkes Ltd
Hindemith: Ludus Tonalis, Schott and Co Ltd
Shostakovitch: 24 Preludes and Fugues for Piano (Preface and Editing by Irwin Freundlich), Leeds Music Corporation, N.Y., Boosey and Hawkes
Stravinsky: Symphony of Psalms (min. and vocal score), Boosey and Hawkes Ltd
Walton: Symphony no. 1 in B♭ minor (min. score), OUP, London

INDEX